D1542602

BROOKS HAYS

BROOKS HAYS

James T. Baker

MERCER

ISBN 0-86554-335-6

B R O O K S H A Y S
Copyright © 1989
Mercer University Press
Macon, Georgia 31207
All rights reserved
Printed in the United States of America

LIBRARY OF CONGRESS CATALOGING-IN-PUBLICATION DATA

Baker, James Thomas.
Brooks Hays / James Baker.
xxv + 218 pp.   15 x 23 cm.   6 x 9″
ISBN 0-86554-335-6 (alk. paper)

1. Hays, Brooks.   2. Legislators—United States—Biography.
3. United States. Congress. House—Biography.   4. Baptists—United
States—Biography.   I. Title.
E748.H387B35   1989
973.9′092—dc20   89-13415
[B]   CIP

CONTENTS

For my friend
FRANCIS MARTIN

PREFACE

Southeastern Baptist Theological Seminary in Wake Forest, North Carolina, established a lectureship in the name of Brooks Hays and announced that its yearly theme would be "Religion in the Life of the Nation." As its first lecturer, a religious leader but also a politician with a politician's love of public recognition, Brooks said in complete honesty that he was more proud of this honor than to have had a building or highway named for him.

Once when Brooks was in Dallas, Texas, to address a Baptist conference on "Christianity and Politics," he was robbed at gunpoint by two young black men who took $175, his wallet, wristwatch, credit cards, and a postage-stamp-sized Bible on microfilm. At a press conference the next morning, he said, "I went back to my hotel and prayed for them. I hope no one will view this as a racial incident. It was a human incident."

These two events vividly portray the essence of this unusual man. He was many things: a lawyer, a lay minister, a congressman, a president of the Southern Baptist Convention, an adviser to presidents of the United States, and overall perhaps the most influential religio-political figure of mid-twentieth-century America. He was a political moderate in a time of extremists, a religious mediator in a denomination known for internecine struggle, a courageous giant in a world of moral pygmies.

Seers, prophets, even saints have been described as people who simply understand the true nature of the world better than the rest of us. If that is so, then Brooks Hays may well qualify to be any one or all three. He understood the nature of man, man's society, and man's world. He understood his country and his church, how they came to be, what they were, what they were still to become; and he not only demanded that they be their best but showed them by his personal example how to be.

This is his story.

ACKNOWLEDGMENTS

A book is never the product of an author working alone. Untold numbers of contributors, advisers, and supporters provide content, structure, and style for the finished copy. Without such persons a book would not go beyond the stage of whim or, at best, dream. This is particularly true of *Brooks Hays*.

For hospitality as I roamed the countryside searching for materials, I am grateful to Francis and Martha Martin of Nashville; Judge Steele Hays of Little Rock; and Bill and Betty (Hays) Bell of suburban Washington.

For technical advice and facilitation, I am grateful to the archivists and librarians at the Southern Baptist Historical Commission in Nashville; the University of Arkansas in Fayetteville; and Wake Forest University in Winston-Salem, North Carolina.

For financial aid, I thank Western Kentucky University in Bowling Green, where I am a teacher, both for a Faculty Research Grant to travel and pursue my research and for a monetary contribution to Mercer University Press to help with publication costs.

For encouragement of every variety, for hosting me in her home, for sharing with me her memories of a hectic but happy life with Brooks, for turning over to me in complete trust the photographs that appear in these pages, I am above all grateful to Marion Hays.

PHOTO SECTION

(All photographs courtesy of Marion Hays)

President Harry Truman with Boy Scout leaders.
Brooks Hays is standing behind President Truman.

Marion and Brooks Hays above Bergtesgaden, Germany, 1951.
They had attended a meeting of European "Protestant Men of the Chapel."

*Marion and Brooks Hays with Ambassador (to Managua)
and Mrs. Whelan, 11 November 1953.*

*Marion and Brooks Hays with a church group
at Barranquilla in northern Columbia,
summer 1957. At the time, Brooks
was the president of the Southern Baptist Convention.*

*The swearing-in ceremony for Brooks Hays's
induction as a member of the
Tennessee Valley Authority Board, 1 July 1959.
He had been appointed by President Eisenhower.*

1959 leadership training workshop involving the Arkansas chapter delegates of Sigma Chi. Marion and Brooks Hays are standing to the right.

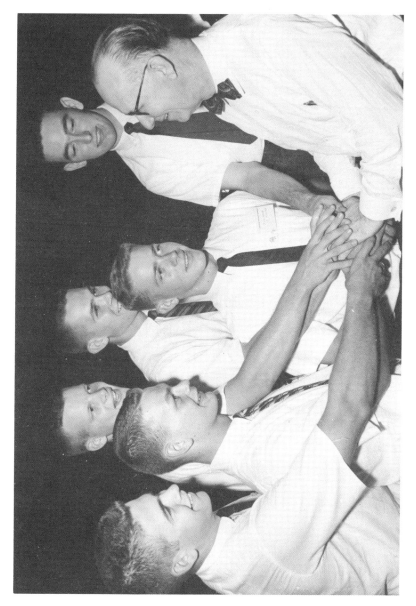

Eleventh annual Valleywide Cooperative Conference, Gatlinburg, Tennessee, 1 April 1960.

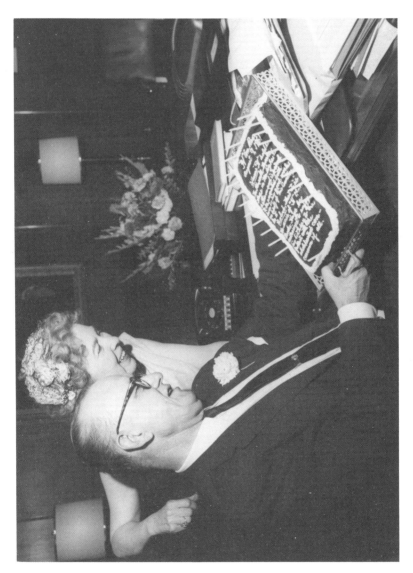

Marion and Brooks Hays examining a birthday cake given to him by his State Department staff, 9 August 1961.

*Judge Bolon B. Turner (Brooks's former law partner)
administering the oath of office to Brooks Hays for service as Special Assistant
to President Kennedy (1 December 1961).
President Kennedy and Marion Hays are observers.*

Brooks Hays during a trip to Africa in April 1963 as a goodwill ambassador for President Kennedy. Here he is meeting with leaders of the Zor Zor tribe in Liberia who made him an "honorary paramount" chieftain.

While Brooks Hays was president of the Southern Baptist Convention,
he was sometimes jokingly called the Baptist "pope."
When Brooks saw this picture, after he and his wife had met the pope,
Brooks said, "Honey, you're adoring the wrong pope!"
(The date for this photo is 23 October 1961.)

Brooks Hays campaigning with some young people, July 1966.

*Marion and Brooks Hays with Peace Corps volunteers at Ibadan,
Nigeria, April 1963.*

National Conference of Christians and Jews award ceremony in Nashville, 22 May 1975. Brooks is holding hands with Minnie Pearl.

Brooks Hays conveying thanks to Mrs. Mamie Eisenhower on behalf of the George Washington University Board (date unknown).

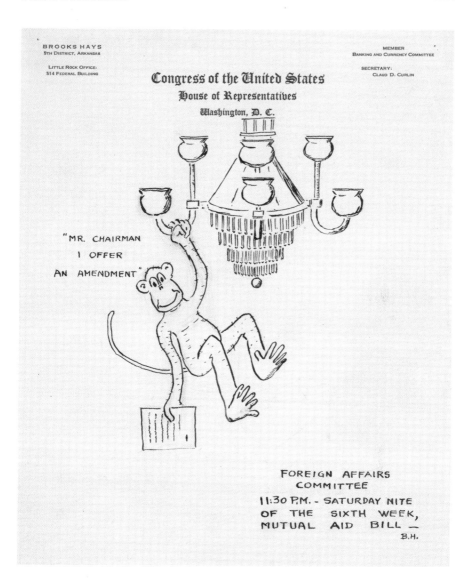

Drawing by Brooks Hays.

ROOTS

The man who would sixty years later stand for a moment as America's most respected moral statesman was born 9 August 1898, a day he would note was full of the numbers 8 and 9. He was born, according to ancient Persian reckoning, a Leo: with the promise that he would be strong, willful, and courageous. He was born, according to the Chinese calendar, a dog: obedient to the established order, loyal to his commitments, faithful to those he served. But he was also born to be a Southern Baptist: to be justified by faith, to be certain of God's love and grace, and to be self-consciously aware that he was to play a role in making manifest the Kingdom of God on earth.

He was named Lawrence Brooks Hays, the Lawrence for Bob Lawrence and the Brooks for Tom Brooks, both men his father's law partners. He would be the only child of Adelbert Steele Hays and Sarah Tabitha Butler Hays. Mr. Hays was called Steele, Mrs. Hays was called Sallie, and by the time their son had been graduated from college he had chosen to be called Brooks. The name Brooks was a natural choice for a young man interested in politics, since the only two Democratic presidents of the United States in the past sixty years had been Steven Grover Cleveland and Thomas Woodrow Wilson, both of whom had used middle names in political careers, as had his father Steele Hays.[1]

Brooks Hays was born in London, Pope County, Arkansas, where his father, in those days more a teacher than a lawyer, had taken a job conducting a summer course at the local public school. The next month the

---

[1]Brooks Hays, *Politics Is My Parish* (Baton Rouge: Louisiana State University Press, 1981) 16.

small family moved a few miles to Atkins and lived there until 1903, when Brooks was five, at which point they moved a third time to Russellville, where Brooks would live until he went away to college in 1915. All three towns are in Pope County; and the fact that various people assumed Brooks was born in each of the towns, an assumption Brooks seldom challenged, gave him an edge in Pope County elections. In the 1928 gubernatorial election, for example, one of his opponents groused, "Brooks'll take the county—can't beat a guy that was born in three different towns."[2]

Pope County is in west central Arkansas, midway between Little Rock and Fort Smith, in the low, blue Ozark Mountains, blessed with clean air, drained by the Arkansas River, a place of great scenic beauty, Democratic politics, and fundamentalist religion. When Brooks was young, black people were a distinct and passive minority. There were few Catholics and almost no Jews, and Baptists and Methodists predominated in a region that bordered Indian Territory and was for decades frontier country.

Late in life Brooks would describe turn-of-the-century Russellville— and thus his early, formative years and life—as a quadrangle that led to and from four buildings, each representing an institution that helped make him what he was. The four buildings were his home, the public school, the Baptist church, and the county courthouse: family nurture, educational enrichment, spiritual nourishment, and opportunity through politics for recognition, power, and service.[3] Perhaps not so odd to those who knew him in his adult life, the church seems to have made the earliest and most permanent, if not always the most positive, impression on him. He would later say that his first memories were of the little Baptist church building back in Atkins, before he was five years old. He would during his lifetime be a family man, a school and college teacher, and of course a congressman, but his most significant and successful role would be that of churchman.

———————

Brooks Hays's paternal grandfather, David Hays, was born and raised near Titusville, Pennsylvania, where America's first oil field was found. Brooks always boasted, with appropriate apocryphal hyperbole, that one of David Hays's brothers had come close to owning that first field and that had this happened the Hays family would have remained in Pennsylvania

———————

[2]Ibid., 3.

[3]Ibid., 13.

to run Standard Oil. Had that happened, he would say with a mischievous twinkle in his eye, he would himself have gone down in history as John D. Hays, wealthy governor of Pennsylvania, and Nelson Rockefeller would have been a rural schoolmaster in upstate New York.

The Hays family did not, of course, gain control of Standard Oil, and David Hays earned his living as a surveyor, bookkeeper, and school-teacher. He left Pennsylvania in the mid-1870s, taught briefly at a school in Lawrence, Kansas, which would eventually become the University of Kansas, then returned to Pennsylvania for a time before heading for Arkansas. There he worked as a bookkeeper in Van Buren before accepting an offer from William Butler to come and teach school in the frontier village of Ellsworth, Logan County, Arkansas. It was in 1879, accompanied by a family that included a seven-year-old son named Steele, that he made the long trek southwest to the edge of Indian territory.[4]

David Hays was a graduate of Allegheny College in Meadville, Maryland, where he had been a classmate of future President of the United States William McKinley.[5] He was a Methodist and a Republican, although he preferred to vote Prohibitionist when he had a choice. This hint of a Republican and Yankee past would cause his grandson Brooks a bit of trouble in his first race for governor of Arkansas in 1928. Brooks faced the issue squarely, however, joking that while the Hays family had indeed once been Yankee and Republican, they had seen the light and come out to God's country and been won over, both by the South and the Democrats. He won the point but not the election.[6]

David Hays was willing to move south because his health called for a milder climate. He seems never to have been a well man; and in 1890, after eleven years in Arkansas, he died, still a young man. But during those eleven years he had taught school in Ellsworth and watched his son Steele develop a permanent attachment to a childhood sweetheart, the daughter of the man who had persuaded the elder Hays to come to Arkansas to teach, the Reverend Dr. William Butler.

This man who would be Brooks's maternal grandfather was also a Republican. William Butler had been born in the hill country of western Ten-

---

[4]Ibid., 1-2.

[5]Brooks Hays, Conversation with Ronald Tonks, May 1975, typeset in 15 parts. Southern Baptist Sunday School Board Archives, Nashville TN.

[6]Hays, *Politics Is My Parish,* 1.

nessee, but as a Union man he had refused to fight for the Confederacy in the Civil War. On the other hand, since all five of his brothers had fought for the South, he had sat out the war in order not to fight against his own family. His grandson Brooks, in his last years, free of the need to please Southern sensitivities, would boast of his two grandfathers and their enlightened attitudes; but during his political career, when he had to have rebel support to get elected, he played it more softly.

William Butler was a graduate of the Vanderbilt Medical College. In 1873, at the age of forty, he moved with his third wife to Arkansas, to practice in Ellsworth, Logan County, on the old military road to Fort Smith. In Ellsworth he served as both a doctor and a preacher. Medicine was his profession, preaching his vocation. He was literally "called" to preach. The local church needed a preacher, but preachers were hard to come by on the frontier. Therefore, the congregation drafted the pious physician to do the job. He served his church, a "Hardshell" or "Old" Baptist congregation, for a number of years, until he was no longer needed. His daughter Sallie, herself a Southern Baptist, a "New" Baptist, was always defensive about his affiliation with the predestinarians, and Brooks himself felt the need to explain that his grandfather was better educated and more enlightened than the people he was "called" to serve.[7]

In 1879 Dr. Butler, the chairman of the school board, invited David Hays of Van Buren, previously of Pennsylvania, to come to Ellsworth to teach. In 1883 Butler ran unsuccessfully, probably because he ran as a Republican, for the Arkansas State Senate.[8] The years 1880 to 1888 were profitable ones for him, and he lived as Ellsworth's most prominent citizen in a two-story white frame house. But in 1893 he lost a good bit of his income and accumulated wealth when Arkansas foundered under the effects of a nationwide panic, a panic that also deeply affected the now fatherless Hays family. Steele Hays, himself unable to go past the eighth grade in school due to his father's illness and death in 1890, now was forced into even deeper poverty. Despite his lack of formal education, he began teaching school. He and Sallie Butler had been married only a short time when Dr. Butler died in 1896 at the age of sixty-three. Both families were now mired in a poverty deeper than either had known since the Civil War.[9]

---

[7]Hays, Conversation with Ronald Tonks, May 1975.

[8]Hays, *Politics Is My Parish,* 3.

[9]Hays, Conversation with Ronald Tonks, May 1975.

Brooks spoke far more often of his father Steele than of his mother Sallie, and it was obvious that this dominate and domineering man deeply influenced his life and dramatically haunted his spirit. Steele Hays, born in Titusville, Pennsylvania, in 1872, may have completed only eight grades of formal schooling; but he was a vociferous reader and had by the time of his father's death and his own marriage educated himself sufficiently to be asked to teach in a series of rural Arkansas schools. In 1901, when he was twenty-nine, he spent a brief period reading law at Washington and Lee College in Virginia, passed the Arkansas bar, and spent the rest of his life as a trial lawyer.[10]

Brooks remembered his father as a powerful orator with a voice so deep and resonant that people in Russellville did not need to go inside the courthouse to hear him plead a case, a lawyer who could reason like a trained logician and who had a mind like a steel trap. His hair was pure white by the time he was forty, yet he kept a youthful face until he was quite an old man. In his white linen suits he was the image of the Southern gentleman. He had great public and personal charm, an advanced sense of humor, and a fine gift for gab. He quite early in life abandoned the Republicanism of his father for the Democratic club of one-party Pope County, assuring himself of private political support from voters. He joined his mother's Baptist church instead of his father's Methodist church, thus securing his claim, which was almost an obsession, to be part of the local establishment.[11]

Steele Hays had only one major weakness, but it caused his family a great deal of grief, kept him from being chosen a leader in his church for many years, and probably cost him his chance at elective office. He drank. Always one to be part of the group, while Steele served as Chief Clerk of the Arkansas House of Representatives at the turn of the century, he spent his afternoons at a Little Rock saloon, developing his political ties and his taste for hard liquor. At last in 1915, when he was forty-three and his son Brooks was about to finish high school, he agreed to go out to Mineral Wells, Texas, to take a cure. It worked, and he kicked his habit. By 1922 he had climbed to what Brooks would call "the peak of moderation and abstention"; but in that year he was rejected in his only race for the United States Congress, in part because his constituency still thought of him as an alcoholic. They trusted him to plead a criminal case but not to represent the

---

[10] Ibid.

[11] Brooks Hays, *A Hotbed of Tranquility* (New York: Macmillan, 1968) 141.

district in Washington. Nevertheless, he stuck to his resolution, and for the last forty years of his life, which ended in 1959, he did not take a drink.[12]

Brooks always harbored ambivalent feelings about his father. He considered him a "gracious" and "awfully good man."[13] He admired his legal knowledge and skills, most of which were self-taught, and his religious sensibilities, which Brooks considered "wholesome," deeply pious without fanaticism.[14] He once wrote, "I have never known a man with a more genuine case of religion." And in a Civitan address in Jacksonville, Florida, in 1951 he described Steele as "a wise and good man, a simple country lawyer who taught his son that a love for justice is a gift of God, that the loving God above has planted it within me."[15] For Steele Hays, religion and politics, while separated by the Constitution, were vitally connected; and this he taught Brooks.

Yet there was undoubtedly about Steele Hays a brutally hard edge, one that both captivated and repelled his more mild-mannered son, in much the same way Hans Luther both captivated and repelled his son Martin in an earlier version of a Protestant leader's formation. Brooks's wife Marion, when she was still new to the family, dubbed Steele "Czar" Hays because of his stern willfulness; and Brooks admitted late in life that he had submitted to the will of the Czar all too often, more than was healthy. He admitted to being too submissive, too pliable where his father was concerned. "A conversation with my father was a monologue," he mused. Steele ordered him not to dance while he was in college, and he obeyed, although he never felt there was anything wrong with dancing. He knew at the time that he should fight this arbitrary order, that he should tell his father that this was his own decision to make, but he could not bring himself to do so. Steele continued to think of and treat Brooks as a boy even after the city of Russellville and the state of Arkansas had come to think of him and treat him as a man. It is likely that Steele never really accepted his son as an adult.[16]

---

[12]Hays, Conversation with Ronald Tonks, July 1975.

[13]Hays, Conversation with Ronald Tonks, May 1975.

[14]Hays, *Politics Is My Parish,* 18.

[15]Brooks Hays, *This World: A Christian's Workshop* (Nashville: Broadman Press, 1968) 106.

[16]Hays, Conversation with Ronald Tonks, May 1975.

Steele teased Brooks privately and kidded him publicly, providing him with a sense of humility and humor, but also causing him some pain. Once when someone asked Steele if he had read Brooks's last book, he joked, "I hope so." When asked whether he would rather Brooks be president of the United States or president of the Southern Baptist Convention, Steele replied, "President of the United States. He's not smart enough to be president of the Southern Baptist Convention." And when Brooks telephoned his father to tell him that he had in fact been elected president of the Southern Baptist Convention, Steele inquired, "On what ballot?" Such stories became part and parcel of Brooks's bag of good humor, but it was obvious his laughter was born of pain. Only in his middle years, when he had come to be his own man, was he able to laugh about such stories. Yet there was genuine love between Steele and Brooks. Just after that telephone call from Chicago when Brooks told Steele he was president of the Southern Baptists, the old man sent him a telegram: "Mother knows and she is proud of her son."[17] A strange, roundabout way of expressing pride. Brooks's mother had died two years before. His father, who could not say how proud he obviously was, would live only two years more.

Brooks Hays's mother, Sallie Butler Hays, takes up much less space in his writings and public addresses than his father. She appears in family photographs as a fair, fragile woman, as refined as her husband is rough, a quiet, unobtrusive Arkansas housewife. Brooks looks more like his mother in these pictures than like his father. His features, like hers, are smooth and rounded, and like her he is taller than average and thin. Had he and his father been brothers, they might have reminded people of Jacob and Esau. Brooks looked more like his mother's son than his father's. While he got his gregariousness and oratorical skills from Steele, he seems to have taken his gentleness from his mother, Sallie.

Sallie Butler was born in Arkansas in 1874, two years after Steele Hays had been born in Pennsylvania. She finished high school while he was already working to support his family, and she attended one term of college at Ouachita Baptist and a year at George Peabody Teachers College in Nashville, Tennessee, before becoming a teacher. She taught school for three years before marrying her childhood sweetheart Steele in 1896 and settling down to be a wife and mother. She died 6 December 1955, near the

---

[17]Ibid.

end of her Congressman son Brooks's year as a United States delegate to the United Nations.[18]

Brooks dedicated the book *This World: A Christian's Workshop* to his father and mother, whom he said had taught him that a Christian must have a social conscience. By pooling their genes and their love they had given him the unique combination of body, mind, and spirit he would need to take him on his long journey to explore the Christian faith and American democracy.

The only other person from his childhood Brooks credited with molding his adult personality was an elementary teacher named Lucy Hill. Miss Hill, one of a legion of spinster schoolmarms who had brought what little learning there was to the early-twentieth-century South, taught Brooks in the fifth grade—and made an indelible impression on him. Miss Hill taught him to love books and learning; and while he never again found a teacher like her, he never lost his love for books or learning. Miss Hill's most famous parallel is Miss Julia Coleman, an elementary teacher in south Georgia whom President Jimmy Carter mentioned in his inaugural address. Brooks once said that he had mentioned Lucy Hill in fully one-third of all the speeches he had made in a lifetime on the political stump and in Baptist pulpits.[19]

Miss Hill had her classes read, memorize, and recite passages from the Scriptures. Brooks always defended this practice, even when as an elder statesman he agreed with the Supreme Court's ban on school prayer. Miss Hill, he explained, taught the Scriptures, particularly the Psalms, as literature. By reading, memorizing, and reciting long passages from the Bible, her students developed an appreciation for some of the world's greatest thought and cadence and honed their public speaking skills. She was so successful in Brooks's case that more than fifty years later, at a presidential prayer breakfast, when a new pair of trifocal glasses prevented him from reading his assigned Psalm 1, he simply pretended he was reading and recited it from memory, having first learned and recited it for Miss Hill in 1908.[20]

Despite finding no more Lucy Hills, Brooks eagerly continued his educational odyssey in the Russellville Public Schools. When he was old he

---

[18]Hays, *Politics Is My Parish,* 2-3.

[19]Hays, Conversation with Ronald Tonks, May 1975.

[20]Ibid.

could still remember that his first school book was *Safe Steps for Little Feet,* a book of Old Testament stories for children, and that throughout grade school he learned his morality from *McGuffey's Reader.* With modest opportunity, he continued to read, study, and prepare himself for whatever life in this new century might have to offer him. His circumstances may have been humble, but his dreams seem not to have been limited by the physical and social parameters of his life.[21]

Brooks claimed never to have dated a girl while in high school. He also claimed that until he was seventeen he was "hardly conscious that boys and girls are different." He was small for his age, barely five feet tall, as thin as a toothpick, and weighed only 110 pounds at graduation. He was only a substitute center on Russellville High School's third team in football his senior year, and he played a grand total of fifty-five seconds the entire season. His parents bought his first suit with long trousers for his high school graduation ceremony, after he suffered death for weeks fearing that he might have to accept his diploma in short pants. Russellville in 1915 had a population of 3,500, and it is a commentary on the condition of education in that day that there were only fifteen seniors in Brooks's graduating class, nine of them boys.[22] Only three of these fifteen went to college, and only two earned degrees. The numbers were continually thinning, with Brooks finding himself a part of an ever dwindling minority.

Home. School. Church. In Brooks's life, from earliest times, church meant a Baptist church. He could never remember a time when he had not attended Baptist services, and when he was old enough to decide for himself he continued to attend them. Yet despite his Baptist roots, despite the fact that Baptists demanded mystical rebirth for salvation, he always freely admitted that he never had a conversion experience. He said that from earliest times he was left cold by the emotionalism of Baptist revivals and that his conversion, if indeed he had had one, had been slow, one step at a time, as he watched the Gospel work in people's lives. He actually made his profession of faith in Christ at a Methodist service, late in 1910, when he was twelve years old. The speaker who persuaded him to make public the faith that had been growing in him over several years was a blind Methodist evangelist named Joe Ramsey. It was Ramsey's sincerity rather than any emotional appeal that won Brooks over. According to Brooks's

---

[21]Ibid.

[22]Hays, *A Hotbed of Tranquility,* 188-89.

own version of the story, he was "a Methodist for twenty-four hours," or until Steele Hays was told.

As in so many of his affairs, his father intervened. The son of Steele Hays was not about to be a Methodist. Although Brooks had tentatively joined the Methodists, he was promptly ordered to withdraw and apply to join the Baptists. In February 1911, Brooks was totally immersed in un-heated water in the Russellville Baptist Church's zinc baptistery. He would always remember the freezing burial and resurrection, his blue skin, and his sincere wish that his father had permitted the Methodists to sprinkle him. He would carry with him throughout life a fondness for Methodists, and from this early experience may possibly have been born the ecumen-ism of the mature Brooks Hays.[23]

Brooks would in his later years recall that the Baptist church in Rus-sellville was as much pain as pleasure for a young man of intelligence and sensitive spirit. His teachers there were for the most part ill-equipped to give him religious instruction. His pastors were frontier Bible thumpers with little education. The Baptist emphasis on local church autonomy meant that there was little denominational power to screen ministerial credentials and encourage sound theology. Sermons were most often de-voted to such pertinent issues as whether or not baptism is required for salvation (this in debate with Campbellites), whether or not footwashing is required of modern Christians (in debate with "hardshell" Baptists), and whether once a person is saved he can fall from grace (in debate with Methodists). He heard more sermons on hell than on heaven and more on what to avoid in life than on what to seek. He would not know a single pas-tor of his hometown church worth emulating until he himself helped call a young seminary-trained man named Clyde Hickerson in 1923.[24]

Yet he continued to attend church throughout his youth, earning a rep-utation for church going beyond the level demanded by his parents. One of his adult friends, Joe E. Culpepper, once told the story that he stopped in Russellville and asked the service station attendant if he had known Brooks when he was a young man. The attendant allowed as how he had, recalled his piosity, and told Culpepper a story. Once Brooks was seen about to catch a bus out of town, carrying a valise in one hand and a Bible in the other. When asked where he was going, he said he aimed to go to New Or-

---

[23]Hays, *Politics Is My Parish*, 274.

[24]Ibid., 5.

leans to see the Mardi Gras. Why the Bible? "Well, if the girls are as pretty as I hear they are, and if everybody has as good a time as I hear they do down there, I thought I might stay over Sunday."[25]

For many years Brooks thought seriously of choosing the ministry for his career. As a boy he attended Chautauqua meetings and heard some of the greatest orators of the new century, men who swayed huge crowds with their memorable sermons, in marked contrast to his pastors. He was particularly captivated by the homilies of William Jennings Bryan and the political idealism of Eugene V. Debs. He would one day joke that all through his youth the men in Russellville made odds on whether he would end up in government or in the church and that when finally he became a lawyer they declared, "The church won."[26] But while he was searching for a path in life, it was no laughing matter.

His deep and abiding interest in politics, according to his own testimony, began with the Easter bunny. When he was six years old he saw an Easter egg bearing the face of Alton B. Parker. When he asked who this man was and was told he had been last year's Democratic nominee for president of the United States, young Brooks announced that he wanted to run for president so he could have his face on an egg. The next Easter he did indeed get an egg with his face on it, and from that day he was in love with politics.[27]

His father saw to it that he became a Democrat, just as he saw to it that he became a Baptist. Steele Hays, the son and son-in-law of Republicans, became a Democrat himself when he was a young man harboring ambitions of high political office, was throughout his life a prominent party regular, and in 1912 was elected prosecuting attorney for a four-county district. His law practice suffered during the race and more so during the term he served, but his zest for the political life inspired Brooks, who sold magazine subscriptions to help supplement the family income.[28]

Steele rose to be Chief Clerk of the Arkansas House of Representatives, and there in Little Rock he introduced his son to state politics. It was during these years that he began spending those convivial afternoons with

---

[25]Hays, *A Hotbed of Tranquility,* 173-74.

[26]Hays, *Politics Is My Parish,* 23-25.

[27]Hays, *A Hotbed of Tranquility,* 3.

[28]Hays, *Politics Is My Parish,* 21.

legislators at Little Rock's Garibaldi's Saloon and was finally convinced by Judge W. L. Moose to go to Texas for a cure. The drinking and its effects, by almost destroying his life, made Steele a Prohibitionist and kept Brooks from drinking until he was in his middle years. But those Little Rock days, when Brooks was in his most formative stage of life, made him thirsty for politics and loyal to the Democratic party.[29]

Brooks always readily admitted that his ancestry was Republican and that had the two families not come to live in a Democratic stronghold, where his father had to join the party in order to hold office, he would probably have been a Republican himself. He said in his later years that had he lived in mid-nineteenth-century America, just before the Civil War, he would have chosen to join the new Republican party of Lincoln. He would have supported Republicans' opposition to slavery and their insistence that the union be preserved. At the turn of the twentieth century, he said, he would have felt more at home with Progressive Republicanism than any other philosophy. He understood, even as he joined and began his climb in the Democratic party, that in Arkansas it stood for white supremacy, that it supported the poll tax that disenfranchised blacks and poor whites, and that it cared little for the have-nots of society, the true majority of citizens of Arkansas.[30]

Brooks cared. His desire to help the poor, the disadvantaged, the sick, and the dying developed early in his life. Although the word *liberal* was not in the Arkansas political dictionary or vocabulary, from his youth Brooks matched the national definition of the word. He found it his hardest task as a boy to go and collect money from three families that lived in his father's rented houses. He was among the very first young Arkansans to advocate social welfare medical insurance and collective bargaining for laborers.[31] As a mountain populist, he found himself in a party unsympathetic to his dreams of social reform. The "Bourbons" of eastern Arkansas had dominated the state's party machinery since the 1870s, when they had ousted black Republicans and restored white Democratic supremacy. Republican excesses just after the Civil War had rendered that party too

---

[29]Ibid., 17.

[30]Hays, Conversation with Ronald Tonks, May 1975.

[31]Hays, *Politics Is My Parish*, 25.

feeble to be a feasible alternative. For Brooks, it was a matter of being a Democrat or never knowing electoral success.[32]

Yet he knew and admitted his party's deficiencies. In later years he would say that the Democrats held power in Arkansas for nearly eighty years—during which time they suppressed blacks, turned deaf ears to the poor, and failed to provide relief during depressions—before they were called to atone for their sins.[33] During the latter part of this time, he was himself first a reformer, then an establishment representative, and finally the very instrument of atonement. The Democratic party is still dominant in Arkansas today, holding all four Congressional seats, both Senate seats, the governorship, and the state legislature. But it is a very different party, with progressive leadership, from the one that ruled Arkansas before the political martyrdom of Brooks Hays in 1958. Brooks was as responsible as any other person or factor for the transformation of his state's dominant party.

Although Brooks would dedicate most of his professional life to politics, calling it in one of his books the "parish" of his ministry to the world, he always kept a balanced perspective on it—and kept a keen sense of humor about it. He loved to tell the story about a North Carolina Congressman named Strange. Strange ordered that when he died his tombstone should read: HERE LIES AN HONEST CONGRESSMAN. When someone asked how people were to know who he was if his name were not carved on the stone, he replied that when they saw that this was the grave of an honest politician they would automatically think, "That's Strange."[34]

In 1915, the year his father took the cure for alcoholism, Brooks was graduated from high school. His father dictated that he enroll at the University of Arkansas in Fayetteville. The tuition would be free, and one of Steele's former public school pupils, J. R. Grant, was a professor there. So in September the obedient son put on the $17 suit he had been given as a high school graduation gift and boarded the train for the most inconvenient, least centrally located, least accessible major university of any state in the union. In Fayetteville, in the mountainous northwest corner of Ar-

---

[32]Ibid., 4.

[33]Ibid., 5.

[34]Hays, *A Hotbed of Tranquility*, 10.

kansas, he was welcomed and settled into place by Professor Grant. Within days he was a seventeen-year-old university man.[35]

Brooks lived for four years in Buchanon (Old Buck) Hall, the school's oldest dormitory, paying $16 a month for room, board, and laundry. The room was unfurnished, and the common bathhouse out back served three dorms. Steele sent him $25 a month, and after paying for his keep he had $9 left. He worked in the university library for 15¢ an hour, and this pittance added another $6 a month.[36] Fayetteville may have been, like Rome, a city built on seven hills, but Brooks had little cash to pursue what few bright lights there were.

He shot up in height during his freshman year. He was just over five feet tall in September, but by Christmas he was close to his adult height of five feet, eleven inches. He continued, however, to weigh barely 110 pounds. He suffered with some patience the usual freshman initiations but ran the gauntlet of upperclassmen's belts so fast that he was jokingly offered a tryout for the track team. He was once taken out, along with the other freshmen, left in the country, and forced to walk barefoot along the rail line back into town. Despite his good nature, though, he was considered something of a prude because he did not drink, smoke, or use profanity. He was in fact given the name "Deacon" by his less pious classmates, and it stuck.

He attended the local Baptist church services each Sunday and taught a Sunday afternoon class for boys at a mission in a poor neighborhood called Rose Hill. He attended and taught classes for the YMCA, which met once a week on campus, and was president of the organization his junior and senior years. But his faith did not go unchallenged. It was tested during his first months in college by his agnostic roommate, a mature man of thirty-one who had come down from the Ozarks to pursue a science major. Brooks and Orland Leach shared a bed, for which they paid $3, and many long hours of theological wrestling. Brooks learned in those sessions the valuable lesson that it is foolish to try to prove logically the claims of Christianity. They are, he began to see, statements of faith. He would meet Leach again after a number of years, after he was in Congress and Leach was a professor in "a great southern college," and learn that Leach had become a Christian. His conversion delighted Brooks, and Brooks always remembered his explanation: "I am

---

[35]Hays, *Politics Is My Parish*, 26-27.

[36]Hays, Conversation with Ronald Tonks, May 1975.

no longer a fraction. I have become an integer." He said that he had found in his own way, by his own methods, that the really vital things of life belong to the realm of spirit.[37] He gave Brooks and his naive college arguments for the faith little credit for his conversion.

Brooks was an active man on campus. He joined the debate team to continue the hobby he had practiced since he was a fourteen-year-old high school champion. He wrote for and later edited the campus newspaper, the *University Weekly,* and he drew cartoons and was later editor of the annual magazine the *Razorback.* He joined every possible club: the military's Scabbard and Blade, the journalists' Pi Delta Epsilon, the debaters' Tau Kappa Alpha, and the scholars' Skull and Torch, which was later recognized as Phi Beta Kappa. His favorite club, the one he kept in touch with throughout his life, was Sigma Chi.[38]

At first he was almost rejected by Sigma Chi because the members considered him too straight-laced. He did not hide the fact that he considered their initiation practices and pranks silly, and he submitted to them with great reluctance. Then after being inducted, not knowing that freshmen were expected to keep quiet during the group gripe sessions, he openly criticized the upperclassmen, his betters, for cursing and was laughed into scorned silence. He might have been drummed out or been forced to resign his membership had not one upper-classman taken his side. "Let 'em laugh," the boy shouted, "damn their souls! I love you, and I appreciate you."[39] The others stopped laughing, Brooks kept quiet, and at last he was accepted for what he was, a pious kid but one who longed for social acceptance.

Brooks's college electives were all in art. He was a compulsive doodler and taught himself to be a competent cartoonist.[40] He placed a long line of his drawings in campus publications and would continue throughout his life to sketch cartoons, some to relieve boredom, some to entertain friends or children. Some were published in newspapers, and others were included in a Washington exhibit. Strangely, however, his aesthetic gifts were all

---

[37]Brooks Hays, Address at Western Kentucky University, Bowling Green KY, November 1968.

[38]Hays, *Politics Is My Parish,* 30.

[39]Hays, *A Hotbed of Tranquility,* 189-91.

[40]Hays, *Politics Is My Parish,* 29.

visual, absolutely none of them musical. The boy and man who could deliver rousing public speeches and sketch rural and city scenes with skill never learned to play a musical instrument and by his own accounts could "barely hum a tune."[41]

It was toward the end of his first semester in college that Brooks met the girl he would eventually marry and remain married to for five months short of sixty years. In separate accounts of that fateful meeting, he and she agree that it took place on 4 December 1915, at precisely 8:00 P.M. They were attending a debate and "Saturday night sociable" sponsored by the university's Periclean Society, held on the fourth floor of Old Main, which still stands on the campus. After gingerbread was served, he stood next to her in a spelling bee. He remembered fifty years later that he was immediately captivated by this Marion Prather, a sophomore studying to be a teacher, a small girl who stood just five feet tall, weighed just ninety-two pounds, and was a Methodist. Brooks, although shy, was undaunted by her superior standing, diminutive size, love for dancing, and alien immersion. He immediately began courting her, pinned her the next year, married her six years later, and through sixty years of marriage seems never to have developed a wandering eye. There was only one woman in his life.[42]

Marriage was out of the question at that time. They were both poor (Marion, whose father had died when she was young, was in school on scholarship), and there were too many miles to go before either one could think of settling down. Marion would finish her college work, during which time she taught the young Bill Fulbright in the university's training school, and teach English in her hometown of Fort Smith for three years before marriage. Brooks would also finish school, during which he would participate peripherally in a world war and be within sight of his law degree before he could set the official date. But from that night at the sociable neither of them had a really serious rival.

The first summer of college, 1916, Brooks wanted to work at a YMCA camp, but his father had already secured him a job teaching school and ordered him to come home. He obeyed. The summer school he conducted was at the village of Sunny Point, Arkansas, and though he was not yet eighteen years old he was given charge of eighty-two kids aged five to fourteen

---

[41]Hays, Conversation with Ronald Tonks, May 1975.

[42]Marion Hays, Unpublished manuscript, "How to Live Dangerously and Enjoy It," I-2. Possession of the author.

to teach for three months in one sweltering room. The job paid $50 a month, a good wage, but Brooks remembered it as the "most miserable summer of my life." The heat was unbearable, discipline was virtually impossible, and he came home every night totally exhausted. To his great relief that summer's cotton crop came in early, and the school closed two weeks ahead of schedule.[43] Brooks would in his lifetime do a great deal of teaching—Sunday school, adult oratorical seminars, university classes—but he would never again teach public school.

During the 1916–1917 school year, with the war in Europe slowly seducing President Woodrow Wilson into joining the Allies, Brooks honed his skills as a debater and campus newspaper reporter. He would recall in old age the speeches he heard made on campus by former President William Howard Taft and Arkansas Senator Joe T. Robinson. Although Germany's image in the press was almost completely negative, Taft urged his young audience not to forget the great contributions made to human culture by individual Germans. Robinson, on the other hand, sprinkled his speech with passages that were viciously anti-German, and these were the parts most rousingly applauded. When Brooks wrote an editorial for the *University Weekly* chiding the students for their prejudice, he was roundly criticized for being unpatriotic.[44] In April the United States entered the war.

During 1917–1918, Brooks's junior year, he reached his peak as a campus leader, a religious teacher at the YMCA, and a champion debater, while other Americans trained for the war in Europe. The campus paper reported on 21 March 1918 that yet another class conducted by Brooks Hays at the YMCA would be called "The Negro Question of the South."[45] Brooks would remember that his audience agreed with him that blacks should have more rights but that they considered the issue moot in a state as conservative as Arkansas. He did little to change their minds, if he tried, and if indeed he was not just as convinced that blacks would never have equality in his state. But the very existence of such a forum makes it quite obvious that, even at this early date, Brooks was one to raise uncomfortable social issues in a religious context and was unafraid of pursuing them to their logical, ethical, and moral conclusions.

---

[43]Hays, *A Hotbed of Tranquility,* 132.

[44]Hays, *Politics Is My Parish,* 38.

[45]*University Weekly,* University of Arkansas, 21 March 1918.

Early in 1918 Brooks was named one of six university debaters, having already helped Arkansas defeat Mississippi A&M during the fall of 1917.[46] On 3 April 1918, the *University Weekly,* calling him a "seasoned" debater, featured his photograph on the front page and announced that he and fellow student Gales Ragsdale had been chosen to travel to Austin, Texas, to uphold the affirmative against the University of Texas in a match scheduled for 8 April. The issue would be "Resolved: That the federal government should require arbitration (with power to enforce decisions) of disputes between organized labor and public service corporations, constitutionality granted." Brooks was quoted in the article (which he may have helped write, since he was on the paper staff) as saying he was anxious to take on and defeat Texas because they had defeated Arkansas in football during the fall semester. This statement made him a hero across the campus because, even in those early days of the pigskin rivalry, Arkansans loved nothing more than football and hated nothing more than losing to Texas. The long competition between the two states and their football squads had just begun. Brooks hoped to make debate an integral part of that competition.[47]

Brooks and Ragsdale journeyed to Austin by train, met the Texas team at the university YMCA auditorium on 11 April, and won the match. They wired the good news home, where it caused a sensation on campus.[48] The two rhetorical gladiators returned to Fayetteville to a tumultuous welcome on 18 April, and at the train station Brooks praised the hospitality, "pep," and good grace in defeat of the Texans.[49] Already he was a budding politician, happily accepting the praise of his constituency, looking beyond the horizon for a broader one.

The moment of glory was short-lived. Even as he debated in a peaceful setting, Americans were preparing to fighting in Europe. That summer Brooks, who despite his dislike of militarism was no pacifist, spent a month at Ft. Sheridan, Illinois, as an uninducted trainee for the army's officer training program. He would later remember being appalled at the way boys were being taught to hate and kill and was thus convinced that war weak-

---

[46]Ibid., 24 January 1918.

[47]Ibid., 3 April 1918.

[48]Ibid., 11 April 1918.

[49]Ibid., 18 April 1918.

ens and eventually destroys man's finer instincts. It is not surprising that he failed to be appointed an officer. But in September he enrolled in the university's Student Army Training Corps. Early in October he was released from his university classes to go to Camp Pike near Little Rock for Infantry Officers' School. That month he was one of fifty chosen as Junior Officers, but he had not yet been shipped out when the war ended on 11 November.[50] Much later he would speculate about what his fate might have been had he not been at the university and had he joined up the year before. He always believed, probably with some justification despite the histrionics, that he would have died in France.[51]

Brooks was mustered out of the army on 6 December 1918, with less than three months' service, in time to return to Fayetteville for the spring semester and earn enough credits to graduate on schedule five months later. But campus life for the young champion debater who had been away in the army, albeit briefly, would never again be tranquil. On 9 January 1919, the *University Weekly* announced that Brooks was resigning as its editor-in-chief, a title he had held, despite his military absence, since his election to it in May of the previous year. He said in his resignation statement that he had served three years on the paper staff and really wanted to devote more time to the YMCA, which he also headed.[52] But there was a good deal more to his resignation than time and priorities. He was about to be embroiled in a major university controversy.

University of Arkansas president, John C. Futrall, had ordered the university nurse, Nina (Ma) Harding, who had worked to save the lives of army officers quartered on campus during the influenza epidemic, to turn over to the university treasury $80 the officers had given her in gratitude for her services. He claimed that since she had served the men on university time and in university facilities the money belonged to the school. This was, of course, a perfectly tailored cause for idealistic students and faculty, and someone called a rally to oppose Futrall and his policy. As a campus leader, debater, veteran, and one of the few senior men left on campus in those days, Brooks was persuaded to speak at the meeting.

He delivered what many in the audience considered the decisive speech. He advised against a student boycott of classes, which had been proposed

---

[50]Hays, *Politics Is My Parish,* 38-40.

[51]Hays, Conversation with Ronald Tonks, May 1975.

[52]*University Weekly,* University of Arkansas, 9 January 1919.

by previous speakers, but he eloquently defended Ma Harding against the greedy president's plan to take her money, and he agreed with previous speakers that the students should file a petition with the Board of Trustees calling for the president's resignation. When the petition reached the board, its members denied all student demands and permitted Futrall to expel several student leaders. Because he had spoken against a strike, Brooks was merely suspended for three days.[53] But the protests continued, and in March the board conducted an official investigation. At a hearing, the president's opponents charged that Ma Harding had been mistreated, that Futrall was not cordial to students when he met them on campus, and that university morale was low, with little school spirit and too much alcohol. Brooks was called to testify about the charges that he had helped formulate, corroborated them all, and perhaps unwisely gave the board names of faculty members who stood with the students and against the president.

After listening to the testimony, the board declared the charges too vague and found for the president on all issues. It took no action to censure Futrall or countermand his orders.[54] The expulsion of the leading students was upheld, and professor of English Roger Williams was dismissed from the university for "conspiracy" with the students.[55] It was forty years later, in 1959, before all student and faculty offenders were officially absolved of their misdeeds. Ma Harding lost her money. President Futrall, described by Brooks as a man who valued money more than people, won his case. Many years passed before he was reconciled with some of the people who had opposed him in the matter, among them Brooks Hays.

In April 1919, while the controversy still smoldered, Brooks was persuaded to return as editor of the paper. The 10 April issue, which disclosed his acceptance, explained that the morale of the staff had been low, thus the absence of recent editions, and that Brooks would be able to give the paper new life. He held his post for only a month, until the next year's editor could be chosen.[56] With school ending and morale still low, with his college career nearing its final tattered curtain, Brooks gave up news

---

[53]Marion Hays, "How to Live Dangerously," V-8.

[54]Arkansas *Gazette* (Little Rock), 27 March 1919.

[55]Hays, *Politics Is My Parish,* 43.

[56]*University Weekly,* University of Arkansas, 10 April 1919.

gathering. His carefree university life, with its debates, religious classes, cartoons, and club meetings, had in effect ended the year before. His senior year had been filled with war, controversy, and disillusionment. His graduation photograph shows a face lean and immature, yet troubled, pouting over unresolved grievances. Brooks was not really ready to leave school, but he knew it was time to move on.

———————

Where he was to go, what he was to do with his life, these were now his big questions. He had spent his college years debating whether to be a lawyer or a minister. The two vocations tugged at his arms with virtually equal pressure. It was an issue that would not be resolved for several months yet, if indeed it ever was, but his next step along the way was determined by his father. In June, Steele Hays told Brooks he would attend law school; and in early July Brooks began packing his bags, preparing to ride a train to the nation's capital and George Washington University School of Law.

CHAPTER 2

GOTHIC ARKANSAS POLITICS

In the middle of the summer of 1919, with Brooks rapidly approaching his twenty-first birthday, at the command and with the help of his father, he caught a train that would in thirty-six hours take him from Russellville to the nation's capital. He had been accepted as a night student at George Washington University School of Law. He had landed a job at the United States Treasury, courtesy of his congressman, H. M. Jacoway.[1] He would work during the day, attend classes at night, and in three years stand for the bar.

He arrived in the District of Columbia on 19 July 1919 (his life was loaded with repeating digits), in the middle of one of Washington's intermittent race riots. The U.S. Cavalry was arrayed along Pennsylvania Avenue.[2] Brooks remembered being frightened, uncertain of his future, and lonely; but he remembered that he loved Washington almost from the first moment he saw it. Late in life he would appropriate Samuel Johnson's dictum on London—"Who does not love the City does not love life, for the City has all that life can afford"—to describe his feelings about the capital.[3] He would, by choice, spend a great part of his life there.

He roomed with Bolon Turner, a friend and classmate at the University of Arkansas, a man who would later be his law partner in Arkansas and much later, when he was Chief Judge of the U.S. Tax Court, swear

---

[1]Brooks Hays, *Politics Is My Parish* (Baton Rouge: Louisiana State University Press, 1981) 45.

[2]Brooks Hays, Conversation with Ronald Tonks, May 1975, typeset in 15 parts. Southern Baptist Sunday School Board Archives, Nashville TN.

[3]Brooks Hays, *A Hotbed of Tranquility* (New York: Macmillan, 1968) 89-90.

Brooks in as assistant to President John F. Kennedy. Brooks, Bolon, and several other "Arkansas boys" lived in an apartment house in northwest Washington. Brooks worked at the Treasury until 4:30 each day, six days a week, and attended law classes from 5:00 until 7:00 each of those evenings. "I just count twenty-dollar bills eight hours a day, six days a week," he wrote his friends, "and on Saturday night I get one of 'em."[4] It was a strenuous routine, forty hours of work and twelve hours of classes a week, and his grades were only average. He seldom made above a C; and he made only one A in three years. It was quite an adjustment for a young man who had made Phi Beta Kappa in college with ease.[5]

He was often homesick. He missed Arkansas. He missed Marion. He had wanted to marry her when he finished his degree at Fayetteville; but Steele had said no, and he had obeyed. Marion had gone back to Fort Smith to teach high school English, where she was rumored occasionally to see fellow teachers of the opposite sex socially. Brooks was unable to go home for holidays, and when he tried calling her on the telephone, he often spent half a day's pay on a conversation that was barely audible. He had no interest in other girls. He would recall the years away from Marion as some of the most painful of his life.[6]

He also had doubts about being a lawyer. He knew right away, as soon as his classes began, that he never wanted to practice law. It would at best be a door to politics, and he liked the idea of politics because for him it was public service. At one point, well into his studies at George Washington, he was in such despair about his career that he poured out his misery to his classmate and debate partner Sarah Tilghman. Sarah, who was working her way through school as a District of Columbia policewoman, would as Judge Sarah T. Hughes of Dallas administer the oath of office to President Lyndon Johnson aboard Air Force One on 22 November 1963. Sarah suggested that he talk with a minister she knew, a Lutheran pastor in Baltimore named John Fleck. After Brooks had explained to Fleck how torn he was, how he loved politics but hated the law, how he wanted to serve mankind and knew that in Arkansas that meant the gospel ministry, Fleck explained to him that God makes no distinctions between vocations, that politics could be his ministry. It was a new idea to Brooks; and he came

---

[4]Ibid., 193.

[5]Hays, *Politics Is My Parish,* 46.

[6]Ibid.

away from the conversation convinced that he could complete his law degree. He would use law as a step toward politics, which would be his ministry.[7]

Despite fatigue, loneliness, and uncertainty about his career during so many of his early months in Washington, Brooks did love the District. The first Saturday night he was in town the older "Arkansas boys" took him, against his better judgment, to the Gayety Burlesque Theater on 9th Street. To everyone's amazement, including his own, he enjoyed himself more than anyone in the group and thereafter was an incurable theatergoer.[8] The big city, with its amusements and politics, was a wondrous place for a boy from the Ozarks. He attended plays and watched politicians. He waited in line for two hours one morning in March 1920 to sit in the Senate Gallery and hear the final debate on the Treaty of Versailles.[9] He watched as even the conservative senator from Arkansas, Joe T. Robinson, spoke in favor of President Wilson's treaty. He left in despair when it was rejected.[10]

He joined the law fraternity of Phi Alpha Delta at George Washington and was invited to the White House in June 1921 to help induct President Warren G. Harding to membership. There he met Harding, former President and then Chief Justice of the Supreme Court William Howard Taft, and General of the Army and World War I hero John J. Pershing.[11] It was his first time to see and meet a president, but it would not be his last. He would meet every one from Harding to Jimmy Carter; and he would hear every one call him by his first name from Herbert Hoover through Carter. He would receive commissions from Truman, Eisenhower, Kennedy, and Johnson; and he would have an executive office in the White House under the latter two.[12] The photograph commemorating Harding's induction into Phi Alpha Delta shows Brooks kneeling with the other law students in the grass beneath the president and his assistants. Brooks is still the thin, brutally serious young man he had been two years before as a college se-

---

[7]Marion Hays, Unpublished manuscript, "How to Live Dangerously and Enjoy It," II-4. Possession of the author.

[8]Hays, *A Hotbed of Tranquility*, 194.

[9]Marion Hays, "How to Live Dangerously," II-3.

[10]Hays, *Politics Is My Parish*, 48.

[11]Ibid., 50.

[12]Hays, *A Hotbed of Tranquility*, 92.

nior. He betrays none of the jovial spirit he was reported to have shown when attending burlesque, the spirit that would one day make him one of the nation's most entertaining political orators. This talent was apparently hiding behind a mask of dedicated scholarship.

Brooks described himself while a law student as a "sermon-taster," by which he meant that he loved to visit various churches on different Sundays, not particular about the denomination, to find the best preachers.[13] The boy who had suffered through poor preaching in Arkansas was now the man free to go looking for the cream of the crop. Washington attracted the very best. Not only were there great pastors, but visiting speakers made the capital one of their favorite stops. Brooks attended services at Foundery Methodist, where he heard a succession of fine orators; First Baptist, where Henry Allen Tupper was pastor and where he once heard William Jennings Bryan preach; National Memorial Presbyterian, where pastor Charles Wood, in Brooks's opinion the city's best preacher, held forth; and Calvary Baptist, led by Will Abernathy, which Brooks considered his home church, both in law school and later when he was in Congress.

He had always loved and would always love good preaching. As a young man he had thrilled to the eloquence of Chautauqua evangelists, both political and religious; and as a Baptist he considered the preaching of the Word the centerpiece of worship. Even as an old man he enjoyed good preaching and at times lamented what he considered the passing of the great age of religious oratory. He blamed the decay of preaching on the changing priorities of modern churches, which want pastors who are more businessmen than teachers. Baptist ministers, he said, spend more time doing public relations and planning financial campaigns than in prayer and study and honing their skills in the pulpit. He suggested that no minister should preach more than one new sermon a week.[14] It is just possible that his love for good preaching, which took him around Washington to different denominations, was a second step in his ecumenical pilgrimage.

In making his rounds of churches, Brooks often saw President Harding, who himself attended Calvary Baptist. Brooks remembered after Harding's death, when the scandal of his having kept a mistress had been exposed, that the president refused to take communion with other members; and he wondered if it was because he felt unworthy to partake. He

---

[13]Hays, Conversation with Ronald Tonks, May 1975.

[14]Ibid.

also remembered how, after Marion had joined him during his last year, Harding had stared at the new Mrs. Hays; and he was astounded, when a Harding biography containing a photograph of the president's mistress appeared, to see how much Marion favored the woman. As to Harding's sexual transgressions, Brooks believed his fellow Baptist was "without venality while making little effort to control carnality." He concluded that Harding "was not hypocritical in seeking the comfort of religion and the forgiveness of God, one of whose commandments he had violated."[15] Brooks himself did consider the prohibition of adultery one of the most sacred of commandments, and he believed that violating it was wrong. He had no use for womanizers.

At long last in 1922, as he neared the end of his third and last year of law school, Brooks was able to end his own womanless existence. Marion Prather had spent almost three years as a high school teacher, waiting for a boy whose father forbade him to marry until he completed his law degree. She had dated other men, one with a bit more than passing interest, and she was having second thoughts about Brooks. He knew it was time to disobey his father and propose, which he did, only to learn, to his dismay, that she would have to give it some thought. Her mother and sister pleaded the case of the boy so far from home, so unpromising, and at last she said yes. Brooks hurried home in late January, between terms, and the marriage was performed on 2 February 1922, another of those dates with repetitive numbers that pop up so often in a review of Brooks's life.

Marion Hays would remember, sixty years later, that this Groundhog's Day was exceptionally sunny, a good omen for marriage if not for an early spring. She would remember the long day and a half train ride back to Washington and the raucous reception they were given at the train station by Brooks's law school colleagues.[16] They moved into a two-room apartment near the Capitol and settled down to five months of wedded bliss amid grinding poverty. Brooks took a job as a salesman for "The Findex" system of business organizers, a punch card system. He never sold a single one, but the company paid him $115 for his efforts. After paying rent and his $18 tuition, he was able to give himself 25¢ a day for lunch and his new wife $7.50 a week for groceries and household needs. She would at times walk an extra two blocks, to a different store, to save a penny on some ne-

---

[15]Hays, *Politics Is My Parish*, 51-52.

[16]Marion Hays, "How to Live Dangerously," II-5.

cessity. Yet despite the hardships of those days Brooks was happier than he had ever been, and his grades that last term were the best of his three years in law school.[17]

The new couple attended church regularly, but they did not agree on denominations. Brooks had often attended the Methodist church with Marion in Fayetteville, and he might have become a Methodist now had he not been afraid it might send his father to an early grave. While she was willing to attend Baptist church with him, Marion would not become a Baptist because the Baptists considered her baptism invalid and would have made her submit to immersion. And so she agreed to go with him so long as she was not pressured to join; and this she did, for sixty years, and never was pressured. Brooks would always claim that for all intents and purposes she was a Baptist, because for years she taught a Baptist Sunday school class and participated in Baptist mission work, but she never relinquished her Methodist affiliation.[18] Neither, by the way, did Ruth Graham, the wife of his friend Billy, who refused to give up her Presbyterianism when Billy became a Baptist.

Marion Hays would prove to be an almost perfect wife for the man Brooks would be. She would organize his private life, give him a secure home, support his career, and keep him humble. Politics, she always secretly believed, was "dissembling."[19] It was healthy for him to spend his life with a woman who faithfully went to his dinners, laughed over and over at his jokes, and took pride in her contempt for his profession. Brooks once mused that Marion believed a subpoena was a kind of sandwich.[20]

In his book *Politics Is My Parish,* in many ways his last will and testament, Brooks included a poem entitled "To a Patient Wife." Written in 1956, at the height of his Congressional career, when he was also deeply involved in religious activities, this poem betrays a good deal of guilt for neglecting Marion. It admits that he had neither the time nor the inclination to do chores about the house or help much with the children; and it begs her that when the grandchildren ask her to appraise his life she should

---

[17]Hays, *Politics Is My Parish,* 54.

[18]Hays, Conversation with Ronald Tonks, May 1975.

[19]Ibid.

[20]Hays, *Politics Is My Parish,* 72.

Be tender, dear, my faults conceal.
   Please make my phony virtues real.

And to sum up his feelings for the woman he had at times in frustration at her bossiness called his "Little Manager," he concludes,

I could have learned, had I not known
   One art, for which I'm famed alone:
You can be sure that loving you
   I never learned, I always knew.[21]

———————————

Brooks finished law school in June 1922 and received his LL.B. degree. By the end of the year he would receive honorary degrees from Salem College in West Virginia and the College of the Ozarks in Clarksville, Arkansas. That summer he was admitted to the Arkansas Bar, an honor he would later denigrate. He would say he had been approved on the strength of a simple oral examination that was more a test of his fitness to be a friendly fellow lawyer than his knowledge of the law. Even in later years, when the Arkansas Bar upgraded the examination by adding a written section, experienced lawyers were permitted to wander into the examination room, discuss the questions openly with the candidates, and help them write their answers.[22] According to Brooks, it continued to be, as it had been in 1922, an induction ceremony for new members of a "good old boys" club; and for Brooks, never keen on the practice of law, it was not a source of pride to be admitted.

Just before leaving the capital for his plunge back into Arkansas life, Brooks clipped a Berryman cartoon from the 13 June 1922 edition of the Washington *Evening Star* and pasted it in his scrapbook. It showed a middle-aged man at his desk and a bespeckled youth, diploma in hand, tapping him on the shoulder, saying, "Now, Dad, you need a rest. I'm ready to take hold." There is no doubt that this expressed Brooks's own feelings, his desire to return home, put his father out to pasture, and start remaking the world. He knew, of course, that this was not likely to happen. He knew Arkansas and its ways, and he knew Steele Hays.

What actually happened was predictable. Brooks passed the bar, as his father expected, and he settled down in Russellville to practice in his fa-

———————————

[21]Ibid., 283.

[22]Ibid., 56.

ther's law firm, as his father also expected. The only real pleasure Brooks found during his first year home came from politics. Almost immediately upon his return he learned that Steele had unexpectedly decided to declare his candidacy for Congress, for the seat being vacated by Representative Jacoway, and Brooks gleefully signed on as his campaign manager. Steele was fifty years old, his son Brooks was twenty-three. Steele seems to have had little personal desire to run, but with friends encouraging him he reluctantly agreed. Brooks would later say that his father lacked the inner urge to succeed at politics. It was an urge Brooks had, and he enjoyed the campaign immensely, even while his father was just going through the motions.

Steele lost the race. His reputation as an alcoholic, though no longer accurate since he had not had a drink for seven years, hurt him in the Baptist Fifth Congressional District. His own church in Russellville did not trust him enough to ordain him as a deacon. His gregarious personality and rugged good looks could not compensate for what was considered to be his weakness for alcohol. Then too there was the Ku Klux Klan. One of Steele's two opponents, Heartsill Ragon, was an active Klansman. Steele had never been a Klansman and made a point of bragging about it during the campaign, so he and the third candidate split the anti-Klan vote, enabling Ragon to win the Democratic nomination in August and thus the general election in November.[23]

Steele ran.third in the race, and Brooks had his first lesson in Gothic Arkansas politics when as his father's manager he had to refuse a request that he "switch" some of Steele's votes to the second-place candidate. To do so would, of course, have helped defeat the Klansman, a good thing, but the idea of playing fast and loose with the people's trust was repugnant to the idealistic young Brooks. He would encounter vote "switching" several times in his own political career, he would never take part in it, and he would always be on the losing end when it occurred.

The Klan was strong in Arkansas in 1922, with outright political control in a few counties, but the Hayses assiduously avoided having anything to do with it. Brooks had, as a matter of fact, been invited by the nephew of the Imperial Wizard to join a student branch at George Washington University School of Law. He declined. Back home in Russellville he was asked by the head of the Arkansas Klan, Ellsworth Combs, to in-

---

[23]Marion Hays, "How to Live Dangerously," III-1.

troduce him when he came to town for a speech. Again Brooks declined, although he did attend the rally.[24] He would admit late in his life, a bit shamefacedly, that in those early days he spoke out against the Klan very sparingly, that his criticism was muted, that he never rebuked fellow Democrats for being members or accepting Klan support, and that his protest against its activities was through his personal refusal to join, to accept support, or to use racism in his campaigns. When asked why, if he did not rebuke the Klan, he did not accept its support, he was scandalized. "Oh well, my great goodness!" he huffed. "I just felt it was an outrageous violation of our standards of tolerance and brotherhood."[25] The times, however, were against him, to the end of his career.

The campaign may have been lost, but it did win for Brooks his father's respect. Although he would have to settle down and take his father's unwanted cases and be a subservient son, he could now kid with his father and debate him on political issues. Their exchanges became legendary. One example, which was repeated every time Brooks introduced Steele at a rally, started with Brooks's saying, "I love every white hair in his old head," to which Steele would reply, "He ought to—he put every one of 'em there."[26] If Steele continued to be, in Marion's words, "Czar Hays," at least Brooks, now a college and law school graduate and a veteran of a political campaign, was the Czarevitch.

His apprenticeship in Steele's law firm would seem to Brooks to be long and tedious. In the fall following his father's defeat in the August primary, he attended the state Democratic Convention in Little Rock and was elected its secretary, the youngest man in history to hold that position. This was heady stuff for a man just turned twenty-four and only four months out of law school. He could see his political career about to take off. But then, back home in Russellville, reality set in. He found himself the very junior partner in the law firm of Hays, Priddy, Hays. His father and his father's partner, A. B. Priddy, saw to it that he knew and kept his place; and they would do so until two and a half years later when the restless, ambitious young man escaped.

He had never really wanted to practice law, and now as his father gave him the dregs of the cases that came to the firm he was convinced he was

---

[24]Ibid., III-3.

[25]Hays, Conversation with Ronald Tonks, July 1975.

[26]Marion Hays, "How to Live Dangerously," III-1.

not meant to be a small town lawyer.[27] Because Steele would not give him important cases, the town's people distrusted him, preferring "the old heads." One man who came in and asked to see Steele, then A. B. Priddy, responded to the news that only Mr. Brooks Hays was available, "I'll just wait for one of the lawyers."[28] Brooks was still his dad's little boy, and even the children in town called him by his Christian name. Once when Brooks was pleading one of the *pro bono* cases, that of a black man whose leg had been cut off by a train, Steele came into the court, took over the case, and made the final plea.[29]

As a result of his relegation to trivial cases, Brooks had plenty of time free to become the firm's public relations man. He did the best he could with a bad situation. He taught himself that charity cases helped him fulfill his ministry. He might have been a prophet without honor in his hometown, but so had Jesus, and after all a prophet is a prophet. He became a kind of civic cheerleader, helping Russellville secure a chapter of the Lions Club, establishing Russellville's first public library, and seeing to it that the city's first public playground was built.[30] All this was done with tact, sincerity, and a sense of humor. In fact, it was at this time that the patented Brooks Hays humor emerged. For years people remembered the time he was defending one of the charity cases, a man accused of disturbing the peace, and the defendant's sons began fighting in the court room. Brooks ran toward the bailiff shouting, "I demand protection."[31] Only once during the two and a half years of his law practice in Russellville did he make any money, and this was $600 for settling a divorce decree. With his earnings, he bought a Ford automobile.[32]

His law career might have foundered in Russellville, but his active religious life did not. No sooner had he arrived home from law school than he plunged into church work. In September of 1922 he was named superintendent of First Baptist's Sunday school, a job quite often given to an unsuspecting newcomer, but Brooks eagerly took it and worked hard at it. In

---

[27]Hays, Conversation with Ronald Tonks, July 1975.

[28]Hays, *A Hotbed of Tranquility,* 144.

[29]Hays, Conversation with Ronald Tonks, September 1975.

[30]Marion Hays, "How to Live Dangerously," III-8-9.

[31]Hays, *A Hotbed of Tranquility,* 145-46.

[32]Hays, *Politics Is My Parish,* 62.

1923 he was ordained a deacon, at last legitimately holding the title he had been given in college. As a matter of fact, he was chosen deacon before his father, who had been passed over because of his alcoholism, and was one of those who helped ordain Steele when he was finally elected.[33]

Church life in Russellville was not always smooth for Brooks, despite his quick advancement. His liberalism, which was unusual for the area, was tolerated; but at times it caused friction. A visiting evangelist once asked the First Baptist congregation to stand as testimony that they would all fight the evil of dancing. Everyone in the building stood except Brooks. Even Marion, who loved to dance and did not consider it a sin, joined the herd and rose to her feet beside him. The next day the evangelist sent a delegation of zealous church members to Brooks's law office to persuade him to join the crusade against demon dance, and he had to turn on his broadest charm to avoid a nasty scene.[34] There was even some opposition to his ordination as a deacon because he had permitted his wife to remain a Methodist. He was accused by an elderly deacon of failing a Biblical requirement for a deacon, that he must be the master of his own household. A Hays ally helped him out of it by pointing out that his accuser, a bachelor, did not himself fulfill the Biblical requirement that a deacon must be the husband of one wife. Everyone, including the bachelor, had a good laugh, and Brooks was ordained.

The direst threat to his ecclesiastical tranquility, however, came when he refused to join the Ku Klux Klan. His pastor, Reverend Jennings, was himself a Klansman, and Brooks once recalled that of all the men in his church only he and his father had refused to join. One Sunday night the pastor invited the local chapter to attend services, and a white hooded band passed silently down the aisle as Jennings glowed and the Hays family looked on in dismay.[35] Brooks weathered the storm, however, and when Jennings moved on in 1923 he helped bring a progressive young graduate of Southern Baptist Seminary in Louisville, Clyde Hickerson, to be the pastor. Hickerson would remain there for twelve years and weather a storm or two himself. But, in the end, he raised the tone of Baptist life in that part of Arkansas and gave Brooks some hope for his church.

---

[33]Hays, Conversation with Ronald Tonks, July 1975.

[34]Ibid.

[35]Marion Hays, "How to Live Dangerously," III-3.

On 23 October 1923, another of those dates with repetitive digits, Marion Hays gave birth to a daughter, delivered by a midwife, and she and Brooks named her Betty Brooks. To this point the young couple had lived with Steele and Sallie; but now they bought a $4,000 house and went to live on their own.[36] The daughter Betty would go on to be a University of Arkansas coed, marry a childhood friend named William E. Bell, and have two children, a son Keith born in 1946 and daughter Caroline Quinn born in 1948. She and her husband and children would be Baptists. She would grow to be tall and thin like her father and lighthearted like her mother. She would be a female deacon and a progressive church woman. She would never look her age and would seem destined to live into her 90s, as did her mother and her mother's mother before her.

In the summer of 1924, chaffing at the bit under his mostly tedious law routine, Brooks jumped at the chance for some excitement. H. W. Applegate of Jonesboro, across the state, asked him to manage his campaign for Arkansas Attorney General. It was understood that if Applegate won Brooks would be made his assistant.[37] Brooks knew that Applegate was a member of the Klan, but so was Applegate's opponent. Therefore, Brooks guessed it would not be an issue in the race, as it was not. Since one Klansman or another was bound to win, Brooks did not feel he was violating his principles by helping one of them. He accepted the offer.

The campaign lasted six weeks, and Applegate won. He offered Brooks the promised job, and the following January Brooks moved his small family to Little Rock. He was now Assistant Attorney General of Arkansas, in charge of Civil Law cases.[38] He would hold the office for exactly two years, until January of 1927, when he would leave for a brief, unhappy stint selling insurance. His work in the attorney general's office gave him his first taste of political power, even if that power was at the behest of someone else. He travelled extensively, was involved in several modestly famous tax cases, and spread his name as widely as he could across the state, keeping an eye cocked for an office he might like to seek for himself one day. During his tenure he advocated a minimum wage for women and helped the state legislature draft a bill to promote county libraries, which when passed was Arkansas' first library law.

---

[36]Hays, *Politics Is My Parish,* 62.

[37]Ibid., 70-71.

[38]Hays, Conversation with Ronald Tonks, July 1975.

One of his cases gave him wide publicity. It involved seven men the acting governor had pardoned from the state penitentiary and the governor
wanted returned. Brooks pleaded the governor's case before the Arkansas
Supreme Court and won by a vote of 3–2. Despite the praise he won for his
work, from governmental officials, the press, and the public, Brooks remembered hating to see the men returned to a prison system he knew was
one of the nation's most brutal. He went to Texas to ask Texas Governor
"Ma" Ferguson to extradite one of the seven; and when "Ma" Ferguson decided she could not do so, Brooks came home emptyhanded, hailed in the
press for trying, and not at all unhappy that the man was still free: a complete victory.[39]

Interestingly enough, at about the time Brooks was appearing before
the Arkansas Supreme Court, his son, who would one day be a justice of
that court, was born in Little Rock. The boy arrived on 3 March 1925 and
was named Marion Steele. He would follow his father by attending the
University of Arkansas and George Washington University School of Law
and by becoming a lawyer. A quiet, almost shy man, he would run for office
only when he was past fifty and then only to seek the seat on the Supreme
Court. He would have a son named Steele III born in 1953 and a daughter
Melissa born in 1955.[40] With his first wife he would join the Presbyterians,
with his second the Episcopalians. As informal and down-to-earth as his
father, with his father's shambling walk, he is not the politician his father
was—and does not regret it.

In Little Rock, where they would make their home from 1925 to 1943
and their headquarters from 1925 to 1959, the Hays family attended Second Baptist Church, which was at that time considered Little Rock's leading church.[41] There Brooks was immediately drafted to teach a Sunday
school class made up of fifteen or so professional men. Brooks would prove
to be an immensely popular teacher, despite his occasional outbreaks of
liberalism, and the class grew to an eventual membership of 350.[42] As it
grew it was moved out of the church to a small building behind the church,
then to a larger one, and finally to one as large as many small-town

---

[39]Hays, *Politics Is My Parish,* 73-74.

[40]Hays, Conversation with Ronald Tonks, July 1975.

[41]Ibid.

[42]Marion Hays, "How to Live Dangerously," IV-1.

churches.[43] It became such a formidable unit that it started meeting for lunch each Wednesday. A year after he took the class it voted to drop its previous name and call itself "The Brooks Hays Class," this over the teacher's protests, and it remained that the rest of his life.

From the beginning the Brooks Hays class was an odd mix of men, everything from fundamentalist Baptists, to liberal Protestants, a few Catholics, and even an occasional Jew. Several men attended Brooks's class before going on to their own churches for the 11:00 worship service. They might have been of different denominations, but they considered themselves all "Brooks's Disciples."[44] Although he never forgot that Little Rock and Arkansas in general were conservative territory, Brooks taught his class "progressive" Christianity.[45] The class gave him an allowance to buy books, and he used it all to buy and read the more liberal theologians. When in 1928 Norman Thomas came to Little Rock and asked if there were any liberals in the city, he was told that there was only one, a lawyer who taught Sunday school at Second Baptist Church.

Brooks tried not to offend conservative sensibilities, but the men admired him for never pulling his punches. He had a number of memorable debates with members, particularly those who were disturbed when he questioned the infallibility of the Bible or racial bigotry, but none of the men ever doubted his sincerity or his Christian devotion, and very few left the class over disagreements with their teacher. His open mind and wonderful wit kept disputations from becoming personal. Brooks always said that the secret of his success lay in the fact that he had no desire to make the men over in his own image, that he preferred instead to reach them with what he believed to be the heart of the gospel, "with the Christian spirit."[46]

Because his occupation was politics and he grew more political as the years went by, Brooks had to struggle to keep politics out of his Sunday school class. Although it robbed him of good examples and subject matter, he tried not to ride any political hobby horses on Sundays. In 1928, during his first race for governor, he had to squash a move among class members

[43]Hays, *Politics Is My Parish,* 72.

[44]Marion Hays, "How to Live Dangerously," IV-1.

[45]Hays, Conversation with Ronald Tonks, July 1975.

[46]Ibid.

to pass a resolution supporting his candidacy. In 1930 he and two of his class members were all in the race for governor, and he had to walk a tightrope to keep from dividing the class.[47] In the 1948 presidential election he supported Harry Truman, his party's nominee, and some of his class members advocated censuring him and changing the class's name. After the election, with Truman carrying the state, the noise died down, and the dissidents sheepishly returned to the fold.[48]

As he observed Arkansas' social problems from the vantage point of the attorney general's office, Brooks grew ever more critical of his Baptist denomination. Baptists seemed to believe that the church's only responsibility to mankind was to bring men personal salvation, that there was no need to do social work to improve men's physical environment. The literature coming to churches from the Nashville denominational headquarters followed a strictly conservative social philosophy. Baptist churches were not the democratic institutions they were said to be because the voices of average members were unheard and unheeded. And Baptists, by being taught that their church was the only true body of Christ, were losing the benefit of sharing religious experiences with other denominations.[49]

Brooks decided to do something about these imperfections. At the 1927 Arkansas Baptist Convention he introduced a resolution to make a study of the needs of rural churches: their poverty, ignorance, isolation. This would be a start toward improving their lot. A committee was named, with Brooks as its chairman. The committee's report the following year was well-received, despite its rather progressive suggestions, but little was done to implement these suggestions. This did not discourage Brooks. At a later convention he introduced a resolution that Arkansas Baptists support the United States' membership in the World Court, and this was also approved, despite the fact that many delegates had trouble deciding what it had to do with spreading the Gospel. Brooks was developing an image as a young religious activist, a bit off center but probably harmless, a fanatic by Arkansas standards but still a sincere man.

In 1928 his image changed. That year he ceased being merely a political appointee and an entertaining religious teacher and jumped into the ring as a candidate for governor of Arkansas. For a year after he left the

---

[47]Hays, *Politics Is My Parish,* 72.

[48]Hays, Conversation with Ronald Tonks, July 1975.

[49]Hays, *Politics Is My Parish,* 66.

attorney general's office he had been sales manager for the Pyramid Insurance Company of Arkansas, headquartered in Little Rock, but he had
realized soon enough that he was not cut out for the secure, dull life of office records and three-piece suits. Early in 1928 he had formed a law partnership with his old George Washington University classmate Bolon
Turner, a partnership that would last for six years, through two races for
governor and one for Congress, through the start of a major economic
depression, until in 1934 Turner took a job with the District of Columbia
Tax Court and Brooks went to work for the N.R.A.[50] Soon after he and
Turner opened their doors Brooks declared his candidacy for governor.

Oddly enough, he had not until just before the filing deadline aspired
to the governorship. Had he not bowed to the wishes of his friend John Carter, who himself wanted to run for attorney general, he would have sought
that lesser office that year. Having ruled the attorney general's race out,
he decided to go for broke and try for the state's top job. On 28 February
Governor John E. Martineau had vacated his office to accept an appointment to the federal bench, and former Lt. Governor Harvey Parnell, now
governor, had shown little interest in running for reelection. The office appeared to be wide open.[51] Eventually there would be seven Democrats in
the field for the August primary, which in Democratic Arkansas was tantamount to election in November, and Harvey Parnell was one of them.
The big money supported him because he was a known and apparently safe
quantity.

Brooks once said that beginning with his race for governor in 1928, "for
a good part of my life election years have been oases";[52] and he ran this
race as all subsequent ones with the gusto of a man slaking the thirst of a
long ride through the desert of law and business. He was only twenty-nine
years old that primary season and had to assure officials that he would pass
the mandatory age of thirty by primary election day in August. He threw
himself into the campaign as only a young man could with an energy appropriate to his age. He was called "the cheerful crusader" in a summer
when Franklin D. Roosevelt gave the name "happy warrior" to Demo-

---

[50]Ibid., 76.

[51]Brooks Hays, *This World: A Christian's Workshop* (Nashville: Broadman
Press, 1968) 45.

[52]Ibid., 46.

cratic presidential candidate Al Smith.[53] He delivered 303 speeches, or as he would later joke, the same speech 303 times,[54] and in two months crisscrossed a state where most of the roads were still dirt. He enjoyed every minute of it. At first the conventional wisdom said, "He's a nice boy. He'll run 4th." But as he gained support and refused to pull his punches he began to be seen as a "trouble maker" and "mud slinger."[55]

Brooks began the campaign by setting out a visionary set of goals for the state: aid to public schools, a state income tax, a state hospital, a runoff for the two highest candidates in each Democratic primary, a plan to attract industry to rural areas, and reform in highway financing.[56] For his platform, as modest as it would later sound, he was labelled an idealist. When the Socialist leader Norman Thomas came to Little Rock during the campaign and was told that the only liberal around was Brooks Hays, he met with Brooks and wished him well but avoided saddling him with negative publicity by a public endorsement. Instead he said in a speech that he had been told six of the gubernatorial candidates were crooks and that one was still young enough to become one.[57]

Typically the election refused to respond to the issues Brooks proposed and focused instead on other matters. For Brooks one was age. He never denied that he was under thirty and tried instead to emphasize his experience and education; but it was a hard issue to quiet. At one point during the long, hot summer, he got sick and his doctor thought he had chickenpox. Coming down with a child's disease would, of course, have confirmed the charge that he was just "a kid," and several of his aids threatened to quit. He was greatly relieved when the rash went away without further damage to his candidacy.[58]

A second issue was his family and their purported wealth. Although Steele Hays had started his adult life in poverty, he was now considered a successful man, rather better off than the fathers of other candidates, and this was used against Brooks. Newspaper ads said that he had been born

---

[53]Hays, *Politics Is My Parish,* 83.

[54]Hays, *This World: A Christian's Workshop,* 44.

[55]Hays, *Politics Is My Parish,* 81.

[56]Marion Hays, "How to Live Dangerously," IV-3.

[57]Hays, Conversation with Ronald Tonks, September 1977.

[58]Hays, *Politics Is My Parish,* 83.

to wealth, with a silver spoon in his mouth, that his father had paid for his schooling and supported him in law. He had served a mere three months in the army and two years as a political appointee. Brooks's ads countered that since he was so honest, since his was the only record among the candidates' that no one could attack, the opposition had decided to make it personal. "Arkansas is following the fine example of Texas and Louisiana," the ads said, emphasizing his rise in public support, "by electing a clean, capable, vigorous Christian Gentleman as Governor."[59] This would be one of the few times that Brooks would overtly use religion in campaigning.

Still another issue was the teaching of Darwinism in the Arkansas public schools. In response to the law in Tennessee that resulted in the 1925 Scopes Monkey Trial in Dayton, the Arkansas legislature had earlier in 1928 proposed a similar law and put it on the ballot for referendum in November. In an address to the United Daughters of the Confederacy, back in the spring before declaring his candidacy, Brooks had gone on record as opposing any move to ban any specific matter from being taught in the schools, including Darwinism.[60] He had said that as a Baptist he believed in the separation of church and state and that he therefore could not support a law that permitted religion to tell the state what is and is not true. But several newspapers had reported the speech under the headline "Sunday School Teacher Opposes Anti-Evolution Bill," and during the campaign Brooks was labelled an evolutionist.[61] It is likely that secretly he was, but it was not politic in the state of Arkansas to be one.

Fortunately for him none of his opponents was able to exploit the issue effectively. He was able to skirt it by saying that he preferred to let the people speak on the subject in November, but it still dogged his steps. After giving a speech on the income tax in Big Flat, for instance, an old man called out, "Yeah, but how do you stand on evolution?" Brooks's fancy answer caused another man there that day to say, "If Brooks is as good a two-stepper as he is a sidestepper, I'll bet he's popular at them Little Rock dances."[62] The referendum, by the way, passed in November, and Arkansas officially banned the teaching of evolution in public schools for the next forty years.

---

[59]Arkansas *Gazette* (Little Rock) 1 August 1928.

[60]Hays, Conversation with Ronald Tonks, July 1975.

[61]Ibid.

[62]Hays, *A Hotbed of Tranquility*, 102.

Only one of the issues Brooks himself raised became central to the campaign; and that one, while later proving him right, worked to raise him above the opposition only to put him down again. It was the state government's support of road bonds. Brooks warned throughout the campaign that certain selfish interests were making big money at the people's expense, that the financial base of the bonds was insecure, and that when the scheme collapsed, honest investors would lose their money.[63] All of which proved all too true at a later time. But in 1928 Brooks was one of the few people and the only candidate for governor to say so publicly. Harvey Parnell openly embraced the Martineau bond scheme, and the people behind it rushed to him with campaign contributions. Brooks spent $25,000 on the campaign, $5,000 of it his own family's money, but he was outspent many times over by forces bent on keeping reform movements of any sort out of power.[64]

It was in this race for governor that Brooks said he first realized the power of his tongue. He learned how easy it was for him to sway large crowds, like the 15,000 who gathered in a Little Rock square for his final address, and how natural it came to say things that people remembered and quoted. At twenty-nine he was a young William Jennings Bryan. But he worried, as he watched the wistful expressions on the faces of people in his crowds, that should the vision he shared with them not come true they would be either disheartened or encouraged to turn to violence. He remembered pulling back, toning down his speeches, for fear he might become a demagogue by exploiting aspirations, that he might climb to power on the misfortunes of his fellow man by raising hopes he could not fulfill.[65] Even the humor he used, and would use the rest of his career, was tempered by the realization that he could injure people with it. He began to turn it, as he would from then on, on himself.[66]

A comparison to Huey Long of neighboring Louisiana is inevitable here. In the same year, 1928, Long was elected governor of Louisiana at the age of thirty-five, having lost the same race four years earlier. Long was indeed a demagogue, using the aspirations of his poor constituents to gain

---

[63]Hays, Conversation with Ronald Tonks, July 1975.

[64]Hays, *Politics Is My Parish*, 81-82.

[65]Hays, Conversation with Ronald Tonks, May 1975.

[66]Hays, *A Hotbed of Tranquility*, 5.

power so he could do battle with big money interests and "Bourbons." It is amusing, if in the end futile, to speculate what might have happened had Brooks been willing to play demagogue and been elected governor of Arkansas in 1928; had he spent a couple of terms reforming or pretending to reform his state while building a political machine; and had he then gone on to the United States Senate in 1932 to help Roosevelt pass New Deal legislation through the 1930s. It is an entirely believable scenario to imagine his being chosen F.D.R.'s vice-presidential running mate in 1944, a Southern progressive just forty-six, and being President of the United States at the end of the war, when his crowning achievement would have been the founding of the United Nations. But, of course, historical fiction is just that.

Brooks always believed that he took the lead in the race two weeks before the primary and that big highway money bought the election from him. He claimed to know of widespread vote buying, and he was convinced that late-reporting counties padded Parnell's margin of victory. Still he ran a strong second on 14 August, carried the city of Little Rock, and easily outdistanced former governor Tom J. Terral. Parnell was awarded 90,000 votes to Brooks's 60,000. Had Arkansas had a run-off for the nomination, he might well have won; but there was no primary, and Parnell was the winner. Despite his loss, he had surprised and impressed a lot of people, and his chances in future elections seemed excellent.[67]

A couple of things that happened during the 1928 campaign demonstrate the character of the young Brooks Hays and predict his future. One was that he took note, as none of the other candidates seems to have done, of the black faces at the fringes of all his rally crowds—and that he was aware that all the better things he wanted for Arkansas would not necessarily benefit them. He was haunted by the way they listened so intently, and he knew that they dreamed of the good life just as whites did, but he was not sure that he would ever be able to help them.[68] Another was the way he reacted when during one of his speeches someone tried to hush a crowd of children. He scolded the man and explained that the children were his natural constituency, that they knew he spoke for them, and that

---

[67]Hays, *Politics Is My Parish*, 86.

[68]Brooks Hays, *A Southern Moderate Speaks* (Chapel Hill: University of North Carolina Press, 1959) 3.

if they could vote he would win in a landslide.[69] Brooks was forever thinking of the future, of the time when children would be adults. Sure enough it was in 1942, when those very children could vote, that he won a seat in Congress. His attitude, of course, brings to mind that of another young man who also loved children and scolded the persons who would silence them. Brooks was, perhaps unconsciously, imitating his Master.

Once the primary was behind him and he did not have to run anymore, Brooks plunged headlong into the 1928 presidential campaign in support of Al Smith of New York and his vice-presidential running mate, Senator Joe T. Robinson of Arkansas. Although the ticket carried the state, Brooks's enthusiasm for it was not popular. His endorsements, which included a number of public addresses and a key statewide radio debate, met with some hostility, particularly when he argued that Smith's Roman Catholicism should not be an excuse for Democratic Arkansas to go Republican. Even his wife Marion and his mother Sallie voted for Herbert Hoover, excusing themselves by saying they were against Smith because he favored repeal of the eighteenth amendment, prohibition. Even Brooks's Sunday school class at Second Baptist felt obliged to protest his support for Smith. But he held his ground. Although he disagreed with Smith's contention that anyone who questioned his religious positions was a bigot, he supported his party's nominee to the end, and he was always proud of having done so.[70]

The year 1929 was profitable for Hays and Turner, Attorneys at Law. Brooks's creditable showing in the Democratic primary the year before brought notoriety and clients to the fledgling firm. Bolon Turner took the more lucrative cases, the ones Brooks considered dull, freeing Brooks to do the more interesting but often *pro bono* ones. One of his friends called it "gathering goat feathers,"[71] but Brooks considered it social work, fulfilling his ministry, and he thrived on it. He served as chairman of the board of deacons at Second Baptist and taught his Sunday school class there. He served as director of the Arkansas Tuberculosis Association and as president of the Pulaski County Children's Home and Hospital. He chaired a committee to plan a new county home for the indigent. He was a member

---

[69]Hays, *A Hotbed of Tranquility,* 12.

[70]Hays, *Politics Is My Parish,* 86.

[71]Ibid., 99.

of the board of directors of the Little Rock YMCA and headed the finance campaign of the Community Fund. He was president of the Arkansas Conference of Social Work, first chairman of the Arkansas Rural Church Commission, and a member of the Baptist State Executive Committee.[72]

He was rewarded for all these volunteer labors by being appointed a referee for the state probate court, bringing even more business to the firm; but he said his greater reward was the satisfaction of knowing he was helping right some of the wrongs he had seen all his life. He had since childhood seen the effects of poverty, ignorance, and disease on the lives of people around him, and he wanted to help soften some of the blows.[73] Yet he knew that this type of volunteer social work had its limits. What he really needed was political power, the power of the vote behind him, to make things change for the better. And running for office was so very much fun.

So it was that only a year and a half after his bittersweet defeat in 1928 Brooks declared on 1 March 1930 that he would try again. He said he had a moral obligation, as the man who had predicted a scandal in road bonds, to continue his crusade, even though he knew a second race would be even more difficult than the first had been. The bond program had not been reformed; Arkansas now had the highest per capita debt in the nation, due to the highway program; the highway commission was corrupt, and Governor Parnell was too weak to do anything about the mess. To remain on the sidelines, he said with vigor, would be to sell out his people.[74]

He was approached by Parnell's supporters and promised that if he would sit out the 1930 election they would all support him in 1932. Should they make good on their promise, he would be governor at the age of thirty-four and have a long career ahead of him. But waiting, for him, meant selling his soul, saying in effect that he supported Parnell; and, of course, Parnell's supporters would expect him to do their bidding once in office. He would not be able to face his followers. He had to run now.[75]

Steele Hays bitterly opposed the decision. He considered it certain political death. For the first time in his life Brooks asserted his manhood and overruled his father. He tried to explain to him that he preferred doing the

---

[72]Marion Hays, "How to Live Dangerously," IV-11.

[73]Hays, Conversation with Ronald Tonks, July 1975.

[74]Ibid., September 1975.

[75]Marion Hays, "How to Live Dangerously," IV-8.

right thing to winning. It did little good. In the end he went to register his candidacy without his father's permission. Brooks would later recall this first rejection of paternal authority and muse about the difference between himself and his father. Steele never understood how thrilling Brooks found the game of politics. For Steele it was a deadly serious business, for Brooks a pleasant holiday. Yet Brooks was the more idealistic of the two and truly believed that politics could lead him to a place of power where he could help people.[76]

Once again road bonds became the major issue of the campaign. "They Have Spent The Money! They Have Not Built The Roads!" ran Brooks's ads in all the newspapers.[77] He seldom mentioned the governor, except to commend him for the way he had accomplished such 1928 Hays plans as a state income tax, a new state hospital, and more state appropriations for public schools.[78] But while he did not criticize the governor, he did blast the governor's administration. His speeches brought the administration into such question that later it would be investigated and found to be the most corrupt administration the state had seen since Reconstruction. "The Public Good Above Private Gain," read banners at Hays rallies. Again, as in 1928, he said too many bonds were being issued, the system would collapse, and the rich would leave the poor holding the empty bag. He made 227 speeches in three months, fewer than in 1928, but this time he used radio to carry his message across the state.[79]

The campaign had its tricky moments. In the heat of the battle Brooks learned on good authority that one of the banks supporting Parnell was about to be closed. He could have used this information against the governor but decided not to do so for fear it might cause a panic and hurt the banking system in general. At another point in the campaign the other antiadministration candidate offered to consolidate forces with Brooks; and when Brooks declined the offer, he accused Brooks of offering him a bribe to drop out of the race.[80] Brooks, of course, denied the charge, but it seemed

---

[76]Hays, Conversation with Ronald Tonks, September 1975.

[77]Arkansas *Gazette* (Little Rock) 13 July 1930.

[78]Hays, *Politics Is My Parish,* 100.

[79]Ibid., 103–104.

[80]Ibid., 106.

to hurt him on election day. He was no longer the pure young candidate of 1928.

According to Brooks's estimates, Parnell's people spent $350,000 to see him reelected, an astronomical sum for the day.[81] On primary election day, 12 August, Brooks received 90,000 votes, 30,000 more than he had received in 1928; but Parnell got 135,000. Brooks had run second again. He had kept his word and run a good race; but now his name was slightly tainted by the hint of bribery, and he was now also considered a loser. It did not appear he would be able to raise money for a third race. At the age of thirty-two he was close to being a political has-been.

In addition to all these depressing developments, the Great Depression was itself now in full swing. Having had no stock in Wall Street, Brooks and his family had not at first felt the immensity of the economic downturn that had started the year before. By late 1930, however, hard times could be felt everywhere and by everyone. Hays and Turner lost clients because people could not afford retainer fees. A joke circulated among Little Rock jurists: "I had a good week. Had one $10 fee, one $15, and two or three little bitty ones."[82] Brooks made hardly anything at law. He made $5 to $10 a session teaching elocution at YMCA buildings in Little Rock, Conway, and Hot Springs. He earned $150 for organizing Lions Clubs around the state one year. His father sent him $15 a week, and he gave Marion $10 of that for groceries. The heady 1920s were over—the bleak 1930s were at hand.

---

[81]Marion Hays, "How to Live Dangerously," IV-8.

[82]Hays, Conversation with Ronald Tonks, September 1975.

CHAPTER 3

NEW DEAL AMERICA

The year 1932 saw Brooks, like most Americans of the day, reach his financial nadir. He had to live and support a family off small retainers, tuition from elocution lessons, and his father's beneficence. Yet he still dreamed of public office, specifically the governorship, and would have declared his candidacy again had his father's law partner, A. B. Priddy, not decided it was his year to run.

Priddy was at first indecisive about the race he had always wanted to make, and at one point he was so sure he would not run that he had Brooks tip off the Little Rock papers that he was out for 1932. Then he changed his mind and declared, and out of loyalty to family and friends, Brooks bowed out of a race he could probably have won. He supported Priddy, even campaigned for him, but did so half-heartedly. Priddy's ignoble defeat in the August primary was a fitting climax to what Brooks would one day describe as a truly "miserable summer" of anxiety and frustration.[1] Once again a gubernatorial inauguration would leave him outside the mansion's front gate.

The summer was not, however, a total loss. As a matter of fact, it saw Brooks win his first statewide election, not the one he wanted to win but one that would help him survive the Depression. He let his friends place his name on the ballot for Democratic National Committeeman; and despite the fact that he refused to campaign for himself, only once making the statement that he stood as an alternative to his Little Rock corporate

---

[1]Brooks Hays, Conversation with Ronald Tonks, September 1975, typeset in 15 parts. Southern Baptist Sunday School Board Archives, Nashville TN.

lawyer opponent, he was overwhelmingly elected.[2] After rejecting a $2,500 bribe by his opponent to withdraw, he carried seventy-three of Arkansas' seventy-five counties and garnered the largest popular vote of anyone in any of the races, including the totals credited to Joe T. Robinson in his re-election to the United States Senate. This proved to Brooks that had he run for governor that year, given the name recognition and public image he had forged in the two previous races, he would have been elected the state's chief executive. He would easily be reelected committeeman in 1936 and hold the office until the Hatch Act, which forbade holding both a government and a political job, forced him to resign in 1939.[3]

Brooks spent the fall of 1932 working for the party's presidential nominee, Franklin Delano Roosevelt. He organized a successful fund raiser, the sale of campaign medallions at a dollar each, and proudly turned over the sum of $4,500 to Roosevelt personally in a St. Louis hotel.[4] He remembered later that he was not particularly impressed with the Roosevelt he met that day. He found him too cautious, given the economic crisis facing the nation, not willing enough to entertain radical ideas, and not particularly statesmanlike. He would, of course, later change his mind on all counts. But he preferred Roosevelt to Hoover, and his support did pay off. Not only did F.D.R. become the president Brooks wanted, bringing the New Deal to America, but he would be a real friend to Brooks Hays. He would keep Brooks in federal jobs throughout the Depression, he would protect Brooks from the eastern Arkansas "Bourbons" who would have destroyed him, and he would have made him a federal judge in 1936 had Arkansas Senator Hattie Caraway not blocked Brooks's nomination.[5]

Early in 1933, however, Brooks was in desperate straits. He had been forced to move his family back to Russellville, and his income was nil. He was in Washington in March 1933, looking for a job with the first Democratic administration in twelve years, and stood in the anxious crowd to hear F.D.R.'s inaugural address. Upon his return to Arkansas he received a call from Frances Perkins, the new Secretary of Labor, offering him a

---

[2]Ibid.

[3]Brooks Hays, *This World: A Christian's Workshop* (Nashville: Broadman Press, 1968) 5.

[4]Hays, Conversation with Ronald Tonks, September 1975.

[5]Ibid.

position with her office.[6] He would have taken it on the spot had there not been one complicating factor. Fifth District Congressman Heartsill Ragon, the man who had defeated Steele Hays for the seat in 1922, had announced that he was vacating his office to accept a federal judgeship.[7] Brooks felt certain, because he had carried the entire state the year before in being elected committeeman, that he could carry his own home district. To do so would mean a new life in Washington and an opportunity to help Roosevelt solve the nation's economic crisis. It was a challenge he could not refuse.

Once again Steele, perhaps recalling his own defeat, perhaps more aware than Brooks that in his insolvent condition he could not hope to run an effective race, advised against running. Brooks once again overruled his father, saying he was sure he could easily carry the district he had won in both his races for governor. He did recognize one problem. The usual procedure for filling an unexpired term in Congress was for a small local committee to meet and select a nominee. This time Governor Parnell, whose candidate was one Sam Rorax of Yell County, announced that he would call a convention to meet in Little Rock to decide the nominee. Smelling a plot to block his nomination, Brooks decided to fight the governor and his plan.[8]

Once again rejecting Steele's advice to drop out of the race and take the federal appointment, Brooks set out on still another crusade, this time to overturn the will of the governor. He visited every delegate who would represent the Fifth District at the convention; and in Little Rock, sure that he had a good chance to win, gave a rousing speech to move that instead of naming the new Congressman at this convention there should be a district primary to name the party's candidate. To the amazement and chagrin of most state officials, the motion passed, apparently giving Brooks the inside track to the nomination; and he confidently filed his candidacy.[9]

He fought for the nomination as if and because he believed his future depended on it. Once again he surprised state officials, who still smarted

---

[6]Brooks Hays, *Politics Is My Parish* (Baton Rouge: Louisiana State University Press, 1981) 110.

[7]Marion Hays, Unpublished manuscript, "How to Live Dangerously and Enjoy It," V-1. Possession of the author.

[8]Hays, Conversation with Ronald Tonks, September 1975.

[9]Marion Hays, "How to Live Dangerously," V-2.

from his victory at the convention, by coming in first on primary night. He had won a plurality but not an outright majority, and his opponents called a midnight strategy session. Sam Rorax was second in the balloting, but he was now seen as too weak to beat Brooks in a run-off. David Terry of Little Rock might possibly beat Brooks, being a native of the big city of the district, so he had to appear to come in second. One Harvey Combs, according to Brooks's story, drove up and down the Arkansas River through the night, ordering local officials to change votes. Rorax balked at being reduced to third place, putting him out of the race; but party leaders prevailed, and Terry was placed second and therefore in the run-off with Brooks. Although Brooks knew of the crime, he had only two weeks to prepare for the next vote, and he decided not to protest, thinking he could win anyway.[10]

He did not. He would remember to his dying day the results of that vote. Because the poll tax kept registration down, the vote was low, with only 9,000 out of a population of 350,000 registering their choice. It would seem from all accounts that Brooks had won the election, leading by a narrow 595 votes until Yell County belatedly called in its tally. There were 1,632 registered voters in Yell, yet the county reported 1,850 for Terry and 616 for Hays, a total of almost 800 above registration. Brooks had carried Yell by 10 to 1 in 1932, and he would carry it by a big margin when he ran for reelection as Democratic National Committeeman in 1936. Terry was a popular candidate, a formidable foe, but it was obvious from the numbers that there was fraud. Brooks went to court to challenge the election, and ballot boxes were impounded; but the Arkansas Supreme Court ruled against his plea, and the boxes were never opened. The case was dismissed, and Brooks was once again a loser.[11]

His faith in the entire political system, particularly local elections and court decisions, was deeply shaken.[12] He said he realized for the first time how unjust politics could be and that he understood now as never before how laborers and sharecroppers felt.[13] For the rest of his life he would rail

---

[10]Hays, Conversation with Ronald Tonks, September 1975.

[11]Hays, *Politics Is My Parish,* 113–14.

[12]Marion Hays, "How to Live Dangerously," V-5.

[13]Hays, Conversation with Ronald Tonks, September 1975.

against this "most fraudulent election in Arkansas history."[14] Yet he would always take pride in the fact that he did not let it destroy him. More than forty years later he would explain that he had survived the calamity because "my faith that this is a moral universe was impregnable."[15] He continued to believe in the democratic process because the people had done no wrong. They were indeed as much the victims of injustice as he was. And yet 1933 left Brooks with scars he had not known after the defeats of 1928 and 1930.[16] The establishment had punished him for his populist challenges to its authority, and he would spend the remainder of the 1930s on the periphery of power, dependent for his livelihood on the good graces of the federal government. He would carry the clouds of defeat over his head for nearly a decade.

David Terry went to Congress in 1933, although it was said that only his wife's dream of Washington society life kept him from renouncing what he considered to be an illegal election; and he served the Fifth District until 1943, when he was replaced by none other than Brooks Hays. In 1942, Terry ran for the United States Senate. Brooks won his House seat, and Terry placed a poor third in the Senate race. In 1944 Terry again made a poor showing, this time in a contest for governor. Yet such was the nature of Arkansas' Gothic political system, where incumbents were generally not challenged, and such was the nature of Brooks's reluctance to risk his family's financial welfare once again for the uncertainty of elective politics that Brooks never considered challenging the rather weak Congressman for the seat that most people knew should have been his ten years before he finally won it.

At any rate, by the latter part of 1933 Brooks had concluded that the Democratic establishment of Arkansas was so fed up with his crusading that it was determined to use any means, legal or otherwise, to keep him from elective office. At the beginning of 1934 he was $8,000 in debt and was failing to earn enough money practicing law to support his family. He had always doubted his fitness to be a lawyer, and now he was convinced it was not his forte. Thus when a second offer came from the Labor Department, with Frances Perkins offering him $4,500 a year to serve as le-

---

[14]Hays, *Politics Is My Parish,* 113.

[15]Hays, Conversation with Ronald Tonks, September 1975.

[16]Brooks Hays, *A Southern Moderate Speaks* (Chapel Hill: University of North Carolina Press, 1959) 16.

gal adviser to the Arkansas National Recovery Administration, he jumped at the chance to have a job with a steady income.

The offer had not been easily won. Arkansas party officials were not about to see the Roosevelt Administration treat kindly the man who had challenged their authority. Brooks had to use every ounce of leverage his Democratic National Committeeman's position gave him to get the appointment. Perkins had at first wanted to make him the state director of the Arkansas N.R.A., but Senator Joe T. Robinson insisted that the job go to one of his close allies. So Brooks, after some maneuvering, was named "Legal Adviser to the State Director of the National Emergency Council and Labor Compliance Officer for the Arkansas Office of the National Recovery Administration." It was a heady title, but still it was merely a federal appointment, not an elective office. Brooks would have to use his considerable imagination and dedication to reform to make it an effective force for good.[17]

As was becoming his style, Brooks responded to the appointment with humor. He told audiences that he had entertained doubts about accepting the job from Mrs. Perkins. It was bad enough taking orders from a woman at home, he joked, and to do it at work as well might prove too heavy a burden. But soon he came to see that his audiences misunderstood him and either chortled at his put-down of women or were offended by what they considered deprecation of the fairer sex. He quickly dropped the quip from his growing body of anecdotes.[18] It has been said that humor is born of suffering, and in his years in political exile Brooks developed a rich store of humor, most of it at his own expense. It would serve his oratorical gift well, keep him humble even when he had become a successful office holder, and make him nationally famous. It would always remain a self-deprecating humor, never harsh or biting, always positive, never used against any other person or group.

Brooks would work for the N.R.A. from early 1934 until the Supreme Court in 1935 ruled it unconstitutional and rendered its symbol, the blue eagle, "the sick chicken." Serving as its Arkansas compliance officer, Brooks traveled across the state, familiarizing himself in detail with the problems of poor people. Having served as president of the Arkansas State Conference of Social Work in 1932, he considered his N.R.A. activities an

---

[17]Hays, *Politics Is My Parish,* 76.

[18]Brooks Hays, *A Hotbed of Tranquility* (New York: Macmillan, 1968) 5.

extension of his dedication to social improvement for the masses. He took every opportunity offered him to settle disputes, working in every case to elevate workers' wages.[19] Arguing that interstate industries' rules forbade the South to put businesses in other parts of the nation at a financial disadvantage by paying inordinately lower salaries than were paid elsewhere, he ruled against several companies that were holding down wages paid to Arkansas workers.[20] In doing so, much to the dismay of the owners, managers, and white employees of these companies, he insisted that higher wages be paid to black as well as white workers.

His most celebrated victory of this sort was in a dispute at a Forrest City garment factory where black women were being paid between $6 and $10 a week for their labor. Brooks convinced the management that if they did not raise wages, and indeed pay workers $5,000 in back wages, the government would likely close the plant for unfairly underselling firms in other states.[21] The management, grumbling about socialists in Washington, caved in and paid both the back wages and the higher weekly wages demanded in the suit Brooks filed.

His reputation as a champion of the poor and minorities spread across the state, making him a hero to some and a devil to others. He was particularly honored by the black community, despite the fact that he had never publicly espoused their causes. One black woman, according to a story Brooks liked to recount, was overjoyed when she heard that Mr. Brooks Hays, that Little Rock lawyer, had decided to take her case in a labor dispute. She waited for him to arrive in her town, saying over and over to her friends, "My Little Rock lawyer done said he would help me. I'm acountin' heavy on my Little Rock lawyer." But Brooks, who was a thin, bespeckled, boyish thirty-six, failed to inspire her confidence once she had seen him. As he got out of his car, she stopped saying "My Little Rock lawyer done come," her face fell, and she began chanting to her friends, "My trust is *really* in the Lord."[22]

In addition to his work with Arkansas' tiny industrial system, Brooks got even more involved, both through his job and through voluntary activ-

---

[19] Ibid., 157.

[20] Hays, *A Southern Moderate Speaks*, 17.

[21] Hays, *Politics Is My Parish*, 116.

[22] Hays, *A Hotbed of Tranquility*, 157.

ities, in the plight of the farmer. In April 1934, he accepted an invitation from Francis Pickens Miller of Virginia to attend a meeting in Atlanta, Georgia, to discuss rural poverty. Out of this meeting came a new organization, the Southern Policy Committee, later called the National Policy Committee, that sought to alert the nation to the social dangers of poverty, racism, and election abuses in America's rural areas. Brooks, as a charter member of the organization, became one of its traveling evangelists, using his speeches for the N.R.A., and later the Agriculture Department, to spread the findings of the committee's various studies.[23]

From 1936 to 1940 the committee met annually to discuss and publish information on Southern and later national rural life, with special emphasis on tenancy; Southern and later national rural industry, with special emphasis on wages, social security, and river projects; and political participation, with special emphasis on eliminating racial prohibitions and the poll tax.[24] At one point, due to his knowledge of the subject, Brooks was asked to write a memorandum on the rural South, its problems and potentials, for Secretary of Agriculture Henry A. Wallace.[25] Brooks would always be careful in later years, however, to tell people not to confuse the Southern Policy Committee with the Southern Conference on Human Welfare. He would, to his regret, attend a meeting of the latter group in Birmingham, Alabama, in 1939. He would leave before it ended its session, but he would be elected an officer in his absence. This would be used against him, to prove that he was a leftist, in his race for Congress in 1942.[26] A social reformer in those days had to walk a fine line between acceptable and unacceptable behavior. He had to be careful about the groups he joined and the people he knew.

Brooks was not always careful. He took chances. Throughout the 1930s he would involve himself in movements and activities to aid the poor of his region. At the time, protected by the liberal national administration, he would not spend much time worrying about political repercussions. He doubted that he would ever run for elective office again. He had nothing to lose. In the 1940s and 1950s, when he was an elected official, a Con-

---

[23]Hays, *Politics Is My Parish,* 119-20.

[24]Hays, *This World: A Christian's Workshop,* 8.

[25]Marion Hays, "How to Live Dangerously," VI-5.

[26]Hays, *This World: A Christian's Workshop,* 8.

gressman from a conservative district, he would seem less radical than he had been earlier. But in the 1960s and 1970s, once again free from the constraints of elective office, he would return to his liberal ways. And if one looks carefully at his public record, even during the 1940s and 1950s, Brooks Hays was still a social and economic reformer, working through the system, watching his words, but still as committed as ever to providing a better life for poor people.

His efforts to forward the goals of the New Deal were often unpopular with the Arkansas establishment of the 1930s. He was considered by the "Bourbons" to be at best a liberal maverick and at worst some sort of Bolshevik. One member of the Arkansas legislature did in fact publicly accuse Brooks of being a Red. Later, when he was in Congress, he would be called a "star gazer and visionary" by conservatives back home.[27] The truth was that he would always be the social worker he had longed to be as far back as college, the social worker he learned to be during the New Deal, the social worker he remained, with muted voice, during his tenure in Congress. He came to see that his calling was to find ways of applying human knowledge to the task of improving the lives of human beings. This was his calling, his parish.

In his gubernatorial campaigns of 1928 and 1930 he had run as a fiscal conservative opposed to big spending, but in the 1930s he strongly supported the New Deal policies of easy credit and government spending. The difference lay, he later explained, in the beneficiaries of such policies. He opposed easy credit for road building because it allowed rich investors to make money at the expense of the poor. He supported spending money to aid social programs because they helped the poor. He believed, as did all populists, that while the rich must be barred from pilfering the public treasury, public money should and must be invested in programs to benefit the poor and disadvantaged.[28] As a boy he had seen poverty grind down men living along the banks of a rich, potentially productive Arkansas River; and as a man he saw New Deal programs make that valley provide a better life for its inhabitants. As a federal employee and as a Congressman, he would use New Deal ideas to help poor people.

Although the work Brooks did to promote higher wages and a better social life for people in Arkansas and across the South brought benefits to

---

[27]Hays, *Politics Is My Parish,* 148.

[28]Hays, Conversation with Ronald Tonks, August 1976.

both black and white citizens, he knew better than to work openly for blacks as a group. This was true during both his years administering federal programs and those in Congress. He always spoke of elevating the standard of living of poor people, not of blacks as such, because to have done so would have led to cries for his resignation. Not even the national administration in the 1930s could save a Southern employee who went too far out on the racial limb. Yet for a man of his day and place Brooks took some unusual risks on behalf of blacks. As early as 1934 he helped found the Little Rock chapter of the Urban League.[29] Later, when F.D.R. asked him to become more involved in social programs for blacks, he became a member of Sears Roebuck President Julius Rosenwald's Commission on Interracial Cooperation. In this capacity he met with black leaders during the 1930s to listen to their problems and ideas and to explain these issues to white leaders. At one meeting held at Alabama's Tuskegee Institute, he became one of the first Southern white politicians of the day to sit down and eat a meal with blacks.[30]

With the closing of the N.R.A., Brooks was in May 1935 offered a job with the Department of Agriculture, under its director Henry A. Wallace, a man he would conclude after close observation to be goodhearted but without much inner strength, too politically naive ever to be a national leader. He came to admire Rexford Tugwell, his immediate superior and a man with whom he would write New Deal agricultural legislation, much more than he did Wallace.[31] He was happy to leave Little Rock after the difficult years there and move to Washington, where he would be a part of the Resettlement Administration, serving as Tugwell's special assistant and dealing primarily with farm tenancy.[32] As the administration's Congressional liaison, he met regularly with Southern Congressmen to work out legislation, in time organizing them into the "Hall's Restaurant Group." With this group he would help hammer out the Bankhead-Jones Bill, which offered liberal loan terms to men of proven agricultural skills to help them buy family-sized farms.[33]

---

[29]Ibid., September 1975.

[30]Hays, Conversation with Walter Brown, May 1975. University of Arkansas Archives, Fayetteville AR.

[31]Hays, Conversation with Ronald Tonks, September 1975.

[32]Hays, *A Southern Moderate Speaks,* 18.

[33]Hays, *Politics Is My Parish,* 122.

As with so many of Brooks's ideas that became law during the 1930s, the Bankhead-Jones program, which passed Congress in June 1937, was called radical and extremist by opponents of the New Deal. Critics said it gave free land to unworthy persons and smacked of communist redistribution of property. In fact, as Brooks defended it, the land that was sold at a bargain and with easy credit to men of proven farming skills was land those very men had lost as a result of the Depression, not land taken from rich landowners. Applicants for the loans were carefully screened and were required to keep up regular repayments, albeit on terms much better than those available from banks.

The only "socialist" element of the program was a clause requiring that those who owned land farmed by tenants treat their tenants with justice and not expel tenants in order to use the land for recreational purposes. This part of the plan reflected Brooks's belief that only those who love the land and want to see it serve the needs of common people should own and operate it.[34] In an address to the annual dinner of the National Christian Rural Fellowship in New York City on 5 December 1935, Brooks had said, "The Christian mind rebels against absentee ownership. The Christian mind rebels against the holding of land by wealthy men for recreational purposes if it be land that is adaptable to family-size farm operation and needed for that purpose. We are going to talk about these practices until they are outlawed."[35] The Bankhead-Jones program helped do just that. Brooks always believed that while several federally sponsored experimental farm colonies got most of the publicity at the time, the program he helped write was the most significant plan of the 1930s for easing rural poverty and the hopelessness of dispossession.[36]

Working in Washington but traveling broadly across the South to observe the Resettlement Program in operation, Brooks learned of conditions far beyond those of Arkansas. During this time he met a young Roman Catholic priest from Granger, Iowa, named Luigi Ligutti. Father Ligutti was a major force in the Catholic Church's program to aid and encourage midwestern farm families, and he was himself a member of the interdenominational Christian Rural Fellowship. Ligutti would one day rise in the Church's hierarchy to serve as Pope John XXIII's adviser on rural life;

---

[34]Ibid., 127.

[35]Hays, *This World: A Christian's Workshop*, 27.

[36]Hays, *A Southern Moderate Speaks*, 18.

and as Monsignor Ligutti he would arrange for his old friend, fellow laborer, and coconspirator to help farmers, Brooks Hays, to have a private audience with the pope.[37]

The Bankhead-Jones program was written but still several months away from passage into law when the election of 1936 came around. Brooks always felt his pulse quicken in election years, and 1936 was no exception, even though he had a secure federal job. He considered running for office that year, wrestled with the decision for quite a time, and finally decided against it. "I am interested in correcting the injustices in the economic order, particularly in the south," he wrote in his journal, "and I am willing to assume a responsibility for protests. But protesters aren't always vote-getters." He knew that his state and its people, most of them poor and needy, were represented by men unresponsive to their needs and opposed to any politician who was. He knew that the older generation considered him a troublemaker, the younger generation considered him a respectable bureaucrat, and both considered him too liberal for Arkansas. He was a man who no longer had enough friends to get him elected. "Should I stay in politics?" he mused. Should he run for office and try to win the power a bureaucrat could never hope to have? "I wish I knew."[38] In the end he remained merely a bureaucrat.

He campaigned for F.D.R. in that day when a federal employee could still play politics. He made public speeches. He debated Alabama lawyer Borden Burr on a regionally broadcast radio show.[39] F.D.R. invited him to ride on his special train from Washington to Little Rock, where the president had been invited to honor the state of Arkansas on the centennial of its joining the Union, as a reward for his loyal service. Brooks and several other Arkansans had dinner with the president in his private car and spent three hours talking with him about the election, rural development, Mussolini, and the Japanese. Brooks remembered how F.D.R. chainsmoked his way through the evening and ate eggs while everyone else had steaks. The president took a special liking to the good-natured young Arkansan, and later he wanted to make him a federal judge, but the nomination would be blocked by Arkansas Senator Hattie Caraway. Mrs. Caraway and her con-

---

[37]Marion Hays, "How to Live Dangerously," VI-4.

[38]Hays, *This World: A Christian's Workshop,* 47.

[39]Hays, Conversation with Ronald Tonks, September 1975.

servative allies would in fact have had Henry Wallace fire Brooks from his job with Agriculture had F.D.R. not intervened and stopped the plot.[40]

The animosity of Caraway's group for Brooks grew out of the other election in 1936, the campaign for governor of Arkansas, when Brooks supported the eventual winner, Carl Bailey, who would himself become an enemy of Caraway. Early in the year Bailey, who had supported Brooks in his races, asked Brooks to support and advise him during the election; and Brooks agreed to do so. Bailey then defeated the Caraway faction's nominee and went on to be a progressive New Deal governor, seeing to it that Arkansas was the first state in the union to adopt a Model Soil Conservation program.[41]

Bailey's relations with Caraway took a turn for the worse in 1937, when Senator Joe T. Robinson died and Bailey decided he wanted to replace him in the Senate. Over Brooks's advice Bailey tried to arrange for a party committee to appoint him to the post, reversing the process Brooks had himself instituted in his race for Congress in 1933. Bailey got his nomination without a primary, but the uproar over his maneuvering encouraged the Caraway faction to run one of its men as an Independent against him, and the Independent candidate won. The debacle did not cost Bailey his governorship, and in fact he was reelected in 1938, but being a Bailey man did hurt Brooks because as a federal employee he was vulnerable to attacks by national officeholders.[42] He was denied a judgeship, and only presidential intervention saved his job.

The Bankhead-Jones Bill of 1937 replaced the Resettlement Program with the Farm Security Administration. Brooks, after surviving the attempt on his political life, went back to Little Rock to become the new administration's regional attorney for Arkansas, Louisiana, and Mississippi.[43] He enjoyed the travel and fieldwork, but trying to keep peace in his Little Rock office gave him a bleeding ulcer.[44] In 1939, with the Hatch Act, he had to resign his place on the Democratic National Committee. Without this base of power he felt even more vulnerable and insecure, adding

---

[40]Ibid.

[41]Hays, *This World: A Christian's Workshop,* 8.

[42]Hays, Conversation with Ronald Tonks, September 1975.

[43]Hays, *Politics Is My Parish,* 135.

[44]Hays, Conversation with Ronald Tonks, September 1975.

to his worries. On 26 November 1940, while in Eureka Springs, he passed out and came close to dying.[45]

An ulcer had erupted. It required four transfusions of blood to save his life. When he was finally out of danger his doctor had some advice: take more leisure time, relax more, and enjoy an alcoholic libation each evening. Brooks was shocked by the latter prescription. He had always been a teetotaler and considered drinking a violation of his Baptist principles. He recalled how alcohol had harmed his father's life, damaged his career, and endangered the family's well-being. But these were doctor's orders, and he complied, if unwillingly. From 1940 on he was a moderate drinker, coining the phrase, "Never less than one, never more than two." He would keep this a secret from his constituents, both religious and political, and would let it be known that in Washington "Brooks Hays Punch" was made from a nonalcoholic recipe. But the man who would represent Arkansas' Fifth District for eighteen years and be president of the Southern Baptist Convention for two terms would be a clandestine, moderate disciple of John Barleycorn.

After what proved to be a rather lengthy recovery from his illness, Brooks escaped the Little Rock office by being named Assistant Director of Rural Rehabilitation in the Farm Security Administration. He would serve there, in the Washington office, from early 1941 until he resigned to run once again for Congress in 1942.[46] It was a new decade, and for Brooks it was time for a change. Federal appointments were less secure now that he was no longer a national committeeman. He knew that only elective office, as insecure as that could be, would give him the power he needed to reform his society. Brooks Hays the social worker, the bureaucrat, was about to become once more Brooks Hays the politician, who would in time become Brooks Hays the statesman.

His years with the New Deal had given him a deep and clear understanding of his native South, its poverty, its potential. He knew from his travels, both within the South and outside it, just how sadly behind the rest of the nation the South—which he always capitalized South—really was. Its educational institutions were weak, its churches preached dubious and debilitating theologies about man's innate corruption, and its ignorance and isolation often produced a shocking intellectual, aesthetic,

---

[45]Hays, Conversation with Walter Brown, May 1975.

[46]Hays, Conversation with Ronald Tonks, September 1975.

and spiritual mediocrity. "None of the South's struggles for survival," he once wrote, "were done in technicolor."[47] The South's story, for Brooks, was no Margaret Mitchell classic novel. It was sad, tragic, but not romantic.

Yet he did have hope for the South. While he was not blind to its weaknesses, he understood its potential. In its natural resources, particularly its descending rivers, lay power, beauty, and prosperity. In its people, toughened by hard times, lay a determination to survive that could be harnessed, with the help of government seed money, for social and economic progress. In its broad devotion to the Christian faith, although it was at times woefully misinterpreted and abused, lay an inspiration and guide for social, intellectual, and economic reform that could revolutionize the whole region. "The Christian religion is one of justice and right dealing," he told the seventh annual meeting of the Christian Rural Fellowship in Nashville, Tennessee, in 1941. "While society's claims [by which he meant property rights and sound finances] must be recognized, the rights of individuals must also be recognized, and it is Christianity's duty to preserve a proper balance between the two."[48] These were the words not of an ivory tower theorist but of a man with nearly a decade of service behind him in the field of social welfare.

Although his federal appointments during the New Deal era provided Brooks with the opportunity to fulfill his social responsibilities, the work he did caused him great frustration. He was at times close to despair and would probably have left government service had he been able to support his family by practicing law. Yet it was at this time that he began cultivating the sense of humor that had always been latent in his personality and would in time become his trademark. Out of pain was born humor, out of frustration came laughter. He would eventually become one of the great wits of Congress and the United States.

Interestingly enough, at one point Brooks toyed with the idea of dropping humor from his public addresses. In 1932, as he toured Arkansas as an aide in the reelection campaign of Joe Robinson, he was impressed with Robinson's political delivery, which was an obvious success. Robinson never used humor. He was completely serious throughout his addresses. When

---

[47]Hays, *Politics Is My Parish*, 20.

[48]Hays, *This World: A Christian's Workshop*, 36.

Brooks mentioned this to him, Robinson explained that humor had no place in serious public discourse. Tell funny stories, use a light manner, and people will remember only the jokes, he said. Brooks mentioned this theory to Marion, saying that he might follow Robinson's example, and she set him straight. He should not listen to that man, she huffed. Humor was his best quality. He needed to use it more and not less. It kept people awake and listening. He should develop it even more fully.[49] Of course he did; and the rest, as they say, is history.

Brooks would in time become as famous for his humor as for his efforts on behalf of social reform or his religious faith. In paying tribute to his career, Francis B. Sayre, dean of Washington's National Cathedral, commented that Brooks understood that "the profoundest ideas are the least pretentious and are best conveyed by the little chariots of anecdote and gentle humor."[50] The humor to which he referred, which had become "Brooks Hays" humor, lay somewhere between that of Abraham Lincoln and Will Rogers: illustrative, apt, telling, and kind.

Brooks never "told jokes" merely to relax a crowd or to entertain. He was never merely an after-dinner speaker. His anecdotes, which were legion, always made a point; and the point each one made was as easily recalled as the anecdote. Yet his stories were never merely illustrative, for they had lives of their own. Perhaps the secret to his success with humor lay in his understanding that "humor, to be truly effective, must be related to a philosophy of life, and should contribute to the expression of ideas."[51] For Brooks humor was a means to an end, never an end in itself. He was one of the few modern orators whose philosophy is as easily recalled as his humor and whose humor is as celebrated as his philosophy.

His stories were always apt. He knew what stories to use and when and where to use them. They always spoke directly to the audience he was addressing. And he knew, from his wide experience addressing widely diverse groups of people, just what would be effective when and where. In addition, he had what students of humor call "presence." His voice, gestures, and body language served his humor well. Audiences knew from his presence that he was a man they could laugh with, and they did. Marion once remarked that audiences sometimes began laughing even before he

---

[49]Hays, *A Hotbed of Tranquility*, 1-2.

[50]Hays, *Politics Is My Parish*, 222-23.

[51]Hays, *A Hotbed of Tranquility*, 3.

got to his humor as such, that they often began laughing before Brooks began speaking. For Brooks humor was a way of thinking, a way of expressing himself, a way of life. Yet he did not believe that a story, to be apt and effective, had to be true. He loved to quote Louis Brownlow: "Never dilute the oil of anecdote with the vinegar of fact."[52].

Bill Angell, a professor of religion at Wake Forest University in North Carolina and one of Brooks's closest colleagues when he directed the ecumenical institute there, believes that Brooks's humor succeeded so well because it was so gentle. As Brooks himself once said, "Humor should never carry a barb."[53] No one ever felt, even if he or she were the subject of one of Brooks's stories, that he or she had been injured, had been a target of someone's anger or ridicule. This is the reason that poor Arkansas farmers could laugh at jokes about themselves, and Washington politicians the same. Brooks, in fact, told most of his stories on himself and on his own people, people who knew he loved them and was one of them.

An example of the kind of self-deprecating story that won Brooks so many laughs and so much love was one about the time his old friend and fellow Southern Baptist layman Owen Cooper stopped in Russellville and asked a gas station attendant if he knew Brooks Hays. The attendant admitted that he did and explained that by holding political office and preaching in churches Brooks was "a ball of fire by day and a bag of wind by night." Brooks told this story hundreds of times, always on himself, and laughed as loudly as his audience with each retelling. Another favorite was the one he told when introduced for a speech by a college dean or president. He would always claim to have known the administrator when the two of them were young men. "We never would have thought, when we were in school, that we would be here today as a dean and a Congressman," he would say. "He thought he would be president of Harvard, and I thought I'd be President of the United States."[54]

Most stories not told on himself were told on his "people," the poor whites of his native Ozark mountains and of the rural South. To illustrate his humorous observation that the Great Depression would not have been so bad "if it hadn't come in the middle of hard times," he would say that after one speech an old man asked him what this Depression thing he kept referring

---

[52]Hays, *Politics Is My Parish*, 223.

[53]Ibid.

[54]Brooks Hays, Address at Western Kentucky University, November 1968.

to meant. "Don't you remember it?" Brooks would say he asked the old man. "No," came the answer. "Well then, do you remember 1932?" The man had to think. "Yeah, I do," he allowed. "That's the year I broke my arm." "You did?" "Yeah. Fell out of a persimmon tree while I was gettin' my breakfast."[55]

Another story, used to illustrate the dangers of misunderstanding and the perils of poor communication, was about a man who called a doctor to come and visit his aging, almost deaf mother. The doctor was new to the town and quite young. The man brought him into his mother's bedroom and shouted, "Mama, this is the new young doctor," and then he left them together. When the doctor had gone his mother called him and said, her face full of indignation, "Son, I wanta tell you about that new young preacher." The man shook his head. "No, Mama, he's not a preacher, he's a doctor." "Oh, well then," the old lady shrugged, "I thought he was awful familiar for a preacher."[56]

Many of Brooks's stories were about preachers, mostly Baptists, since he was himself a laypreacher and a Baptist. One story, used to illustrate his church's tendency to legalism and perhaps also to emphasize finances over morals, was about a preacher who ran away with $200 from the church treasury. He was caught in Little Rock, but he had spent the money. Someone asked one of his deacons whether the church planned to prosecute him, and the deacon replied, "Nope, we're gonna keep him here and make him preach it out, every last penny of it."[57] A story that featured the opposite type of preacher, but perhaps the same type of Baptist, recounted the time a preacher was riding in his carriage through the woods on a Sunday night and was held up by a highwayman. The preacher handed over the $11 in his wallet. "That all you got?" the robber said as he eyed the preacher. "That's all that's mine," the preacher replied. "There's $300 in this bag, but it belongs to the Baptist church I pastor, and to get it you'll have to kill me." The robber sighed. "Here, take back your $11. I'm a Baptist myself."[58]

Baptists caught the brunt of Brooks's religious humor partly because he could kid his own church without charges of bigotry, partly because he

---

[55]*Washington Humor*, featuring Brooks Hays (recording).

[56]Hays, *A Hotbed of Tranquility*, 170.

[57]Ibid., 167.

[58]Ibid., 166-67.

could so clearly see his own church's shortcomings, and partly because he believed that by using humor he could draw attention to those shortcomings and perhaps help effect reform. He was particularly embarrassed by the Baptist tendency to avoid ecumenical affiliation and cooperation, and he used one story to illustrate the Baptist tendency to place denomination above church. A deacon of a Baptist church in a small town opposed a move to merge his town's two tiny churches, one Baptist and one Christian (Disciples of Christ) by declaring, "I've been a Baptist all of my life, and nobody's gonna make a Christian out of me."[59] Another story had a Baptist preacher, after admitting that he had failed to win converts in a small town revival meeting, saying to a friend, "But I sure fixed it so nobody else'll get 'em."[60]

Seldom did Brooks speak humorously about other denominations. There might be an occasional Methodist story, his wife and a considerable portion of his constituency being Methodist, if addressing a Methodist group. And as he moved into national politics, he developed a collection of gentle Catholic stories. Since so many Catholics were Democrats and thus, in a sense, a part of his "family," they were a legitimate target for his humor. One such story had two Catholics discussing a third. "He's changed over to the Republican party," one said. "Can't be," said the other, "I saw him in mass last Sunday morning."[61]

But Brooks was extremely cautious about telling Jewish stories. Jews were, of course, rare in Arkansas. As Brooks became a national figure the horrors of the Nazi Holocaust were becoming known, so that he feared that even the most innocent quip might be interpreted as being anti-Semitic. Only one Jewish story can be found in his collection, and before he used it he had to be assured by his aide Warren Cikins, himself Jewish, that it would not be offensive. In the story a rabbi, dressed in Old World habit, wearing a black suit and hat and a beard, was jeered by a group of little boys as he walked down a Little Rock street. "What's the matter?" he said to them. "You've never seen a Yankee before?"

Brooks was almost as sensitive about telling humorous stories about blacks as he was about Jews. He did on occasion relate true stories about his dealings with blacks, and in the early days he was not above imitating

---

[59]Ibid., 167-68.

[60]Hays, *Politics Is My Parish,* 7.

[61]Hays, *A Hotbed of Tranquility,* 175.

their dialect, just as he imitated the dialect of poor whites. Southern blacks were after all, despite their political disenfranchisement, a part of his "family." But he refused to tell a story that might confirm white prejudices or hurt the feelings of blacks. Some of his poor white characters do bear resemblances to blacks, however, and it is possible that he told what Southerners called "nigger jokes" in whiteface. One was about a boy hired to clerk at a general store during the Depression. His boss, leaving for a time one day, told him about the coffee under the counter. "It's only for our special customers," he explained. "They know to ask for bird seed, which is the code for coffee." So when a well-dressed lady came in and asked for her birdseed, the boy looked under the counter and saw two kinds. With people listening to the conversation, he improvised, "Do your bird perk or do he drip?"

Brooks had no more qualms about poking fun at ignorance in any form than he did about lampooning Baptist practices. Perhaps just as he hoped he could change Baptists for the better, so he hoped he could make people change by facing them with their ignorance. At any rate, his kidding was always gentle and done with compassion. And it always bore the ring of truth, even when he refused to dilute the oil of anecdote with the vinegar of fact.

A new period in Brooks's life began in April 1942, when Fifth District of Arkansas Congressman David Terry, the man who had defeated him in 1933, decided to surrender his House seat to run (unsuccessfully as it turned out) for the United States Senate. Brooks immediately began dreaming of running for the seat, and he went to discuss it with Steele. The old man turned thumbs down on the idea, as he had done so often before when Brooks wanted to enter a race, putting on a dramatic show of opposition. He took off his glasses, took out his teeth, and began to cry over and over, "You'll put me in my grave, you'll put me in my grave."[62]

At first Brooks thought he would just override Steele's veto, as he had done twice before, but after talking with his mother he agreed to give his father the final say. The next day, after talking it over with some of his political cronies, Steele changed his mind and gave Brooks his blessing. He did remind him that this would be his last chance to win elective office, that if he ran and lost this time his political career would probably be over;

Hays, *Politics Is My Parish,* 138.

but he told him that this race would be between a dog and a rabbit. For the dog, Brooks's opponent, the present Lt. Governor Bob Bailey, it would be merely a race; but for the rabbit, Brooks, it would be a matter of political life and death.[63] This would give him the edge. Brooks announced on 12 April.

Bob Bailey was also from Russellville, but he was as different from Brooks as night is from day. He was uneducated, loaded with prejudice, and used grammar that even the people of northwest Arkansas found offensive. Brooks led Bailey almost from the start, and in desperation Bailey made the mistake of attacking Brooks personally. He began talking of Brooks's three previous defeats, calling him a loser. Brooks countered with speeches, delivered with mock humility, saying there was nothing dishonorable about defeat, that the truly honorable man persisted through defeat to victory. He played for sympathy, using humor, when he referred repeatedly to "my God-given right to persist."[64] Bailey had played right into his hands. He was outwitted.

As the primary day neared, Bailey grew even more desperate. He knew he needed an emotional issue, since personal attacks seemed not to phase Brooks, and so he resorted to the age-old issue of race. He began calling Brooks, the man who had helped found Little Rock's Urban League and had won higher wages for black workers, a "nigger lover." He specifically accused Brooks of consorting with leftists and race mixers by attending the 1939 Birmingham Southern Conference on Human Welfare. On the Saturday before the primary, a hot day in the middle of the summer, full page ads in area newspapers accused Brooks of planning to alter the Negro's status by joining and being elected an officer in an organization whose aim it was to overthrow the Southern system of government and way of life. At this late date it was too late for Brooks to explain either his racial policies or the fact that he had left the Birmingham Conference once he understood its nature, and this before he was elected without his consent to an office.

There was nothing to gain and everything to lose by starting a crusade for equal rights. No blacks were registered to vote in the district, and to advocate political rights for blacks would have meant sure defeat. So he kept quiet about his racial policies and showed newspaper men proof that

---

[63]Hays, Conversation with Ronald Tonks, September 1975.

[64]Hays, *A Hotbed of Tranquility,* 28.

on the day he was elected an officer and the day when all the radical proposals were passed in Birmingham he was speaking in New Orleans. "I was
in New Orleans," was his brief, simple explanation. If he had been in New
Orleans, he could not have been at the Birmingham Conference. It was
simplistic, but it worked, and he won his race.[65]

The day before the primary election, 26 July, a full-page ad appeared
in the Arkansas *Gazette* and other papers defending Brooks against Bailey's charges. In it Brooks's supporters said their candidate would be surprised to see this page because he was too gentlemanly to answer such
smears. It echoed the statement Brooks had made earlier that he was in
New Orleans the day the Birmingham Conference passed its resolutions
and did not mention the fact that he had been elected an officer. It printed
a resolution passed in 1941 by the Methodist women's Society of Christian
Service: "Race as an issue is the refuge of demagogues who, as candidates,
must divert attention from their own records and from the greed of special
interests supporting them for office."[66] Nothing was said about Brooks's
well-known opposition to racism or about the way blacks in Arkansas were
oppressed and disenfranchised by government policy. The Hays camp
played it perfectly. Brooks was himself perhaps no longer as pure as he had
once been, but neither was he as naive. This time he wanted to win, and
he did.

The lesson of the 1942 election would teach him to mute his statements
and activities on behalf of blacks. He would work for the next fifteen years
for his white constituency. He would be by Arkansas standards a racial
liberal, but he would insist on calling himself a moderate. He would do what
he could for blacks without alienating his white constituency. All of this
until the year 1957, when Little Rock Central High School and its crisis
called the young Brooks Hays back to center stage.

Brooks beat Bob Bailey 16,000 votes to 12,500. He carried Little Rock
and Yell County. In fact, he carried all but one county in the district. He
was able to send money he had not spent back to contributors. It was a bittersweet victory. He knew that he had been elected by 16,000 people out
of a district population of more than a third of a million. He knew that Arkansas was still not a democracy because on election night officials in the
one county he lost offered to switch enough votes to give him a clean sweep

---

[65]Hays, *Politics Is My Parish,* 143.

[66]Arkansas *Gazette* (Little Rock), 26 July 1942.

of the district, an offer he refused.[67] Still he was able to find humor in the process. He recalled that in 1928 he had been referred to as the Boy Scout candidate. Now in 1942, he joked, all those Boy Scouts were old enough to vote, and they had elected him to Congress.[68]

In November Brooks easily defeated the Republican opposition, and in January he became a Congressman. He was about to be a part of America's legislative history during the middle third of the twentieth century.

---

[67]Hays, *Politics Is My Parish,* 142.

[68]Hays, Conversation with Ronald Tonks, September 1975.

CHAPTER 4

MID-CENTURY CONGRESSES

Brooks Hays was a member of the United States House of Representatives from 1943 to 1959, at the midpoint of the twentieth century, from the early stages of World War II through the early stages of the Civil Rights Movement. He represented the Fifth Arkansas District in the Seventy-eighth through the eighty-fifth Congresses, working primarily with legislation in the fields of economics, foreign affairs, rural life, and civil rights. He came to be identified by a title he shared with very few other Congressmen: a states' rights liberal.

Brooks wanted desperately, when he first arrived in Washington as a newly elected official, to be appointed to the House Agriculture Committee, hoping to use the expertise he had gained during his work for the New Deal to plot legislation to help the farmers of his district, the state of Arkansas, and the entire rural South. But a Congressman from eastern Arkansas already sat on this committee, and tradition said that only one member from a state should be on any committee, so he had to choose again. His next choice was Foreign Affairs (in the Senate called Foreign Relations because, as Brooks once joked, senators are too dignified to have affairs); but here again he was denied his wish. A "more glamorous" newcomer, J. William Fulbright, also of Arkansas and a former Rhodes Scholar, wanted Foreign Affairs; and as Brooks later explained, "I yielded to him as an Oxford-trained student of international affairs."[1] So Brooks got his third choice, Banking and Currency, "that prosaic panel" as he would always call it.

---

[1]Brooks Hays, *Politics Is My Parish* (Baton Rouge: Louisiana State University Press, 1981) 153.

Although it was his third choice and he continually made light of its work, he would serve on Banking and Currency for eight years and would later admit that it was one of the best experiences of his life.[2] It required him to make his first systematic study of economics and formulate his own personal philosophy of how the American economy should work. He had always been considered a sound money man, from his early years as a crusader against those poorly managed Arkansas road bonds, yet he had also been a New Deal Democrat who believed that the government should finance social programs for the poor. As a member of Banking and Currency he would consistently oppose, under both Democratic and Republican presidents, spending increases for the Washington bureaucracy, yet he would support the expansion of social welfare programs. His experience on Banking and Currency would authorize him to say that men and women who are uneducated and unhealthy cost the nation more than it costs to educate and keep them healthy. It would give authority to his unwillingness to support free enterprise schemes if they did not include programs of human service. Because he was on record as an advocate of fiscal integrity, he could say, "I will go in any direction that a sound interpretation of the basic Christian idea of concern for disadvantaged people leads me,"[3] and have conservatives support his programs for the disadvantaged.

From 1943 to 1951, as he served on Banking and Currency, he found himself dealing first with wartime price controls, then postwar living costs, and finally commodity concessions. Most important for his constituents, and he believed the nation as a whole, was the effort he put into drafting legislation on farm credit and agriculture.[4] He was a founding father of the Arkansas River Valley Program, which changed the face of his district and brought his people their first measure of prosperity. In addition, he saw to it that surplus government land was made readily available to returning veterans willing to be family farmers.[5] Overall, even though he was not dealing directly with agriculture or with foreign affairs, the work he did

---

[2]Brooks Hays, Conversation with Ronald Tonks, October 1975, typeset in 15 parts. Southern Baptist Sunday School Board Archives, Nashville TN.

[3]Ibid.

[4]Ibid., August 1976.

[5]Brooks Hays, *This World: A Christian's Workshop* (Nashville: Broadman Press, 1968) 11.

touched these areas enough to make his first four terms challenging and fulfilling.

Yet through the 1940s he continued to harbor dreams of dealing with international matters. In 1951, as he began his ninth term, he was able to move over to Foreign Affairs. There he proved an aggressive supporter of the United Nations and a strong advocate of foreign aid. He believed that foreign affairs should be conducted in a completely bipartisan way, and he often found it easier to work with Republicans than with his fellow Democrats, many of whom were conservative, isolationist Southerners. During this second half of his Congressional career he was, in the Eighty-second Congress, made a member of a Select Committee to Investigate Tax Exempt Foundations. In 1955 he was a U.S. delegate to the United Nations. In the Eighty-third and Eighty-fourth Congresses he was a member of the special Committee on Intergovernmental Relations. And in 1958, during what would be his last full year in Congress, he was appointed by House Speaker Sam Rayburn to a special blue ribbon committee to study the problems and potentials of astronautics and space exploration.

Throughout his Congressional career, during his early maverick days and during the New Deal 1930s, Brooks was known by his Congressional colleagues if not by his constituents back home as a liberal, a states' rights one to be sure, but a liberal nonetheless. He was a strong opponent of the poll tax, which he rightly believed effectively disenfranchised a majority of voters throughout the South. He preferred, as a believer in states' rights, that the various states repeal this tax for themselves; but when he finally admitted that this would never happen, he began to advocate a constitutional amendment prohibiting it. He never let the "Bourbons" back home deter him from making this case over and over.[6] Nor did he let them silence his advocacy of social programs for the poor, human rights for all Americans, and a strong United Nations that could deal with war.[7]

He kept his political fences mended back in the Fifth District, and even those who did not understand his liberal voting record could not deny that he worked hard for his people. He wrote a weekly "Washington Letter" that was printed in all the newspapers of the district, and he regularly gave a Sunday radio talk on all district stations. And so a man who was probably

---

[6]Marion Hays, Unpublished manuscript, "How to Live Dangerously and Enjoy It," VII-4 Possession of the author.

[7]Hays, Conversation with Ronald Tonks, August 1976.

too liberal for his district, who had to disguise his liberalism by calling himself a moderate, was politically unassailable for sixteen years. He was considered a veritable institution in central Arkansas, and it would come as a shock to everyone, there and elsewhere, when he was defeated by the emotions of 1958. Many of his constituents who voted against him then would later say they would never have done so had they dreamed he could be defeated.

First-term Congressmen in 1943 made $10,000 a year, enough to support a family in Washington but not enough to permit regular visits home. Brooks drove to work and back each day. The very first day, when he parked in the Capitol lot, a policeman eyed his license tag. "So you're from Arkansas," he said. "Can you read?" Brooks allowed as how he could. "Then read that sign," the cop said and indicated one that said "Reserved for Members of Congress." "Can you read?" Brooks grinned and handed him his card. "Sorry, Congressman Hays," the cop said and with a bow moved on.

From the beginning Brooks established his reputation for humor. He would often repeat the story of the first time he ever addressed the Speaker of the House. "Mr. Speaker, will the gentleman from Georgia [it was Carl Vinson] yield?" he piped. "I am happy to yield to the distinguished gentleman from Arkansas," Vinson responded. Whereupon, being overwhelmed by the great compliment he had been paid, unaware that this was merely House protocol, Brooks promptly forgot the question he had wanted to ask.[8] And colleagues would be just as amused at his story about his maiden speech, a roaring five minutes' worth, which the *Congressional Record* mistakenly attributed to Arkansas representative Oren Harris. When Brooks castigated the clerk, then apologized for losing his temper over the matter, the clerk replied, "That's all right, Mr. Hays, you should have heard Mr. Harris."[9]

By 1948 Brooks was known as Washington's best storyteller-humorist since Chauncey DePew.[10] Because he believed that the "softening process of laughter helps you with the thread of serious thought that comes later,"[11]

---

[8]Brooks Hays, *A Hotbed of Tranquility* (New York: Macmillan, 1968) 21.

[9]Ibid., 76.

[10]Arkansas *Democrat Magazine* (Little Rock), 23 May 1948.

[11]Hays, Conversation with Ronald Tonks, September 1977.

he became a master at softening his audiences, those on the floor of the House as well as those out on the hustings. Representative Chester Gross of Pennsylvania once ridiculed the state of Arkansas by saying that all they produced down there were dogs. On the House floor Brooks retorted, " If all the cows in Arkansas were one cow, she could stand with her front feet on the great plains of the West and her hind feet in the Dominion of Canada and with her tremendous tail could wipe icicles off the North Pole. If all the hogs in Arkansas were one hog, he could stand with his front feet in the Gulf of Mexico, his hind feet in the Atlantic Ocean and with his mighty snout could dig another Panama Canal. If all the dogs in Arkansas were one dog, he could stand on the loftiest peak of the Ozark Mountains and raise a howl that would blow the rings from off the planet Saturn, and all the possums in Pennsylvania could not grease his upper lip." Later, out on the Capitol steps, Brooks presented Gross with an Arkansas hound dog named Henry.[12] A commentator once said, "There are Democrats, there are Republicans, and there is Chester Gross." He might have added "and Brooks Hays." While Brooks was often critical of the flowered political oratory that he had heard as a young man, so often empty of meaning, he knew how to use it for comic effect.

Among his fellow Congressmen and the Washington establishment, Brooks was almost as well known for his art as for his humor. Since childhood he had enjoyed a facility for drawing, and in college all his electives had been in art. Off and on, in spare moments through the 1920s and 1930s, he had done sketches. But in Congress, during the long and sometimes tedious hearings and debates, he was able to fine-tune his talents. He often entertained his Congressional colleagues with his cartoons, always commentaries on contemporary events, often on committee proceedings. Once one of them even affected the proceedings. A committee meeting seemed to go on forever one day, with members offering amendment after amendment to the bill before them, until Brooks drew and passed around the table to the chair a cartoon showing a monkey hanging from a fancy chandelier saying, "Mr. Chairman, I offer an amendment." The chair, seeing more than a grain of truth in the commentary, quickly brought the session to a close.[13]

---

[12]Unattributed magazine article, Brooks Hays Collection, University of Arkansas, Fayetteville.

[13]Hays, *A Hotbed of Tranquility*, 82.

A number of Brooks's cartoons were published in newspapers and magazines, the most memorable being a picture of the White House in mourning the day after President Roosevelt died, with the caption "Resquiescat in Pace." His reputation thereafter grew to the point that the Congressional Club, an organization of Congressmen's wives, sponsored exhibitions of his work in 1947 and again in 1948. Some were pen-and-ink drawings, some oil paintings, some scenes of Arkansas and some of Washington, the two places he knew best. One of the paintings from the 1948 exhibit, a view of Union Station Plaza, appeared in *Life* magazine.[14] Brooks would always think of art as a mere avocation and never really take it seriously, but it proved a valuable way of easing tension and served him well as a creative outlet for his political frustrations. He would continue to draw even into his old age, entertaining his children, his grandchildren, and even President Kennedy's daughter Caroline in the White House.

In Congress Brooks was a committed Democrat, loyally voting with his party leadership on most issues. Once when Douglas Branch, pastor of First Baptist Church, Rocky Mountain, North Carolina, misspelled his name "Hayes" in their correspondence concerning church matters, Brooks wrote back, "We used to say in Arkansas that if it were spelled Hayes he was either a Republican or illiterate, and I don't want to be classed either way."[15] But this was of course a joke, and though he was a loyal Democrat, he was not a purely partisan politician. There were so few Republicans in the Fifth District, indeed in all of Arkansas, that they did not threaten him. In Congress he found that he got along as well with Republicans as with Democrats. He became a close friend of Republican Representative Walter Judd of Minnesota, a man with whom he often disagreed but shared a common religious faith. He also continued to meet with his old "Hall's Restaurant Thursday Dinner Group," which he had helped found in 1936, a mixed bag of legislators and administrators of both parties. He was particularly convinced, as we have seen, that foreign policy should be formulated without partisan squabbling.

Perhaps Brooks's most widespread Congressional image, however, was that of lay religious leader. He was first and foremost Mister Baptist, a tireless supporter of liberal religious causes, a self-trained moral theologian. He held offices in his denomination, regularly spoke in church ser-

---

[14]Arkansas *Democrat Magazine* (Little Rock), 23 May 1948.

[15]Letter from Brooks Hays to Douglas Branch, 4 April 1957.

vices across the country, and was an expert on the degree to which church and state can and should be mutually supportive and exclusive. He was believed to be a teetotaler. As noted earlier, there was even a drink, a mixture of orange juice and ginger ale, served at his home for parties called "Brooks Hays Punch." Brooks had, of course, not been a teetotaler since 1941, but it served his purposes that his Arkansas constituents and Southern Baptist brothers should consider him a nondrinker. Therefore, he never questioned the image publicly. His slogan, "Never less than one, never more than two," was a well-kept secret among family and close friends.

As a believer in prayer, Brooks never considered Congressional invocations a violation of the separation of church and state. It was he who, virtually alone among the minority Democrats in the new Congress in 1947, encouraged Washington Presbyterian pastor Peter Marshall to take the Senate Chaplaincy when Marshall feared he might insult his predecessor by accepting the post. Brooks was called on to give one of the memorial addresses at Marshall's church when the young minister died in 1949.[16] Yet Brooks was extremely sensitive to the charge that he used religion to get votes. In his Congressional races he tried hard to discourage his supporters from mentioning his church work, and as a member of the Thursday Congressional Prayer Group he persuaded his colleagues to close their meetings to outsiders so that no one would be tempted to bring guests and play on religion.[17]

Brooks had been in Congress only a year and a half when he was given the opportunity, in September of 1944, to visit wartime Britain and France. He had faced no primary opposition from fellow Democrats that year, and the Democratic primary was tantamount to election in November. Republicans had in fact told him, "We like what you're doing," and they planned no challenge in the fall general election. Brooks always believed that Arkansas Republicans benefited by keeping their numbers small so that each party member got a large share of funds when the national G.O.P. sent money down the pipe.[18] About the only political excitement of the year for him came when Bill Fulbright wanted to run for Hattie Caraway's Senate

---

[16]Hays, Conversation with Ronald Tonks, October 1977.

[17]Ibid., August 1977.

[18]Ibid., August 1976.

seat and asked Brooks to approach her about it for him. Brooks answered with a story about an Indian who had six wives and was ordered by the federal government to get rid of five. "You go tell 'em," he told officials.[19] Brooks thought Bill should tell Hattie himself. Fulbright did, and he went to the Senate. Otherwise it was a quiet year for Brooks, and he was able to accept the offer to go to Europe.

He flew, accompanied by Walter Judd, on a British Airways four-motor hydroplane, a "flying boat," which required two days to reach the British Isles, a total of almost twenty-four hours. They went from Baltimore by way of a North Atlantic base to Foynes, Ireland, Brooks arriving without a passport he was supposed to have received before takeoff.[20] After some quick diplomatic negotiations he was finally allowed to proceed to a London still being harassed by buzz bombs, short on all kinds of necessities, blacked out each night. While there he kept busy. He lunched with U.S. Ambassador John Winant and British Foreign Minister Anthony Eden, spent a weekend at Clivedon with Lord and Lady Astor, and attended Parliament, where he heard Churchill speak.[21] He himself addressed the Royal Institute of International Affairs, where he joked that he had also been born in London—Arkansas.[22]

From London he crossed over to Normandy, following the route American soldiers had taken during the invasion just three months earlier. He spent three days in France, making the first contact of any outsider with French Baptists since 1940; and on 22 September 1944, he lunched with Dwight D. Eisenhower at Allied Headquarters in Paris. This was to be the beginning of a long, mutually beneficial friendship. Although Brooks would not be able to support Ike when he ran for president, remaining loyal to the Democrats and supporting his friend Adlai Stevenson in 1952 and 1956, he would make every effort to support Eisenhower's legislative proposals. He would mediate the dispute between Ike and governor of Arkansas Orval Faubus during the Little Rock Central High School racial crisis of 1957. Ike would then appoint him to the Board of Directors of the Tennessee Valley Authority when Brooks lost his House seat in 1958. All this despite the

---

[19]Marion Hays, "How to Live Dangerously," VIII-1.

[20]Hays, *This World: A Christian's Workshop*, 50.

[21]Marion Hays, "How to Live Dangerously," VII-8.

[22]Hays, *A Hotbed of Tranquility*, 206.

fact that Brooks confided to close friends and family that he considered Ike of very average intelligence, a characteristic he felt Ike shared with a later Republican president, Ronald Wilson Reagan.

Upon his return to the States late in September, Brooks granted a number of news interviews, both to the secular and to the religious presses. The Arkansas *Baptist* carried the story of his contact with French Baptists. The Arkansas *Democrat* reported details of his trip, including the way he felt as bombs fell around him in London and how he had been forced to wash his clothes in basins. Whether the *Democrat*'s headlines, "Hays Frightened by Buzz-Bombs; Does His Own Laundry,"[23] was intended to be as amusing as its more imaginative readers believed it to be is not clear. The publicity, however, strengthened Brooks's hold on the Fifth District electorate. He had been recognized as a religious, socially conscious Congressman who took care of local needs, but now he was seen also as a courageous statesman of international stature. He would easily win reelection every other November until 1958.

Because he was now known as a card-carrying patriot, the American Legion asked him to help them put together an economic package to benefit returning veterans. From 1945 through 1947 he would spend almost all his time on the project. He became a cosponsor in the House of the legislation that would be the G.I. Bill of Rights after Senate compromise.[24] In the process of his work for the bill, he sent out a questionnaire to veterans asking what they most needed to reestablish normal lives and discovered that 600,000 of them wanted to return to family-sized farms. He joined with his Senate colleague Bill Fulbright in drafting legislation for this purpose. The Hays-Fulbright program, which sold farm-sized plots of surplus government land at bargain prices to veterans with farming backgrounds, was strongly opposed by Frank Hancock, director of the Farm Security Administration. But Hays and Fulbright offered it as a patriotic gesture of gratitude to the men who had saved the nation, and it was passed.[25] Reminiscent of the program he had sponsored during the 1930s to make land available for sharecroppers to purchase, the Hays-Fulbright program was, according to Brooks, one of his greatest achievements.[26]

---

[23]Brooks Hays, Conversation with Ronald Tonks, 24 August 1976.

[24]Hays, *This World: A Christian's Workshop*, 3.

[25]Hays, *Politics Is My Parish*, 149.

[26]Hays, Conversation with Ronald Tonks, August 1976.

Brooks was unopposed in his first reelection bid in 1944, but in 1946 two returning war veterans, Lt. Col. Parker Parker and Major Homer Berry, challenged him for his seat. This was, of course, the year that returning vets all across the nation reached out for power, the year in which Richard Nixon of California and John Kennedy of Massachusetts were elected to the House of Representatives and Joseph McCarthy of Wisconsin was elected to the Senate. Brooks had kept his fences mended, however, and his constituents were satisfied with his work. He defeated Parker and Berry—"Parker Parker and Berry Berry" as his House colleague Wright Patman called them—quite handily, rolling to a clear majority in the three-man race.[27]

Brooks attacked postwar problems, both domestic and foreign, with relish. He worked hard for the Marshall Plan to revive the economy of western Europe. He called it a distribution of seed money that would eventually yield great benefits for America as well as the rest of the world. He called it the political equivalent of foreign missions and told audiences that a poor blind man in his district told him that the Marshall Plan was "our Christian duty." He told people that he hoped in the future the churches and the government would coordinate their world aid programs for better effect.[28]

Brooks had taken his first big political risk as a Congressman when he voted in 1943 to end the Martin Dies Committee, later called the House UnAmerican Activities Committee, which had been appointed in 1938 to uncover foreign subversion in the United States. He had been one of only ninety Congressmen to vote against the committee, the only one from Arkansas, and he had received extensive criticism at home in Arkansas for it.[29] In 1946, John Rankin of Mississippi introduced the resolution to give HUAC a new term, this without House Speaker Sam Rayburn's approval, and Brooks was the only House member from the Deep South to vote no. Again there was grumbling back home, but Rayburn was so grateful that he put Brooks on the Democratic Patronage Committee.[30] He was at the same time a black sheep and the teacher's pet.

He did not fare so well the next time he voted liberal on an issue his district considered important. He was the only member of the Arkansas

---

[27]Hays, *Politics Is My Parish,* 158.

[28]Ibid., 166-68.

[29]Marion Hays, "How to Live Dangerously," VII-16.

[30]Hays, Conversation with Ronald Tonks, October 1977.

delegation and one of only a half dozen from the entire solid South to vote against the first version of the Taft-Hartley Bill, which sought to limit the power of labor unions to refuse governmental arbitration. He received seventy-five telegrams and stacks of letters from home, all of them protesting his support of collective bargainers, many of the messages abusive; and he said that had there been an election in 1947 he would probably have been kicked out of office.[31] But he rode out the storm, hoping his constituents would know that he was doing what he thought best, and he was relieved when in conference the three provisions of the bill he opposed were removed. He did vote for the final version of the bill and even voted to override President Truman's veto of this bill so odious to liberal Democrats.[32] He was back in good graces at home, and with a clear conscience.

By Arkansas and Southern standards Brooks was a liberal, by national standards a moderate. He knew, and so did his colleagues, that a true national liberal could not survive political tests in Arkansas. There were times he would have voted liberal but simply could not afford to do so. He would not be able to be the true liberal he wanted to be until events conspired to drive him out of office in 1958. Meantime, as a representative of the people in the Fifth, he had to be cautious and do what he could to make the nation a better place without losing the support back home he needed to remain in power. He was not above playing the patriotic game to mask some of his more unpopular activities, as when he sponsored the legislation that changed the Statue of Liberty's island in New York harbor from Bedloe to Liberty Island[33] and later sponsored legislation to erect a memorial to veterans of the war in the Pacific. This is not to say that his efforts were insincere, only that they were politically savvy.

In 1948, as in 1944, Brooks was unopposed for renomination. In his diary he described how it felt to be unopposed by recalling how a sheriff of Yell County had put it: "You don't have to laugh when you ain't tickled."[34] But he did run into trouble that year when he publicly supported Harry Truman in his bid for reelection to the presidency. At a public meeting in Little Rock, a Mr. Wooten openly castigated Brooks for defending Tru-

---

[31]Ibid., August 1976.

[32]Ibid.

[33]Ibid., October 1977.

[34]Hays, *This World: A Christian's Workshop,* 64.

man, whom Wooten called a communist sympathizer and race mixer. Woo-
ten was, by the way, supporting Dixiecrat presidential candidate Strom
Thurmond. Brooks refused then or any other time to strike back in kind.
He told Wooten and his cronies that he respected their opinion, even though
he could not agree with them, and their snarls died down. Truman lost the
Fifth District, but he carried Arkansas, and the complaints slowly stopped.
Even members of Brooks's Sunday school class, many of whom had bit-
terly resented his support for Truman, soon forgave him his trespasses.[35]

Truman asked Brooks why he had encountered such opposition in Arkansas. Brooks assured him, perhaps incorrectly as it turned out, that the
problem was not race, despite Truman's civil rights proposals, but economics. Many Arkansans were Democrats in name only—in economic matters
the wealthier ones were Republicans, Brooks explained. He regaled Truman with the story about a man who, when visiting a friend for dinner,
asked how long his cook had been with him. "She's never been with me,"
the friend replied. "She's been against me from the start."[36] But it should
have been obvious to Brooks, even in 1948, that the National Democratic
party and its Southern wing, for eighty years solidly loyal, were beginning
to part ways. The Dixiecrat movement was just a first step. There would
be periodic reconciliations but no permanent healing, particularly as presidential nominees grew ever more liberal. Only Kennedy and Carter would
carry the South for the Democrats between 1948 and 1988. The issue, even
if Brooks would not say so to Truman, was race.

Knowing how poorly Truman's civil rights plan was received in the
South, yet knowing that Truman believed it had led to his reelection and
would doubtless propose it to the Eighty-first as he had to the Eightieth
Congress, Brooks made a fateful decision: to formulate, write, and propose
an alternative plan. Early in 1949, only six months after battling for Truman in a state that hated his plans for the racial reorganization of the nation, Brooks introduced to Congress his own plan to bring racial justice to
the republic without pushing the white South beyond its limits of toleration. Soon to be labelled the "Arkansas Plan" after the home state of its
author, it called for equal justice before the law but left enforcement to the
states and carefully avoided any mention of integration.

---

[35]Hays, Conversation with Ronald Tonks, August 1976.

[36]Ibid.

The Arkansas Plan will be discussed in some detail in chapter 6, but its three major proposals were to wipe out the poll tax by a constitutional amendment, to declare lynching a crime but let the states prosecute cases, and to create a federal board to encourage without forcing fair employment practices. By today's standards, by the standards of what came after it, the Arkansas Plan sounds pathetically modest; but in its day, proposed by a representative from the South, it was strong enough to turn a few heads toward Brooks Hays, making him a center of attention. His life and career, whether he knew it or not, were about to change.

On 1 April 1949, *U.S. News* published an article on the resistance of the solid South to integration and featured the Arkansas Plan, with a photograph of its author, as the only sane and workable compromise any Southerner had proposed.[37] Truman met with Brooks in private and told him that he considered it a good plan, definitely a step in the right direction, and that he would sign it if it passed Congress. He had made promises during the campaign, however, to support a stronger bill, and for political reasons he could not publicly endorse the Arkansas Plan.[38] It was hotly debated for a time, criticized by Northern liberals as being too weak and by Southern conservatives as being too strong, and at last it was dropped. It was too moderate for either extreme; and in 1949 the middle ground was too narrow to support any civil rights bill.

Brooks turned to other matters. After a conversation with the man who was perhaps his best friend on Capitol Hill, Senator Mike Monroney of Oklahoma, Brooks introduced a resolution to install a prayer room in the Capitol. While he believed in the Baptist principle of the separation of church and state, he also believed that representatives of the people, like the people themselves, needed a quiet place to pray for divine guidance in their work. He said, in defense of what some might call an element and example of the American Civil Religion, that with all due respect to what Jefferson had called the impregnable wall between politics and religion "to be impregnable it need not be impenetrable." While neither church nor state should try to give the other orders, they need not be enemies. He was proposing a room for personal, not private, devotion.[39] But House Speaker Sam Rayburn saw things differently, feared that it would be seen as an

---

[37]"Portrait," *U.S. News,* 1 April 1949, 28.

[38]Hays, Conversation with Ronald Tonks, August 1976.

[39]Hays, *Politics Is My Parish,* 175.

effort to use religion for political purposes, and put an end to the idea—for the moment.[40]

Brooks had to wait four years to try again and two more before the room was completed. In 1953, after the Eisenhower landslide brought in a Republican Congress, the new leader Joe Martin would respond favorably to Brooks's renewed request for the room and tell him to draw up a bill. He would write it, introduce it, shepherd it through Congress, and be named Chairman of the Prayer Room Committee, the only Democrat to chair a committee in the Eighty-third Congress.[41] The room, which would open to fanfare in March 1955, had once been the Congressional barroom. Its stained glass window, donated anonymously by a Los Angeles window maker, featured symbols of Catholicism, Protestantism, and Judaism, along with a picture of George Washington kneeling in prayer.

According to the rules Brooks drew up to satisfy politically and religiously sensitive Congressmen, the room was to be completely private. No Congressman could be photographed praying there or even coming or going to and from it. No meetings could be held there, no constituents taken there. It was to be purely for prayer. Still Brooks got his due recognition for the idea and for carrying it through to reality. Under the heading, "For Congress, A Place to Pray," *U.S. News* wrote, "A Sunday school teacher in Congress is realizing an old dream." There followed the story of Brooks's efforts to give representatives a chance to seek divine guidance.[42]

Brooks had only token opposition for reelection in 1950; and as the Eighty-second Congress convened in 1951, he surrendered his seniority on the Banking and Currency Committee to move to Foreign Affairs. He was ready to turn his attention to a wider world.

―――――――

Brooks had always advocated a bipartisan approach to foreign policy, believing that party politics should end at the water's edge, and now on the Foreign Affairs Committee he was able to put his theory into practice. He teamed up with Walter Judd to make public appearances in which they brought international issues before American audiences. Judd, who could be bitterly partisan about his conservatism, would often speak—too long,

―――――――

[40]Hays, Conversation with Ronald Tonks, October 1977.

[41]Ibid., August 1976.

[42]"For Congress, A Place to Pray," *U.S. News*, 25 March 1955, 14.

Brooks complained gently—on the need for Congress to have a larger say in foreign affairs. Then Brooks would speak, in what time remained, on behalf of a stronger United Nations. In 1949 the two had sponsored House Concurrent Resolution 64: "to support and strengthen the United Nations, and to seek its development into a world federation open to all nations with defined and limited powers adequate to preserve peace and prevent aggression through the enactment, interpretation, and enforcement of world law."[43] The resolution, opposed by such organizations as the Veterans of Foreign Wars, said by them to be unpatriotic, had failed; but Brooks and Judd had continued their crusade. Judd, who had been a medical missionary in China, had changed his mind about parts of the resolution after the 1949 communist victory in mainland China, but events in Korea the next year made him a supporter of the United Nations once more. He and Brooks were complementary partners.

In 1951 Brooks found himself walking a political tightrope for a time when Truman fired General of the Army Douglas McArthur. He agreed with Truman that McArthur's insubordination was intolerable and that he had to be relieved of his command in Korea; but he had to be careful not to criticize a hometown boy, McArthur having been born in Little Rock. Word spread that Brooks opposed inviting McArthur to address a joint session of Congress, and Brooks took some pains to deny it, reminding his constituents that, in fact, he had been the first Congressman to suggest the idea. What he failed to say was that he had done so in 1945, at the end of the war, six years before the struggle with Truman over the Korean Police Action.

Two other events stand out in Brooks's first couple of years on Foreign Affairs. He cosponsored and introduced to Congress the Hays-Devereaux Bill, which set aside land and money to erect a memorial to the battle on Iwo Jima in honor of Pacific veterans. Sculptor Felix de Weldon recreated in bronze the image Associated Press photographer Joe Rosenthal had captured as the American flag was raised on that island after the bloody and costly battle to capture it from the Japanese.[44] And Brooks also went on a fact-finding mission to West Germany to study U.S. policies of postwar occupation. Chancellor Konrad Adenauer was disturbed about these policies and was calling for changes. Brooks was part of a team, all mem-

---

[43]Hays, *Politics Is My Parish,* 161.

[44]Ibid., 178.

bers except him coming from the North, that met with Adenauer to discuss problems. In the meeting Brooks explained that he should give Americans, "these Yanks," a bit more time. He explained that he was from a state that had once been occupied by Yankees, but now he loved them.[45] The humor was apt and appreciated by both sides, and Adenauer later commented that Brooks had helped them all relax and get down to business.

The year 1952 was again easy on Brooks as an incumbent. He was renominated and reelected with only token opposition, as he would be in 1954 and again in 1956. But it was not an uneventful year. In January he stirred a minor controversy when he and an Illinois Democratic Senator suggested publicly that both the Democratic and Republican parties nominate Eisenhower for president. Brooks later apologized and admitted that it was an ill-advised suggestion, that he was just thinking of ways to keep the nation united in what would likely be a devisive year. He explained that he had, of course, expected the Democrats to win Congress. When Eisenhower declared himself a Republican and won that party's nomination, Brooks fell into line to support the Democratic candidate, his old friend Adlai Stevenson.

That same year Brooks's article "Faith Steadies the Politician" appeared in the *Christian Century* and was read into the *Congressional Record* by Walter Judd.[46] The Congressman who had held major office in the largest American denomination—vice president of the Southern Baptist Convention in 1950—was now beginning to gain a constituency far beyond the Fifth District. That summer the Democrats, knowing of his moderate position on civil rights, which he considered a moral issue, named him to the Platform Committee for its national convention. He hammered out the language that would please few but offend even fewer and could be adopted by the American political party with larger numbers but less cohesion than its rival. His language helped hold that party together, despite losing, through the campaign.

As Brooks spent more and more time on foreign affairs, his opinions grew firmer and more widely known and appreciated. In 1954, as the French lost control of their empire in southeast Asia, he called on the Eisenhower administration to take an active part in the settlement there.

---

[45]Ibid., 173.

[46]Brooks Hays, "Faith Steadies the Politician," *Christian Century* (10 June 1952): 698-99.

He did suggest seeking China's help in setting up negotiations, which was anathema to Secretary of State John Foster Dulles, and he even advocated trading with Communist China in nonstrategic materials; but he stood against admission of China to the United Nations, which would have meant the expulsion of Taiwan. Just as he was on race a "states' rights liberal," so he was in foreign affairs a "cold war liberal"—a man with more vision than most of his contemporaries but still a man of his times.

As a result of his interest in and contribution to American foreign affairs for two Congressional terms, Brooks was in 1955 named a U.S. delegate to the Tenth General Assembly of the United Nations. He threw himself wholeheartedly into a job that others might have considered routine and made a special study of every issue that came before him. He made speeches and wrote reports on Korean reconstruction,[47] technical assistance to lesser developed countries,[48] and the fund for economic development.[49] He was particularly intrigued by the problems of third world nations in Asia and Africa and encouraged the more-developed nations to help these countries as a way of binding the human race more closely together and thus keeping the peace. He insisted that instead of calling these countries "underdeveloped" that they be called "less developed," since even the more-developed ones had pockets of severe underdevelopment. And he argued that when more-developed countries aid less-developed ones both benefit from the exchange.

His tenure was not all serious, however, and there were times of laughter. The Brooks Hays mark of humor was left on the Tenth General Assembly, as it was left on mid-century Congresses. One particular moment was long remembered by participants. When the Soviet Union introduced a resolution to have its puppet state of Outer Mongolia admitted to the United Nations as an independent nation with a vote of its own, Brooks stood to argue that the United States might well try to have Texas admitted as Outer Arkansas.[50] It is not known whether or not the Russians laughed. Texans did so reluctantly.

Once again in 1956, as in 1952, Brooks was asked to help write the civil rights plank for the Democratic National Convention's platform. Civil

---

[47]*U.S. Department of State Bulletin,* 24 October 1955, 672-73.

[48]Ibid., 14 November 1955, 804-808.

[49]Hays, *Politics Is My Parish,* 163.

[50]Hays, *A Hotbed of Tranquility,* 227.

rights was becoming an increasingly important subject for the two parties; and the Democrats, still deeply divided between their Southern conservative and Northern liberal wings, needed Brooks's moderate touch. In the late spring of 1957 he was elected president of the Southern Baptist Convention, and that summer he earned the gratitude of the Eisenhower Administration—particularly Ike's Chief of Staff Sherman Adams—by reversing himself on a foreign aid package. In July 1957 the House Foreign Affairs Committee seemed determined to deny Ike the three-year foreign aid appropriation he had requested. It tentatively approved a one-year plan instead. But Brooks, as *Time* magazine called him "the pivot," was uneasy about the one-year decision. His year at the United Nations had made him aware of the need for long-range planning.[51] After a call from Adams asking him to reconsider and a weekend to think it over, he changed his vote and thus reversed the decision. The committee approved the Eisenhower plan, as did Congress. Eisenhower called to thank Brooks personally.[52]

Brooks, Adams, and Eisenhower would meet again in the near future, when the Little Rock Central High School racial crisis exploded two months later. Brooks would try to mediate the squabble between the Republican national administration and Democratic governor of Arkansas Orval Faubus. Once again Brooks would earn Ike's respect and gratitude, if not that of his Democratic constituency back home. Late in 1957 he wrote to his father to tell him that he had been approached about a federal judgeship. In the letter he recalled how he had been blocked from the bench by Hattie Caraway when Roosevelt wanted to make him a judge twenty years before and how he had ruled himself out when approached earlier in the 1950s. Now he was interested. He would talk with Bill Fulbright and maybe John McClellan,[53] Arkansas' two United States senators.

Times had changed. Earlier in the decade he had been secure in his House seat. But after mediating the Central High controversy there were smoldering threats to unseat him, and he feared one of them might just succeed. As president of the Southern Baptist Convention, he was a moral leader, and perhaps politics seemed just a bit too worldly for him. The bench might give him the wider forum he sought for his ethical pronouncements.

---

[51]"About Face," *Time,* 15 July 1957, 17.

[52]Hays, Conversation with Ronald Tonks, August 1977.

[53]Letter from Brooks Hays to Steele Hays, December 1957. Brooks Hays Collection, University of Arkansas, Fayetteville.

He saw that in the era of the Warren Court, the federal judiciary had become the major arena of social reform. And he was almost sixty years old, perhaps ready for a more leisurely pace. In the end, however, he heard no more about the federal appointment. He guessed his nomination had been blocked by one of the Arkansas political establishment figures, and he suspected John McClellan, whom Truman had once told him was "a mean son of a bitch."[54] At any rate, he returned to his House seat and prepared for the election of 1958.

Late in 1957 the Russians sent up Sputnik, the first man-made earth satellite; and in 1958 Sam Rayburn appointed Brooks to a newly created blue-ribbon committee, one that would look into America's need to explore space. Rayburn was said to have considered the space business a passing fancy and to have said that the committee's work was a waste of time; but the panel took its work seriously, set up an agency to develop a space program, and eventually helped establish NASA, the National Aeronautics and Space Administration.[55]

The year 1958 also found Brooks joining Maine Congressman Frank Coffin on a Special Study Mission to Canada. Brooks had always been interested in hemispheric solidarity, and he was eager to look into problems that existed between the two North American neighbors. He listened as Prime Minister John Diefenbaker complained of the trade imbalance between the two nations and excessive American ownership of Canadian oil, mining, and manufacturing industries.[56] The Hays-Coffin Report, which was published and had a great impact on Canadian-American relations during the next decade, called for mutual understanding and cooperation to solve problems and resolve differences. It led to the establishment by Congress and Parliament of a joint Canadian-American committee to oversee trade disputes and a better climate of cooperation between the two nations in a number of economic areas.[57]

Brooks met Diefenbaker's wife while in Canada and learned that she was the daughter of a Baptist minister. He invited the Diefenbakers to attend the 1958 Southern Baptist Convention in Houston, where he would

---

[54]Hays, Conversation with Ronald Tonks, September 1975.

[55]Ibid., August 1976.

[56]Hays, *Politics Is My Parish,* 177.

[57]Hays, Conversation with Ronald Tonks, September 1977.

preside, but at the last minute they could not come. Diefenbaker did attend the joint meeting of the Southern and American Baptist Conventions in Atlantic City, New Jersey, in 1965, as Brooks's guest. The long arm of Brooks Hays, religious leader and politician, continued to mold both political and religious events for a long time after he left office.

As Brooks faced reelection in 1958 he had reason for optimism, despite the animosities he had stirred statewide for his efforts to mediate the crisis at Central High School. Although he was being called an integrationist, a race mixer, even a "nigger lover," he had over the past eight terms earned the respect and even love of his constituents. He was the father of countless bills that helped them economically; he was president of the Southern Baptist Convention, with which a plurality of them were affiliated; and he was known to be an authority on world affairs. Even his enemies, which were few, believed him to be politically invulnerable. Most people in the Fifth District thought that he had made a mistake by taking Ike's side in the Little Rock mess, had gone too far out on a shaky limb, but while they would not mind giving him a warning, they did not really want him to lose. It might be a difficult year, but it would end, as usual, with a victory.

He appeared to be right when the results of the Democratic primary in June were in. His opponent, Amis Guthrie, was an avowed segrationist and ran a racist campaign against him. Guthrie, who in 1955 had been a charter member of White America, Inc., a group that later merged with the White Citizens Council, called Brooks a race mixer and said that since race mixing was unconstitutional all its proponents were communists. Brooks responded, in his moderate way, by explaining that he had the year before merely tried to keep peace and order, that he had not tried to alter Southern patterns of life. He also said that he had not been consulted about sending federal troops into Little Rock.[58] But he refused to speak ill of Negroes, and when he was told that he should match Guthrie's oratory he said, "I am not a hater. If my district wants a hater, I'm not the man."[59]

Today these words almost sound like Brooks was daring his constituents to turn him out of office, but at the time *Newsweek* magazine heard

---

[58]Brooks Hays, *A Southern Moderate Speaks* (Chapel Hill: University of North Carolina Press, 1959) vii-viii.

[59]"Victory Without Hate," *Newsweek*, 23 June 1958, 28.

in them the challenge of a true statesman for his people to turn from racism to humanitarianism. And he was temporarily vindicated. He won the primary against Guthrie 43,000 votes to 28,000;[60] and in his district winning the Democratic primary had always been tantamount to reelection. The Republicans had not even nominated an opponent for November. He felt he had weathered the storm. In 1960, if he chose to run again, there would be other issues. The worst was over. The dust would now settle. He would later admit that once he had defeated Guthrie he got cocky. He spent very little time in the district between June and October, preoccupied with church work, sure of reelection.[61] He moved about the country, a national, international, religious leader, leaving the home fires untended.

On 12 September 1958, however, two news items provoked the voters of the Fifth District. One reported that the United States Supreme Court had just ruled that Little Rock schools must desegregate without further delay. The other, complete with photograph of Brooks posing with a group of black ministers, reported his attendance at the National (Black) Baptist Convention in Chicago.[62] Passions in Little Rock and westward, making a connection between the two stories, were enflamed against Brooks. Within days Little Rock Central High School had been closed for the remainder of the school year, and the populace was on edge. Still Brooks went about his larger duties, unaware of what was happening at home. Then just eight days before the general election of 4 November, Dr. Dale Alford, a Little Rock eye surgeon, announced that he would oppose Brooks in the election as an independent write-in candidate.

Although Governor Orval Faubus would always deny involvement in this challenge, saying at the University of Arkansas in 1975 that he had in fact discouraged Alford from running, that if he had wanted to hurt Brooks he would have entered an opponent in the primary, it seems certain that he and his cronies set the plot in motion. Having the year before cast his lot with segregationists, both in Arkansas and across the South, Faubus simply could not tolerate Brooks's moderation to stand in contrast to his own actions. Faubus did apparently have second thoughts about the effort after he had talked with the sheriff of Conway County, but by then it was too late to force Alford's withdrawal. Faubus's field generals, led by

---

[60]Marion Hays, "How to Live Dangerously," X-7.

[61]Hays, Conversation with Ronald Tonks, August 1976.

[62]Hays, *Politics Is My Parish*, 184.

aide Claude Carpenter, who took a leave of absence from the Public Service Commission to run Alford's campaign, had already plotted the method
of attack and could not be persuaded to change their minds.[63]

Brooks, although embittered by the way was ambushed and sent down
to ignoble defeat, would always harbor a tender spot in his heart for Orval
Faubus. He had spent several days with him during the Little Rock Central crisis, and he felt he knew him well. He considered him a talented man,
potentially a good man, who had a profound weakness, a need to be popularly approved regardless of the way he earned the approval. He seemed
to be almost a classical Greek tragic hero. In 1958 he would win and Brooks
would lose; but in history Brooks would be the winner and Faubus the loser.

Dale Alford had, as a member of the Little Rock School Board in 1955,
voted to approve Superintendant of Schools Virgil Blossom's desegregation plan. He had been, however, the most racist member of the board and
had been persuaded to approve it only by being convinced that it was the
minimum plan that the law would allow. Now as a candidate for Brooks's
House seat he had a chance to capitalize on public disapproval of the plan
he had helped pass. Having once been a radio announcer in college, the
forty-two-year-old Alford adapted well to the new technique of television
campaigning. Since the bulk of the Fifth District's population lay within
viewing distance of Little Rock, his eight-day campaign was manageable.

In his ads he reminded veterans that Brooks had opposed a plan to raise
benefits for their non-service-related disabilities. He reminded postal employees that Brooks had not supported their appeal for an immediate pay
raise. Since Guthrie's attacks on Brooks had proved vain, Alford did not
try to convince people that Brooks was evil. Instead he referred to him as
a well-meaning, fuzzy-headed do-gooder, a "national" Democrat, a moderate in a segregationist state. He criticized him for not praising the work
of Arkansas' great governor. In short, he said in so many words that Brooks
was no longer in touch with the sentiments of his people. He should be
turned out to pasture. Near the end of the campaign he announced that at
every polling booth there would be men with stickers bearing the name of
Dale Alford and an X. All the voter had to do was take one and stick it on
his ballot to register a protest to the Brooks Hays way of conducting business and to restore traditional Southern values.

A week before the election Brooks hurried home from a Baptist meeting to face his worried staff. Some of his advisers told him to say publicly

---

[63]Ibid., 181-82.

that he was a segregationist. Otherwise, he might lose the election. "I can't say that," he told them, "for the simple reason that I am *not* a segregationist."[64] He might not have favored forced integration, and he may have deplored the use of troops to see court orders carried out, but he would not stoop to say that he believed in the old patterns of discrimination. Having always been able to persuade the people of his district of his way of thinking, or at least persuade them that he was doing what was best for them, he believed he could still count on his old methods. He found that racism knows no reason. People would no longer listen. He appealed to Alford's party loyalty, reminding him that he had pledged, by voting in the primary, that he would support the party's nominee in November; but his words fell on deaf ears. He protested that the use of stickers was unconstitutional, but the governor's office had the attorney general declare them legal.

Political advertisements in the Arkansas *Gazette* on Monday, 3 November, the day before the election, are revealing. The one for Faubus, who was seeking reelection as governor, identifies him as Friend of the Working Man. The one for Alford asks, "What Does Brooks Hays Stand For?" and recalls the fact that he attended the Birmingham Conference in 1939, where resolutions sought to overturn the Southern way of life. The Brooks Hays ads, not as positive as one might expect, reminded voters that Alford had voted to integrate the Little Rock schools at a board meeting on 24 May 1955. These were the last hurrahs before Tuesday, 4 November 1958.[65]

The turnout for the election, as usual in one-party Arkansas, was low. Brooks had received 12,000 more votes in the June primary than Alford did in the general election. In June 71,000 persons had cast ballots, in November only 61,000. Yet Alford beat Brooks by 1,100 votes, 31,000 to 29,900. On 5 November the Arkansas *Gazette* would offer the headline: "Election Officials Distribute Stickers For Alford, But Nobody Seems To Care"; and on 6 November Alford would claim that his was a states' rights victory. In all the papers there was shock that such a thing could have happened.[66]

Brooks would claim much later that he knew of approximately 3,000 illegal ballots that were cast. He would say that since the Arkansas con-

---

[64]Ibid., 188.

[65]Arkansas *Gazette* (Little Rock), 3 November 1958.

[66]Ibid., 5-6 November 1958.

stitution did not approve "stick-ins," and certainly not ones that were
handed out by election officials, all of Alford's votes were illegal. He would
say that since Alford had voted in the Democratic primary, he had violated
his promise to support the party's nominee in November. But these charges
came twenty years after the fact, when as an elder statesman he reconsid-
ered the events from afar. At the time he was surprisingly diffident about
the outcome of the election, and as late as a decade later he would say, "I
was defeated because of my position, and that was the high point of my career."[67] He seemed almost glad to lose—for the right reason.

He knew on election night that he was out and had little chance to reverse the vote and perhaps should not try. "I had these basic impulses," he
would say much later, "that grew out of my political philosophy which was
not the popular position."[68] The Fifth District wanted a die-hard segregationist, it did not want him any longer, and he was ready to step aside.
The people believed he was bad for them, he explained to his friends, and
"I can no longer represent the district."[69] He was surprised, when he called
Alford to congratulate him, to hear a secretary answer, "Congressman Alford's Headquarters." When Alford came on the line, he called Brooks "Mr.
Hays," even though he had called him by his first name when earlier that
year he had fitted him for the very pair of glasses he wore that night.[70]

The Fifth District was in a state of shock. A majority of the constituents would have agreed with the woman who told the press, "If I'd known
Brooks was in any real trouble, I wouldn't have voted against him."[71] Most
voters considered their stick-in for Alford merely a protest, a way of blow-
ing off some steam, and they were surprised and sickened by the result of
their collective anger. At his postelection news conference, the largest of
his political career, Brooks was pensive and chastened but not without his
famous sense of humor. He told of discussing the outcome with his eighty-
six-year-old father Steele, who was more disgusted than angry. It was time
to quit anyway, Steele had told him, but he would have preferred to lose

---

[67]Brooks Hays, Public Address, Peabody College, Nashville TN, 13 March 1968.

[68]Hays, Conversation with Ronald Tonks, August 1976.

[69]Harry Ashmore, "They Didn't Want a Man of Reason," *Reporter* (27 November 1958): 21.

[70]Hays, *Politics Is My Parish,* 187.

[71]Marion Hays, "How to Live Dangerously," X-10.

to a more prestigious opponent. He told Brooks, and Brooks told the press, that he felt like the man who, having been kicked by a donkey, pleaded with the doctor to keep him alive long enough for him to catch pneumonia because he did not want on his tombstone: "He was kicked to death by a jackass." That night on the NBC Nightly News David Brinkley repeated the story, and his coanchor Chet Huntley was so convulsed with laughter that he could not complete his sign-off.[72]

That same night on CBS, Eric Severeid devoted his editorial to the Hays defeat, as did radio newscaster Edward P. Morgan, who commented that Brooks had lost for his principles. These were only the opening salvos in what was to be a virtual orgy of praise to a fallen hero. The 1958 election had seen a Democratic landslide overall, with thirteen new Democratic senators; yet one of those new senators, Eugene McCarthy of Minnesota, allowed as how the loser Brooks Hays had been given more press coverage than all the winners combined.[73] Brooks was right to say that this was the high point of his career. He had lost, but "my moral position was impregnable."[74] A host of Americans, both Northerners and Southerners, were about to agree.

Brooks received a telegram from John Kennedy and a letter from Richard Nixon, both offering condolences. Brooks and Nixon were to exchange such condolences for some years, Brooks to Nixon when he lost the presidency in 1960 and in 1962 when he lost his race for governor of California, Nixon to Brooks again in 1966 when Brooks failed in his bid to be governor of Arkansas. In 1968 Brooks wrote Nixon that their letters of condolence were now ended, since "you have quit losing and I have quit running."[75] Neither was true, of course, because Brooks lost another election in 1972, and in 1974 Nixon was forced to resign the presidency. This latter event Brooks called a "tragedy" and hoped Nixon would one day be reconciled with the human family.[76]

It was not just politicians who mourned Brooks's defeat. He received more than 4,000 letters expressing everything from sorrow to outrage over

---

[72]Hays, Conversation with Ronald Tonks, August 1977.

[73]Ibid.

[74]Ibid., August 1976.

[75]Brooks Hays, Public Address, Western Kentucky University, Bowling Green KY, November 1968.

[76]Hays, *Politics Is My Parish,* 193.

the results of the election. On *Face the Nation* he commiserated with the mourners, but still he saw some humor in it all. When Howard K. Smith asked him whether he had known how deeply Arkansans opposed integration and how much trouble he was in, he said that he had known and had tried to warn others. He compared his plight during the past year to that of a man considered by his friends to be a hypochondriac. On his tombstone when he died he had carved, "I told you I was sick."[77] Few others were laughing. A cartoon in the Washington *Post* showed Faubus standing behind Brooks, stabbing him in the back, saying, "I said I wouldn't stand in your way."[78] Harry Ashmore, in an article called "They Didn't Want a Man of Reason" written for the *Reporter,* compared the Hays defeat on 4 November to that of the only other Democratic incumbent to be defeated in races for the House, Coya Knutson of Minnesota. Mrs. Knutson, he explained, lost when her husband complained publicly that her political career was ruining their marriage. Hays was just as much a victim of alienation of affection, that of an entire district.

Ashmore wrote that Brooks stood with the Bible when he declared racism to be wrong and with Edmund Burke when he said that the man who cannot persuade his constituents of his philosophy should relinquish his seat. Brooks may have paid the supreme political price for his moderation, this Hays admirer said, but things might still turn out for the best. Now he was free to speak his mind openly on the racial crisis and other matters; now he was better known nationally than ever before; and now in this larger forum his loss had given him he would be a tremendous force for good.[79] Brooks Hays the politician was becoming Brooks Hays the statesman.

Soon the defeat in Arkansas was being referred to as a political martyrdom by national magazines; and the martyred Brooks Hays was being held up as a hero to the cause of racial moderation. *Time* told his story— along with that of Mississippi Governor James P. Coleman, who had gone to Arkansas to campaign for him that last week, and who was now under severe attack from racists at home—to illustrate what was happening to Southern moderates.[80] *U.S. News* featured Brooks in a question-and-an-

---

[77] Hays, *A Hotbed of Tranquility,* 45-46.

[78] Hays, Conversation with Ronald Tonks, August 1976.

[79] Ashmore, "They Didn't Want a Man of Reason," 20-21.

[80] "Attack from Behind," *Time,* 17 November 1958, 22.

swer format, and there he explained his moderation. While he was not an integrationist, he said, he was a constitutionalist, one who believed that the courts must be obeyed, and such moderation had cost him his political life. He said he was depressed and saw no immediate hope of improvement in Southern attitudes, but he said he refused to surrender to despair.[81] *Newsweek* featured his part in the Newport, Rhode Island, meeting (see chapter 6), when he had brought Eisenhower and Faubus together, and quoted him: "I was so disturbed, I was indifferent to my political future."[82] Brooks was emerging as the one Southern politician with enough moral scruples to do what was right for the nation.

There were numerous suggestions, from writers and other politicians, that Brooks contest the election. He considered it, but he decided not to do so, he said later, because at first he did not know about the subsequently revealed voting irregularities and because he felt that with his district so badly divided he should perhaps just step aside.[83] But he did permit John F. Wells, publisher of the weekly newspaper the Arkansas *Recorder,* to start a campaign to have Congress investigate the election. Wells was no friend of Hays, having several times taken him to task in editorials, but he was convinced that this election had been won by fraud. The Faubus conspiracy to unseat Brooks, he felt sure, had been accomplished by vote buying, stuffing ballot boxes, and the illegal use of name stickers.[84] He wanted to have the election declared invalid and the seat vacant until a new election could be held.[85]

Wells did get the attention of the House Special Elections Committee, and there was an investigation of sorts; but about all Wells got for his troubles was an award the next year for "Courage in Journalism." His efforts did not help Brooks. *Commonweal* magazine, describing Brooks as the "nationally known Protestant lay leader whose views on race are normally described as moderate," warned Congressmen who might be vulnerable to racists at home that for their own good they should support the

---

[81]"What Happened in the Election," *U.S. News,* 14 November 1958, 97.

[82]"Casualty," *Newsweek,* 17 November 1958, 30.

[83]Marion Hays, "How to Live Dangerously," XI-1.

[84]"Conspiracy Charged," *Newsweek,* 29 December 1958, 16.

[85]Hays, Conversation with Ronald Tonks, August 1977.

investigation;[86] and a number of prominent religious and political leaders gave such support. But Southern Democrats were not supportive, and the Democratic leadership, particularly House Speaker Sam Rayburn, showed little interest in the case. The conventional wisdom was that the party could be held together only by following the "Southern strategy" of not threatening segregationists. Most Republicans, except for Vice-President Richard Nixon who promised to support the investigation, fell in line behind their ideological brothers, the Southern Democrats.[87] The investigation turned out to be a whitewash.

The Committee did go to Little Rock, ostensibly to look into the election, but it refused to hear testimony from people ready to admit fraud. Its members said that a citizen protest such as this was not as significant as a protest from a candidate. Had Brooks himself filed the protest, had he pushed for the investigation, they would have given it more time and attention. Since he had not, they felt they were meddling in local political affairs. Majority leader John McCormack, soon to be Speaker of the House, promised Brooks that the House Administration Committee would look into the matter after Alford was seated. Thomas P. O'Neill of Boston, also to be Speaker of the House, made a strong bid to prevent Alford's seating, knowing that afterward it would be virtually impossible to unseat him; but Alford took his seat, and McCormack's promised investigation never materialized. In politics, Brooks would say, possession is nine-tenths of the law.

Alford would serve only two terms, from 1959 to 1963. In 1962 a redistricting plan combined his district with that of the powerful and popular Wilbur Mills, and he decided not to make the race. Instead he ran against his mentor Orval Faubus for governor, lost, and in 1964 supported Faubus for his sixth term. When I tried to contact Dr. Alford to ask his comments on the 1958 election, he refused to see or even talk with me by telephone. Still a practicing optometrist in 1987, he had his secretary refer me to his 1959 book *The Case of the Sleeping People*. All he had to say, the message to me read, was in those pages. All those pages had to say, basically, was that he ran in 1958 to warn the people of Little Rock about the communist menace of the civil rights movement.[88] Whether he believed that during

---

[86]"Election Dispute," *Commonweal*, 19 December 1958, 306.

[87]Hays, Conversation with Ronald Tonks, August 1977.

[88]Dale Alford, *The Case of the Sleeping People* (Little Rock AR: privated printed, Pioneer Press, 1959).

his brief political career he had sufficiently warned them will perhaps never be known.

So Brooks Hays left Congress, and nothing in his years of elective office so became him as the leaving of them. In later life, after he had had time to reflect on those years, he would have both pride and regret. He was sorry it had taken him and the other Arkansas representatives so long to make the Arkansas River Project operational and that, while it had done so much good for so many people, there were still pockets of severe poverty along its shores.[89] He regretted not pushing harder, after it encountered opposition, for the strip mine control bill he had proposed early in his career.[90] And he sadly admitted, despite his image as a champion of civil rights, that in truth he had been too much a man of his time and place to fight for civil rights as his religious convictions often urged him to do.

He was never a committee chairman. The seniority system saw to that. He would have been nearly seventy-nine years old, in 1977, before he could have chaired Banking and Currency, and even older before he could have chaired Foreign Affairs. But he compensated for his lack of parliamentary powers by being a prodigious sponsor of bills, "people oriented" he called them, that caused House action. Once when Representative Jack Anderson of California was asked how the Hays Bill was faring, he replied, "Do you mean the Hays River Bill to save Arkansas, or the Hays Rural Industries Bill to save the South, or the Hays Foreign Relations Bill to save the world?"[91] This was the image of the Congressman Brooks Hays, a veritable whirling dervish of legislative energy, a man who believed that good laws and programs made life better for the people, a social worker in politician's clothing.

Nor did his involvement with Congress and its legislation end when he surrendered his seat in 1959. Brooks served Presidents Kennedy and Johnson as liaison with Congress, using his contacts and skills at negotiation to help them accomplish their ambitious legislative goals. He served as consultant to the House Ethics Committee in the late 1960s. He founded the Close-Up organization to bring young Americans to Washington to see

---

[89]Hays, *Politics Is My Parish*, 170.

[90]Hays, Conversation with Ronald Tonks, August 1976.

[91]Ibid.

the government at work first hand. And in 1970 he and Walter Judd founded the Former Members of Congress, an organization designed to make the knowledge and skills of former members available to Congress and the public, with Brooks serving as its first president from 1970 to 1972.

Brooks was a natural philosopher, curious, reflective, willing and able to speak his mind; and as such he contributed a few lines to the book on human, and particularly American, political thought.

For example, on leadership. He once said that in his early years he had believed it mattered little who was elected to office, that the nation, with good laws, could survive bad leadership, but that over the years he had come to see that the best of laws administered by less than virtuous men will be unjustly executed.[92] He said he considered the Congressmen with whom he served for sixteen years to be generally but not unanimously virtuous. "Their standards," he once said, "are about what you would find among 535 bank presidents, or 535 presidents of Rotary Clubs, or 535 stewards in the Methodist Church, or 535 deacons of the Baptist Church." He did not say 535 ministers. If he found a common failing in the Congressmen he knew, himself included, it was their tendency to say and do exactly what their constituents wanted them to say and do, regardless of their own convictions, regardless of what was best for their constituents.[93] He was analyzing this tendency in 1950, long before he was himself faced with a choice between conviction and expediency when the racial crisis came.

Politics for Brooks was quite often the painful act of choosing between "alternatives, neither of which is ideal," thus making costly moral choices.[94] Choosing the right course, if it does not agree with popular opinion, can lead to defeat; but Brooks believed, as he once told students at Rutgers, "One should never equate success with the ability to get more votes than someone else in a given election."[95] For Brooks, as the title of his last book indicates, politics was a parish, a religious vocation; and as the title of another of his books indicates, the world is the Christian's workshop. "The business of politics," he told the seventh Congress of the Baptist World Al-

---

[92]Letter from Brooks Hays to Hugh Brimm, 11 September 1950. Brooks Hays Collection, Baptist Sunday School Board, Nashville.

[93]"Interview," *Christian Science Monitor,* 14 October 1950, 4.

[94]Hays, *This World: A Christian's Workshop,* vii.

[95]Hays, *A Hotbed of Tranquility,* 230.

liance in Copenhagen in 1947, "is much more than manipulating mass sentiment for particular economic and social ends; it is one of the most satisfying expressions of faith in the efficacy of New Testament teachings."[96]

In 1956, as chairman of the Christian Life Commission, Brooks addressed the Southern Baptist Convention in Kansas City. He warned his audience to avoid the assumption that the church has nothing to do with political action.[97] He would doubtless be appalled today to see how such sentiments have been used to justify the clerical involvement in conservative Republican politics. He had something quite different in mind when he wrote, ". . .the spiritual and moral basis for a free society is found in the universal forces of justice and liberty and love. The great adventure of politics is merely to bring man's laws into alignment with the divine or natural law. It is that simple."[98] What he meant was that the Christian love for mankind should be translated into social programs to help that part of mankind that cannot help itself. If it is simple, it is simple Walter Rauschenbusch and not simple Jerry Falwell. For Brooks, "It will be a great day for the world when religion, education, and politics recognize that the three constitute a tripartite responsibility for the redemptive and humanizing forces in this earthly existence."[99]

---

[96]Hays, *This World: A Christian's Workshop,* 115.

[97]Ibid., 122.

[98]Hays, *Politics Is My Parish,* 279-80.

[99]Ibid., 277.

CHAPTER 5

S0UTHERN BAPTISTS

B rooks Hays's race for Congress in 1933, that ill-starred affair that kept him from trying again for elective office for nearly a decade, ended in the city of Conway, country seat of Faulkner County. The final rally, an outdoor spectacle, was sponsored, organized, directed, and led by local ministers, most of whom supported Brooks because of his well-known religious convictions and involvement. Brooks was leery of the meeting because he feared that religion and politics would be mixed in an inappropriate way. Ultimately, he agreed to appear on the condition that the preachers not try to exploit religion for political purposes. His words fell on deaf ears.

One minister opened the meeting with prayer, another closed it with prayer, both petitioning God for a Hays victory. Brooks was introduced as "our candidate [the preachers' candidate, perhaps God's as well] Brother Brooks Hays." Brooks could never be sure how many votes religion won him that day, but he was pretty sure the rally required his opponents to steal Conway, a town they had expected to win squarely, in order to take Faulkner County away from him.[1] Brooks tried to downplay his religion that day, hoped that the preachers' performances would not affect voters either way, and thereafter always resisted the temptation to use religion to win votes.

Some critics would say that Brooks did, in his own more subtle ways, use religion to forward his political career. It is true that he was a religious man, publicly so, and that he said publicly that he let his religious faith influence his political behavior. He probably used religion to forward his

---

[1]Brooks Hays, *A Hotbed of Tranquility* (New York: Macmillan, 1968) 30-31.

political goals, probably more so than even he was aware. While he warned politicians, himself included, not to claim God's support for their various schemes, he let his constituents know about his deep religious commitment and convictions, said openly that he let his faith influence his behavior, and argued that politicians can and should let church and state interact for the improvement of human life without violating the principle of separation of church and state.[2]

To his way of thinking, religion cannot and should not be hidden or ignored, even in the life of a politician, particularly in the life of a politician, because as he liked to quote Carlyle: "A man's religion or his no-religion is the most considerable part of him."[3] He believed with W. E. Hocking that "It is only religion, reaching the ultimate solitude of the soul, that can create the unpurchasable man, and it is only man unpurchasable by any society, that can create the sound society."[4] An article Brooks wrote in 1952 for the *Christian Century,* America's most influential Protestant magazine, still stands as his best statement on politics and religion—indeed, as one of the best ever written by an American statesman. He admitted at the start that religion has often been and can easily be exploited by politicians and that this has made intelligent, critically minded Americans rightly suspicious of any politician who speaks openly about and practices publicly his religious faith. But he said that this was a pity because he considered it imperative both for religion and for the political process that responsible public officials be able to discuss religion without inhibition.

He said that early in his career he determined never to identify his own candidacy or program with "a righteous cause," never to claim that he was God's man or religion's candidate. While he had at times believed that he was morally right about this or that and had taken risky stands to prove his confidence, he had never used divine approbation to gain advantages at the polls or in legislative sessions. He explained that he prayed over public affairs but only to know what was right, never to win a victory. George Washington, he explained, understood that there can be no public morality without prayer and religion; but Washington also knew that

---

[2]Brooks Hays, Conversation with Ronald Tonks, October 1977, typeset in 15 parts. Southern Baptist Sunday School Board Archives, Nashville TN.

[3]Hays, *A Hotbed of Tranquility,* 231-32.

[4]Brooks Hays, *Politics Is My Parish* (Baton Rouge: Louisiana State University Press, 1981) 261.

prayer and religion should only be used to extend public morality, not to further any particular political program. He said that he found it helpful, as a politician seeking to do what was right, to paraphrase St. Paul at Miletus: "Neither do I count my *political* life dear unto myself."

He went on to recall his 1933 race for Congress and its fraud, and he admitted what a test of faith it had been for him. He said he had prayed as he entered the courtroom for the hearing to determine the election's validity but that his prayer was not to win, simply to avoid being cynical if he lost. As he walked away a loser, he said, he was at peace. "My faith in God and in my fellow man survived that bitter experience," he wrote. "Indeed it was that faith that pulled me through." He also recalled the first year he served in Congress, when his constituents at home had pressured him to vote a certain way on an issue and he had felt he had to vote another way. He was afraid his decision might cost him his reelection in 1944. Again he had prayed for peace of mind, not for political success. He got both the peace and the success as he was reelected, and at that point in his career he believed, as he still did in 1952, that "the eternal God is indeed our certain refuge, and underneath us are the everlasting arms."[5]

Churchmen were pleasantly surprised to hear such words coming from an Arkansas Congressman who was also a prominent Southern Baptist lay minister. The name Brooks Hays would each following year become more closely associated with thoughtful religious and political reasoning. He would continue to practice his religious faith and his political craft in the most public of places. He would continue to do what he considered right, regardless of repercussions and consequences. He would eventually find himself at center stage in a drama watched by the world; and his performance there would make him both a political martyr and something of a religious saint.

Brooks was first and foremost a Baptist. The Baptist denomination of Protestantism, which was born in England but has reached its greatest numerical strength in the American South, molded his character, his philosophy of life and conduct, and his public image. By choosing him as their leader twice in the late 1950s, Southern Baptists both recognized his dedication and worth to the denomination and gave him a forum wider than most politicians ever have to discuss ethical and moral issues. Although

---

[5]Brooks Hays, "Faith Steadies the Politician," *Christian Century* (11 June 1952): 698-99.

he was "Mister Baptist" to the nation, he reached beyond the usual Baptist limitations to be what all Baptists have the potential but few have the courage to be. There are reasons.

Brooks's father Steele was the first Hays to become a Baptist. All those before him were Methodists. The Butlers, his maternal forebears, were Baptists, with his grandfather serving for years as a Baptist preacher; but Brooks's mother was baptized only after Brooks was born.[6] Brooks was persuaded to make his faith public, "was saved"—as the Baptists say—by a Methodist evangelist, and was in the process of joining that church until Steele ordered him to become a Baptist. He married a Methodist and made no effort to make her change her affiliation, although husband and wife both attended Baptist services all their lives. Perhaps knowing that his own Baptist roots were none too secure and seeing his wife's serene faith made him the ecumenist he would be throughout his life.

Brooks always spoke with some bitterness of his boyhood church in Russellville, Arkansas. One has to wonder how he came to develop such a strong faith with such an unattractive initial experience with the Baptists. His pastors were uneducated racists, his teachers barely literate, and the church services unnourishing and at times embarrassing. Indeed from these early experiences came a lifelong reluctance to trust a certain type of Baptist preacher, the man with little education, burdened with the prejudices of his heritage. And he would always consider even the better educated, more sophisticated, large church pastors of his adult years too much like businessmen to trust them with his deepest secret fears and hopes. From boyhood days he was a bit anticlerical, exceptionally so for a Baptist, and he believed strongly in the very Baptist doctrine of the priesthood of every believer. From his childhood through his old age he tended to nourish his own soul through prayer, reading, and social service rather than leave the job to professional practitioners.

He wrestled for a long time, through college and well into law school in Washington, with the question of whether or not to be a minister. The Lutheran minister in Baltimore convinced him that the law and public service, which he later translated into politics, could be just as much a ministry as the pastorate. But it is entirely possible that had he had more positive ministerial role models as a boy he might have opted for the ministry. Had he done so, of course, the political world would have been much

---

[6]Hays, Conversation with Ronald Tonks, October 1977.

poorer; and perhaps even the Baptists would not have benefited as much by Brooks the minister as by Brooks the lay leader. That fictional Russellville neighbor who said "The church won the argument, so Brooks went into politics"[7] may have been right in ways the creator of the story, Brooks himself, could never have understood.

At any rate, instead of a cleric Brooks became a lawyer, a politician, a public servant. He taught Sunday school, served as a deacon, held denominational offices, and preached widely; but for him ministry was primarily politics. As he phrased it, "Politics is my parish." As early as his first races for governor (1928, 1930) and Congress (1933), he considered public office a way of fulfilling his ministry. In his very first race for governor, in 1928, his newspaper advertisements identified him as the "Christian Gentleman" running for the state's highest office. While he never again used such overtly religious language to describe his attitude toward politics, he continued to consider politics a religious vocation.

In 1941, after eight years as a federally employed social worker, in an address to the Christian Rural Fellowship in Nashville, Tennessee, Brooks examined his Southern Baptist version of the social gospel. Quoting St. Paul, "The husbandman that laboreth must be the first to partake of the fruit," he argued that property owners had an obligation to let those who work the land enjoy the first fruits of the land, adequate to their needs.[8] He made no suggestions for socialist reapportionment of land already held by owners, but he made it clear that men should not be permitted to keep recreational land idle while other men go hungry or homeless. Here he demonstrated his dedication to the political ministry by speaking out as a secular evangelist for the noble cause of God's noblest creature. Later as Congressman, with the power of elective office behind him, he worked more moderately but with the same ministerial zeal for social causes.

As a Congressman, he slowly turned his attention to world affairs, and in this field as well he considered politics his secular ministry. His sermon theme was world peace. In his world view the United States was called to play the role neither of domination nor of withdrawal but that of peace maker. He told a meeting of Civitan International as early as 1951, when

---

[7]Brooks Hays, *The Baptist Way of Life* (New York: Prentice-Hall, 1963; Macon GA: Mercer University Press, 1981) viii.

[8]Brooks Hays, *This World: A Christian's Workshop* (Nashville: Broadman Press, 1968) 39.

he was first joining the House Foreign Affairs Committee, in the deepest days of the cold war that led to McCarthyism, that since the love of justice is a God-given human attribute it is logical to assume that the Russians and Chinese have it just as we do, that this common quality can be the basis of peace among nations. A Baptist who believed that Jesus came to bring peace on earth to men of good will, Brooks would work the rest of his life as an evangelist for world peace, which he believed could be achieved by human beings acting on God-given instincts and dreams, whether they recognized those gifts as God-given or not.[9]

Brooks was widely known by Baptists and other Christians involved in social work, outside his home state as well as in Arkansas, long before he was elected to Congress; but his Congressional seat gave him a much wider forum, a wider ministry. As we have seen, less than two years after he entered Congress he made his impressive wartime trip to Britain and made religious periodical headlines by meeting there with Baptist World Alliance president J. H. Rushbrooke, then crossing over to the continent and making the first American Baptist contact with French Baptists since the Nazi conquest of Paris in 1940.[10] Four years later, in 1948, he was made a member of the Southern Baptist Social Service Commission, which would later be called the Christian Life Commission, and would serve on that most liberal and socially minded Southern Baptist board, helping it become the most admired and vilified agency of the convention, until 1960. He would be its chairman from 1955 to 1957 and would encourage its members to explore a number of trails, particularly in the area of racial brotherhood, which caused periodic uproars among conservative Southern Baptist brethren.

In 1950, at the urging and organization of two Southern Baptist ministers who knew and admired his type of secular ministry, Brooks was elected vice-president of the Southern Baptist Convention. Reverend Bruce Price, who had known the Hays family as a boy growing up in Russellville, first suggested the idea to Brooks and pressed him to permit his name to be entered in the contest; and Reverend James Wesbury made the nomination at the Chicago convention. Brooks was elected second vice-presi-

[9]Ibid., 103-106.

[10]Hays, Conversation with Ronald Tonks, August 1976.

dent and served one term. He made no effort to move up to president right away. He was not present for his election in Chicago, but in 1951 he attended the convention in San Francisco at his own expense to show that he appreciated the honor.[11]

Why neither Brooks nor his supporters made an effort to nominate him for president of the convention in 1951 or soon thereafter is not clear. He was busy in Washington just then, having moved to a new House committee, and perhaps he felt he had enough denominational responsibility with the Christian Life Commission. At the time he was appointed to the commission, it was already trying to formulate policy concerning the racial problems of the South. Brooks heartily agreed with its other members that race was the most important social issue facing Southern Baptists—a white denomination, the largest Protestant one in America, located primarily in a region of the country containing more than half the entire black American population. The 1947 convention in St. Louis and 1948 one in Memphis heard Christian Life Commission reports on the problem. While the first report, called a "Charter of Principles for Race Relations," did not mention the integration of schools or public facilities, it was an unusually progressive document, coming as it did from a denomination composed of white and mostly conservative Southerners. As long as three years later, at the Chicago convention of 1950 when Brooks was elected second vice-president, two Texas delegates railed against a proposal that Negroes be addressed as Mr. and Mrs. But in 1947 and 1948, Christian Life Commission reports were calling for an end to prejudice and for the establishment of community good will between the races. The commission advocated extending to Negroes the right to vote, serve on juries, and receive equal treatment before the law, in other words their constitutional rights. While Brooks did not originate the commission's research and advocacy in this area, he would as a member help perpetuate and accelerate it. He found in this work a ministry he was not fully free to fulfill as a representative from Arkansas.

As Brooks found himself dealing with the political fallout of the 1954 Supreme Court decision declaring public school segregation unconstitutional, his Christian Life Commission reported to the convention meeting in St. Louis that it found the *Brown vs. Board of Education of Topeka* decision compatible with Baptist Christian principles, commended the court

---

[11]Ibid.

for giving the South time to adjust to the new reality, and urged Baptists to stand for peace and moderation in the period of transition before them.[12] In this report, which caused major consternation among delegates from the Deep South, the commission was doing its best to fulfill its role of helping Southern Baptists apply the teachings of Christ to human social problems. Brooks would say later that while he did not necessarily agree at the time with the report's assumption that the court's decision was constitutional, he did agree with its call for justice and brotherhood and was in full agreement with the commission's attempt to educate Southern Baptists concerning the religious dimensions of the racial crisis.

In May 1955, Brooks was once again reelected to the commission, and at the Ridgecrest Baptist Assembly in July he was made its chairman. He would serve as chairman for two years, until he was elected president of the Southern Baptist Convention, and would see to it that this was one of the commission's most active, productive, and controversial periods of service. One of his first acts as chairman was to help the commission apply for and receive a $15,000 grant from the Fund for the Republic to provide Southern Baptist pastors with information about the Supreme Court's desegregation order. Brooks was not fully aware when he suggested making the request, helped write the proposal, and enjoyed accepting it from the fund what a storm of protest he was stirring.

The Fund for the Republic, headed by former University of Chicago president Robert M. Hutchins, was underwritten by the Ford Foundation. Since 1952 it had made outright grants to organizations seeking to educate the public on a number of matters of national concern. Its purposes were to eliminate restrictions on freedom of thought, to promote liberty and equal opportunity, and to foster a better understanding of the United States Constitution. Its board agreed with Brooks that Southern Baptist pastors, if properly educated about the current racial crisis, could render immense service by helping maintain an atmosphere of sanity in the South. No sooner had the grant been made, however, than the fund came under intense national scrutiny and brought the wrath of Southern Baptist conservatives down on the head of the Christian Life Commission.

The first attack on the fund came early in 1955 from radio commentator Fulton Lewis, Jr., and in July Congressman Carroll Reece of Ten-

---

[12]Brooks Hays, *A Southern Moderate Speaks* (Chapel Hill: University of North Carolina Press, 1959) 201.

nessee attacked it on the floor of the House of Representatives, calling it a left-wing subversive organization. Then in 1956, just after it made the $15,000 grant to the Christian Life Commission, the House UnAmerican Activities Committee decided to investigate its activities. Immediately, a hailstorm of hysterical protest from Southern Baptists descended on the commission. The commission's executive officer, A. C. Miller, was called before the Southern Baptist Convention's Executive Committee in June 1956 to defend taking the money. He tried to explain that since the commission was not adequately funded by the convention, since it received no convention money at all for education on the race issue, it had to seek outside funding. Brooks tried to help Miller later in the year by saying publicly that while he did not agree with everything the Fund said and did, he considered it and its directors thoroughly American in their attempts to promote the public good.

All such defense, well stated as it was, proved useless as H.U.A.C. continued to probe the Fund. Grassroots Southern Baptists raised holy hell about the way a convention agency had accepted funds from a "subversive" organization. "The Selma Baptist Association" of Alabama, led by one Jack Trammell of Sardis, after studying certain "trends" in the Southern Baptist Convention, called on the Christian Life Commission to return the "tainted" $15,000. Trammell would go on to press his cause and would make it a motion at the Southern Baptist Convention of 1958. But already by November 1957, with Brooks now president of the convention, A. C. Miller was so hard pressed to explain the scandal that he asked Brooks for a statement from the United States attorney general to the effect that the Fund had never been on the Justice Department's list of subversive organizations. H.U.A.C. did finally issue its report on 30 March 1958, concluding that while it found some of the fund's liberal notions unpalatable, it could find no evidence of subversion or lack of patriotism and preferred to spend its time on more obvious enemies of the nation. The report, released by Representative Francis Walter, said that the Fund did little educating and recommended that it lose its tax-exempt status, but it could find no major fault with its work. This allowed Brooks and the Christian Life Commission to say that the Fund had been investigated merely to determine its tax status, but the howls of protest from certain ambitious Southern Baptist fundamentalist politicians continued to be heard.

They continued in large measure because, in the field of race relations as in other areas of public moral concern, the Christian Life Commission continued to deal with sensitive issues and to speak out as the gospel and not as Southern tradition dictated. The commission spent most of its energy addressing traditional Southern Baptist concerns with traditional Southern Baptist approaches and drew traditional Southern Baptist conclusions. Along with forums and reports on labor relations, the commission in Brooks Hays's time held forums on obscenity in literature and films. Along with sessions and reports on race relations came sessions on alcoholism and gambling. Brooks wrote to A. C. Miller on 5 November 1957, saying that in every speech he made he emphasized the time the commission spent on such things as alcoholism and obscenity because "I think it is good to have the attention of our Baptist people directed to the fact that we are not confining our interests to race problems."[13] But racists in the Southern Baptist Convention seemed to hear only the commission's statements on race. By raising the issue of race relations, by dealing with it from a Christian perspective, the commission was forcing Southern Baptists to face a problem most of them would just as soon have ignored. It was courting a hostile reaction.

For his part, Brooks seemed to grow more liberal on the race question as he helped the commission and the convention deal with it. He still called himself a moderate regarding race relations, still questioned whether the Supreme Court's desegregation order was wise or even constitutional, but he grew ever more convinced that the gospel demanded Christian brotherhood among the races. He knew from observing the actions and statements of other Christian denominations that Southern Baptists were lagging behind the church as a whole in its racial attitudes and practices. He kept a file on the pronouncements of the other denominations and their leaders and used it to gauge Southern Baptist progress. In 1955 he had said flatly that Southern Baptists needed to take more aggressive action to answer the civil rights challenge and that the commission must take the lead.

At the 1956 Southern Baptist Convention in Kansas City Brooks defended, without using notes for his speech, a Christian Life Commission document supporting the right of submerged people all over the world to strive for their rights.[14] His remarks were commended by the National Council of Churches. Though the statement was condemned by rural pastors, most of whom were not in attendance and heard about it second or

---

[13]Letter from Brooks Hays to A. C. Miller, 5 November 1957. (unless otherwise indicated, all letters are from the Brooks Hays Collection, Baptist Sunday School Board, Nashville, Tennessee.)

[14]Hays, *A Southern Moderate Speaks,* 204.

third hand, Brooks was reelected chairman of the commission. After the 1957 report of the commission to the convention in Chicago, a report that said, "Prejudice against persons or mistreatment of persons on the grounds of race is contrary to the will of God,"[15] Brooks moved that it be received rather than be approved by the delegates, and it was. He was also elected president of the convention.

As noted earlier, during this time Brooks was more confident of the theological requirements of Christian brotherhood than of the constitutional demands of social integration. He seems also to have been more confident that Southern Baptists would understand his racial liberalism than that his congressional district would. In 1956 he let himself be pressured into signing the Southern Declaration of Principles, usually called the Southern Manifesto, which defended traditional Southern racial segregation as against court-ordered integration.[16] But the next year, having been elected president of the convention after defending the Christian Life Commission's liberal racial statement, he intervened to keep the Little Rock crisis from becoming a tragedy. The year after that, still president of the convention, guided by a conscience tuned to the principles of the gospel the commission quoted, he refused to declare himself a segregationist and lost his congressional seat. In the case of Brooks Hays, as he himself believed, the more truly religious a politician is the more he can be depended upon to do the right thing.

In the story of Brooks's expanding ethical sensitivities, the name A. C. Miller stands out. Miller, who directed the Christian Life Commission during the days when it sought to deal with race relations, when uneducated and/or power-hungry Baptist preachers sought to have it disbanded, must have been a remarkable man. He encouraged, helped write, and defended the series of commission reports on race that upset so many conservatives in the convention. He was responsible for issuing a 1957 pamphlet called "Integration," written by Southwestern Baptist Theological Seminary's T. B. Maston, which caused the Louisiana state paper the *Baptist Message* to demand that the convention abolish the commission.[17] He made the convention face its obligations to morality in a time when even a Home Mission Board book on denominational work among blacks, *The*

---

[15]"Portrait," *Newsweek,* 10 June 1957, 76.

[16]Hays, *A Southern Moderate Speaks,* 206.

[17]*Baptist Message,* 8 August 1957.

Long Bridge, was forced out of Baptist bookstores. A courageous man with an unusual degree of ethical foresight, he doubtless influenced Brooks's thinking on racism.

Yet strange to a modern ear sound the words of a letter Miller wrote to Brooks in 1957. Having described the vicious verbal attack one conservative, racist Southern Baptist pastor had made on the commission, Miller concluded by quoting the Nashville daily paper's cartoon "Hambone." "Hambone" appeared regularly in Southern papers in those years, featuring a small Negro man, a perfect stereotype, who spoke words of folk wisdom in a black dialect. That day "Hambone" said, "Men wid a closed min' ain' so bad—pervidin' dey jus keeps dey *mouf* closed, too."[18] The words were indeed appropriate to conclude a letter about racist remarks, but the fact that Miller quoted them without apparently noticing the racism of the cartoon itself demonstrates just how racist the society in which he and Brooks worked was. It was a difficult time to be a moderate, to avoid compromising Christian values, in a conservative denomination; but Brooks and Miller, of all the men working to establish lines of racial brotherhood, would come closest to doing so. In Brooks's case, it would make him a man of destiny—and of history.

––––––––––––

In July 1956, soon after being reelected a second year as chairman of the Christian Life Commission, Brooks received a letter from Bruce H. Price, the Russellville native whose middle name was Hays for Brooks's father, who was now pastor of the First Baptist Church of Newport News, Virginia. Price had organized the effort to make Brooks a vice-president of the convention in 1950, and now he was suggesting a move to make Brooks the convention president.[19] Price said that he had discussed the idea with Jim Wesbury—pastor of Morningside Baptist Church in Atlanta, Georgia, the man who nominated Brooks for vice-president in 1950—and they agreed it was time for such a move. Price would be elected president of the Southern Baptist Convention's pastors' conference in May. Brooks responded to Price's letter saying that while he was honored by his thought, he felt that with his Congressional duties and work with the Christian Life

––––––––––––

[18]Letter from A. C. Miller to Brooks Hays, 30 June 1958.

[19]Letter from Bruce Price to Brooks Hays, 30 June 1957.

Commission perhaps it would be better not to pursue the plan any further.[20]

Price let the matter lapse for a time, but in March 1957 he wrote to Brooks again, renewing his offer to organize a nomination.[21] This time Brooks responded favorably and even went so far as to suggest that Price ask evangelist Billy Graham to nominate him.[22] Price answered by saying that Graham, who was a member of a Southern Baptist church but spent most of his time on interdenominational evangelistic crusades, was considered by many Baptists not strictly "one of us." He suggested asking J. D. Grey, pastor of the First Baptist Church of New Orleans, Louisiana, and a past president of the convention, to offer the nomination.[23] That same day, without waiting for Brooks' reply, Price wrote to Grey asking him to do the honors, carefully explaining that he was not trying "to start a campaign" for Brooks.[24]

J. D. Grey politely refused. He used the excuse, whether it represented his real feelings or not, that as a past president of the convention he considered it inappropriate for him to lend his influence to any particular candidate. Brooks was of course a somewhat controversial figure in the convention—a politician by trade, chairman of the liberal Christian Life Commission, a layman in a church led mostly by ministers—and to place his name in nomination involved a certain amount of personal risk and daring. But Price was undaunted. He next wrote to Paul Caudill, pastor of the First Baptist Church of Memphis, Tennessee, asking him to nominate Brooks, telling him that he was Brooks's first choice.[25] For two weeks Price stewed, with no answer from Caudill, deciding at one point that he might have to nominate Brooks himself, before word finally came that Caudill was willing to do it.

The Chicago convention in May 1957, though held in a Northern metropolis, was typical of the Southern Baptist annual meetings of the 1950s. The crowds were large and loud, the business was conducted with amazing

---

[20]Letter from Brooks Hays to Bruce Price, 5 July 1956.

[21]Letter from Bruce Price to Brooks Hays, 30 March 1957.

[22]Letter from Brooks Hays to Bruce Price, 4 April 1957.

[23]Letter from Bruce Price to Brooks Hays, 9 April 1957.

[24]Letter from Bruce Price to J. D. Grey, 9 April 1957.

[25]Letter from Bruce Price to Paul Caudill, 18 April 1957.

informality, and pastors milled about looking for old friends and new churches. Unlike the conventions of more recent times, however, there were only scattered, minor plots to change the convention's structure and direction, no busing in of unqualified hordes to vote particular ways on certain staged issues, no real efforts to pack denominational committees with ideological purists. As to the election of convention presidents, candidates tried hard not to appear to be running for the office, past presidents tried not to exert undue influence on the choice, and there was only infrequent griping about outcomes. The controversial Christian Life Commission report on race relations was received by the delegates, despite its liberal slant, and Paul Caudill placed the name of Brooks Hays, one of its authors, in nomination for president of the convention.

Brooks and Ramsay Pollard of the Broadway Baptist Church of Knoxville, Tennessee, received the most votes on the first ballot and went into a runoff. An apocryphal story, which Brooks often told in later years, had one delegate responding to Brooks's initial success, "We don't want a politician to be president of the Southern Baptist Convention," to which the man next to him replied, "Don't worry, Brooks ain't enough of one to count." The second ballot was to be by standing vote, but by this time Brooks was so nervous that he had left his seat near the front of the auditorium and gone out into the lobby to avoid seeing it. He was there only a few moments when he was called to come forward to accept election. Ramsay Pollard, the man he beat, would hold the office at a later time. The first thing Brooks did after acknowledging his election was hurry out to call Steele Hays in Arkansas. When told of the victory, Steele is supposed to have said, "On what ballot?" But later in the day Brooks received a telegram from him, telling him that he was sure Brooks's mother, who had died in 1955, knew of it and was proud of her son.

Brooks was only the sixth layman in the 113 year history of the Southern Baptist Convention to be elected president. He followed Jonathan Harelson (1889-1898). W. J. Northen (1899-1901), E. W. Stephens (1905-1907), Joshua Levering (1908-1910), and Pat Neff (1944 and 1946, there having been no convention in 1945). To date there has been only one layman president since Brooks, Owen Cooper (1973-1975). The minute word of Brooks's election hit the papers, he began receiving messages of congratulation from religious and political leaders. His papers at the Southern Baptist archives in Nashville contain telegrams and letters from scores of Baptist pastors and denominational leaders, spokesmen of other denominations, and Congressional colleagues such as Hubert Humphrey, Estes Kefauver, and John Sparkman. Paul Butler, chairman of the Democratic party, and Federal Bureau of Investigation Director J. Edgar Hoover also sent best wishes. Arkansas Senator J. William Fulbright wrote to congratulate Brooks on the honor the Southern Baptists had conferred on him, but then added, "Or perhaps I should say the honor which you have conferred on the Baptists by accepting this appointment."[26]

One of the more unusual letters came from Director of the National Association for the Advancement of Colored People Roy Wilkins, who congratulated Brooks on his victory and suggested they meet one day in Washington for coffee.[27] Brooks, who within three months of this day would be embroiled in the Little Rock Central High School crisis and sixteen months later become one of the civil rights movement's martyrs, thanked Wilkins for his letter but made no mention of the offer to meet.[28] Brooks was after all still a member of Congress, responsible to the citizens of a conservative district, and a meeting with Wilkins would probably not have been good politics. Brooks seems, in fact, despite his growing sensitivity to racial issues, not to have trusted the NAACP; and during the Little Rock crisis he would consider the local chapter more a part of the problem than of the solution. But it is a pity that at that moment he did not feel free to meet with a man who could have helped him immensely in the difficult days to come. He was still a leader at the discretion of an Arkansas congressional district and a religious denomination, neither of which was up to his own social awareness and resolve.

Not all Southern Baptists were happy about Brooks's election. Some leading pastors found his assumption of symbolic power disturbing. Former SBC president R. G. Lee, pastor of the Belleview Baptist Church of Memphis, Tennessee, an arch conservative, confided to an intimate that it was "too bad" Brooks was president because he was a well-known "liberal." However, in a 3 June letter Lee promised to pray for Brooks and give him advice if he asked. Lee was one of the first prominent Southern Baptist pastors to lament the "liberal trend" of the convention and to start a counter trend toward fundamentalist crusading. Later in his life Brooks would express some bitterness at Lee, his attitude, and the fundamentalist leaders who followed him. Brooks would describe himself as a "Rauschenbusch Baptist," one who took the theological position of the New York

---

[26]Letter from J. W. Fulbright to Brooks Hays, 13 May 1957.

[27]Letter from Roy Wilkins to Brooks Hays, 12 June 1957.

[28]Letter from Brooks Hays to Roy Wilkins, 24 June 1957.

City Baptist minister who founded the Social Gospel Movement, rather than a "Lee Baptist," one who was intolerant of any deviation from the fundamentalist, obscurantist approach to theology. Brooks later recalled how Lee had once called Lyndon Johnson a liar for saying that the heart of the gospel is the fatherhood of God and the brotherhood of man. That is precisely the heart of the gospel, Brooks huffed, giving some indication that he was probably the person who wrote that line into L.B.J.'s speech.[29]

At his first presidential news conference Brooks pledged a renewed devotion to the time-honored Baptist principles of Biblical theology, religious liberty, and evangelism. "The Bible is our chart," he told the press; but he would, in true Baptist form, be a democratic president, refusing to force his own interpretations of the Bible on anyone else. He said he believed in religious freedom, within the denomination, in the nation as a whole, and in foreign countries where it may or may not be guaranteed; and he intended to fight for it in all three places. No "ecclesiastical authority," he said, should ever insinuate himself between the reader of scripture and God. Finally in a bow to an issue dear to Southern Baptist hearts, though one must wonder how dear to his own, he said he hoped Congress would soon decide to ban serving alcoholic beverages on commercial American aircraft.[30]

Brooks began his presidency with a visit to the Southern Baptist Executive Committee in Nashville on 19 June 1957. He told its members that he had always conducted his work as a Congressman much the way he would have conducted his ministry, had he been ordained. His work in government, like the pastoral ministry, had both a pastoral and a prophetic dimension; and he would try to use both forms of ministry to serve the convention as he tried to serve his Arkansas constituency. He went on to pledge his support of Biblical theology, religious liberty, and evangelism, the three pillars of Southern Baptist life. Then he warned them, in words that would later sound prophetic, that in him they had a controversial president. He promised not to invite controversy, and certainly not to embarrass them, but he wanted them to know that by doing his duty he might raise some dust.[31] Perhaps he was referring only to his attitudes toward racial brotherhood, or to the fact that fundamentalists considered him

---

[29]Hays, Conversation with Ronald Tonks, August 1977.

[30]*Baptist Press,* June 1957.

[31]Hays, *This World: A Christian's Workshop,* 127.

a liberal, and that either of these matters might cause trouble. He could hardly have foreseen what would happen to Little Rock—and to himself—within three months.

The controversies of his Southern Baptist presidency, however, had more to do with Southern Baptist polarity than national political polarity. The most immediate stir, Brooks's first controversy, came in late June, when he spoke at his home church in Washington, Calvary Baptist. Religious News Service reported that he promised as president of the Southern Baptist Convention to help close the gap between Southern Baptists and their Northern brothers in the American Baptist Convention, as well as to participate in ecumenical endeavors with other Protestant denominations. He had attended the American Baptist Convention's Philadelphia convention in early June and had heard the reading of letters collected by New Testament scholar W. W. Adams about "vicious competition" between Southern and American Baptists in "frontier states" like Illinois and California, with Southern Baptists demonstrating some rather un-Christlike behavior.[32] Calvary Baptist, whose pastor Clarence Cranford was to serve as president of the American Baptist Convention the next year, was, like most Baptist churches in the District of Columbia, aligned with both conventions. As such it was the appropriate setting for Brooks to advocate a new spirit of cooperation. But as soon as the report was distributed, Southern Baptist state papers were deluged with criticism of his statement, many calling for his resignation.

Brooks responded by saying that he could not recall using the term *ecumenical* in his address but that if he did he meant it in a broader sense than that of denominational merging. When that clarification did not still the storm, he issued a further correction, saying that he was not an ecumenicist if that meant a man who was willing to compromise church doctrine or one who favored church union or uniformity. "I am a Baptist," he said, playing to his audience, a man who believed wholeheartedly in the principles that made Baptists distinctive. He promised never to compromise his commitment to "individual soul liberty, church autonomy, and believers' baptism." He also hinted that the R.N.S. had misquoted him.[33]

This latter excuse brought a quick reprimand from R.N.S. chief editor Louis Minsky, who pouted that R.N.S. was unnecessarily damaged by an

---

[32]Minutes of American Baptist Convention, Philadelphia, June 1957.

[33]Brooks Hays, Form Letter sent to those protesting R.N.S. story.

unjust accusation.[34] Brooks explained to Minsky that Glenn Everett, who had covered the address and written the story, had told him in a letter that the R.N.S. rewrite of his story had misinterpreted his original statement; but Minsksy still complained that if Brooks felt he was misquoted or misinterpreted, he should have come to them with a request for clarification and/or retraction, not go public with an accusation that he had been misquoted. Minsky stood by the accuracy of the story, and his only correction was to say that Brooks, even though he was president of the Southern Baptist Convention, spoke only for himself, not for all Southern Baptists. Slowly the story died.

Not so its revelation, new to many Southern Baptists, that their new president belonged to a church affiliated with the American Baptist Convention, and worse, that his wife Marion was not even a Baptist. One Ralph H. Bartlett wrote to Brooks ordering him to get out of Calvary Baptist, with its liberal theology and racial policies, or resign his presidency.[35] Brooks responded to Bartlett that he was a member of Second Baptist Church of Little Rock, which was affiliated only with the Arkansas and Southern Baptist Conventions.[36] But such obfuscation failed to halt the criticism, and finally Brooks had to issue a statement explaining that Calvary had two categories of members: Members of the Church and Members of the Congregation. He said that he was one of the latter, which meant that he was, in Southern Baptist terminology, under Calvary's "watchcare."

As to his wife's affiliation, he made no attempt to deny that she was a Methodist, just as he had not when her alien baptism had threatened to keep Russellville Baptists from ordaining him a deacon in 1923. However, he did mention in every response that she was a faithful worker in the Baptist Women's Missionary Union, that she had taught Sunday school classes in Baptist churches for thirty-five years, that she attended Baptist services with him, and that she had raised their two children to be Baptists. Despite these disclaimers, protests against a Southern Baptist president harboring a Methodist wife continued for the two years of his presidency. Only having been divorced and remarried or retaining a common law wife would have caused him more grief.

---

[34]Letter from Louis Minsky to Brooks Hays, 28 August 1957.

[35]Letter from Ralph Bartlett to Brooks Hays 24 May, 1958.

[36]Letter from Brooks Hays to Ralph Bartlett, 26 May 1958.

The loudest and most prolonged protests, however, came over the issue of race. These protests came in a steady stream from the moment he took office until his term ended. They came for the most part from the Deep South, where the largest black population lay, where resistance to any form of integration was most strident. Ebenezer Baptist Church of Cardova, South Carolina, for example, wrote to him and still protested the Christian Life Commission's 1954 report to the convention in St. Louis, which had concluded that the Supreme Court's desegregation order was !n harmony both with the Constitution of the United States and with the Gospel of Christ. Ebenezer told President Brooks Hays, who had himself doubted in 1954 whether the court's decision was truly constitutional, certainly prudent, that it would henceforth send its funds not to the Southern Baptist Convention's cooperative program but to an organization supporting segregation.[37] The Healing Springs Baptist Church of Blackville, South Carolina, sent Brooks its resolution protesting the Christian Life Commission's 1957 report and announcing its intention no longer to use convention literature, "whose purpose it is to spread socialistic and communistic propaganda to our youth."[38] Pastor Frank Sutton of Newberry, South Carolina, asked Brooks to answer certain specific theological questions, to prove his orthodoxy, dedication to Southern traditions, and qualifications to be president of the convention.

Brooks respectfully declined to answer Sutton's litmus-test questions, saying inquisitions were un-Baptist. He did answer all the letters of protest concerning the race issue with a form letter, patiently explaining that the convention in Chicago had "received" and not "adopted" the Christian Life Commission's report, that Baptists had the right to disagree with the commission and with each other on race, that the Christian Life Commission served as a much-needed "conscience" for the convention, and that he would gladly come anywhere he was invited to discuss the racial crisis and the churches' response. But it was soon evident that he would not be asked to come, that it would be risky to discuss race in such states as South Carolina, Georgia, Mississippi, and Louisiana. The letters he received on the subject during the summer of 1957 are amazing to read, now that thirty years have made them a part of history. The misspelled words and tortured grammar serve to emphasize the racial bigotry of people supposedly

---

[37]Letter from Ebenezer Baptist Church to Brooks Hays, 7 July 1957.

[38]Letter from Healing Springs Baptist Church to Brooks Hays, 16 August 1957.

dedicated to Christian love. Only one bright spot appears in the gloom of this ream of letters and that in the form of correspondence from Pastor J. Dan Williams of the Northgate Baptist Church of Greenville, South Carolina. Williams applauded Brooks's efforts to help heal the South's racial wounds. "Many of us in South Carolina stand with you in the effort to find a sensible and Christian way through these difficult problems facing us in the Southland," Williams concluded.[39] Perhaps other pastors who approved of his work simply failed to write.

Brooks seemed to take strength from the attacks. He was not particularly spoiling for a fight; but feeling as he did that he had the majority of Southern Baptists behind him, as he would feel he had the majority of his congressional district behind him that same year, he decided to meet the question of race head on. Gone was the wavering politician who just a year before had signed the Southern Manifesto, and in his place stood the statesman who would walk chin up into the Little Rock Central High School crisis. The change well could have been achieved by his election to the Southern Baptist presidency, with the responsibility for moral leadership he felt it required.

In August 1957, the Southern Baptist magazine *Royal Service* wrote to ask if he would write an article on either "The Ministry to Minority, Racial and National Groups" or "The Christian and the Alcohol Problem." He could have played it safe and pleased a lot of Baptists by choosing the second topic, but he chose the first, saying that while the latter was important he did not want the first to be neglected. And on 30 August the United Press reported his call for churches to live up to their "three clear duties" in racial matters: to keep free and unfettered the prophetic voice of the pulpit, to support nonviolent approaches to ease racial tensions, and with Christian courage to correct specific examples of racial injustice.[40] He concluded by encouraging interdenominational meetings to resolve local race problems, which of course only further inflamed the segregationist Baptists who considered cooperative work with other denominations the equivalent of lying down with the Devil.

As a result of being always in the spotlight over the issue of race, an issue that he had thought was long buried rose from its grave to haunt Brooks. Louis Hollis of Jackson, Mississippi, circulated to all Baptist state

---

[39]Letter from J. Dan Williams to Brooks Hays, 11 November 1957.

[40]United Press report, 30 August 1957.

papers the story of how in 1939 Brooks had attended that meeting in Bir-mingham and been elected vice-president of that race-mixing, communis-tic Southern Conference for Human Welfare. Not since his 1942 race for Congress had anyone raised this issue. In response Brooks permitted Bruce Price, who volunteered to serve as his point man on this matter, to release a letter explaining, as he had done in 1942, that after arriving in Bir-mingham Brooks had taken issue with the discussions and decisions of the conference, left town, and was elected a vice president *in absentia,* without his consent, and had never served in the office. Brooks's defenders, using Price's letter as ammunition, labeled all subsequent charges about the Birmingham Conference "religious McCarthyism." The issue slowly faded.

Brooks's defense of the Christian Life Commission's 1957 report con-tinued to wrankle grassroot sensibilities and bring out the worst of racist protests. A former Texas prison official named R. R. Pyle, who identified himself as a "Baptist seventy years, a deacon thirty-five," wrote to Brooks: "I am sure that 'God' did not intend for the colored and White Blood should be mixed. . ." It would be a "tradgedy" if we as Baptists should ". . . Breed our clean White boys and girls to Black bad smelling Negroes."[41] Carey Daniel, pastor of the First Baptist Church of West Dallas, Texas, vice pres-ident of the Dallas White Citizens' Council, and cousin of then Texas Gov-ernor Price Daniel, wrote to Brooks: "I hereby register the strongest possible protest against the race-mixing and mongrelizing activities of the 'Christian Life Commission.'" He added that his church was cutting off funds to the cooperative program until there was a radical change in pol-icy, meaning that the commission no longer be funded; and he enclosed for Brooks's edification a copy of his latest book, *God the Original Segrega-tionist.*[42]

Daniel's book followed a thesis that slaveowners and segregationists had propagated and defended for more than two centuries. The Negro is the descendant of Ham, the son of Noah whom God cursed, and as Ham's descendant he is destined to draw water and chop wood for other races for-ever. Brooks wrote to A. C. Miller, "This is as bad as anything I have seen." Such trash gave legitimacy to the Christian Life Commission's race rela-tions effort "to make sure that perverted interpretations of the Bible on

---

[41]Letter from R. R. Pyle to Brooks Hays, 1 June 1957.

[42]Letter from Carey Daniel to Brooks Hays, 3 June 1957.

this subject do not go unchallenged."[43] The Daniel book, he lamented, was being circulated in the halls of Congress. It made him even more certain that he could not be associated with this kind of racism, and it added to his conviction that as leader of his denomination he must stand for an enlightened attitude toward the race question.

The letters continued and increased in numbers after Brooks intervened to bring Faubus and Eisenhower together at the time of the Little Rock Central High School crisis in September 1957. Jack Trammell, who identified himself as a member of the committee on resolutions of the Selma (Alabama) Baptist Association, sent Brooks the names of eleven articles and/or publications distributed by the Southern Baptist Convention supporting this vicious thing called integration. He also sent copies of class notes taken in a Southwestern Baptist Theological Seminary class on social ethics that called for, among other things, laws to outlaw lynching. Brooks, he said, should see to it that these publications and lectures cease.[44] Even letters written by literate persons, with correctly spelled words and logical diction and paragraph construction, such as one from a lawyer and member of the Springfield, South Carolina, Baptist Church, said that "the welfare of both races will be best served by keeping them separate," and that if the Southern Baptist Convention continued in its drive for integration it should be dissolved and replaced by local associations of Baptists with like minds.[45]

Some of the letters got emotional. E. D. Estes of Jackson, Mississippi, wrote Brooks: "Where do you stand on this nasty mess? Come clean with us!" He had loved Brooks for thirty years, he said, and he was tired of hearing ugly things said about him. "Please tell us," he begged, "that you are trying to save us from integration."[46] Ralph Kolb of Sumter, South Carolina, wrote to say he wished the last convention had chosen some humble pastor as its president because Brooks was leading Southern Baptists into strange ways. "When the communists fail in their efforts to mongrelize the white and negro races," he theorized, "they may then try to drive a wedge between the two." Then he warned, "You, who are chosen to be our reli-

---

[43]Letter from Brooks Hays to A. C. Miller, 27 August 1957.

[44]Letter from Jack Trammell to Brooks Hays, 6 December 1957.

[45]Letter from Springfield S.C. Baptist Church to Brooks Hays, 10 August 1957.

[46]Letter from E. D. Estes to Brooks Hays, 13 February 1958.

gious leaders may have to answer to God for failing to warn the Nation" of the calamity to come.[47] It would seem that Mr. Kolb failed to see that the Christian Life Commission's attempt to educate Southern Baptists on the racial issue was this kind of warning. At least it was not Mr. Kolb's kind of warning.

The letters reflected a real fear among Southern Baptists in the Deep South that integration of schools, which they perceived Brooks Hays favored, would mean the end of their way of life. When a number of churches in Mississippi called for him to resign his presidency and the state convention considered cancelling his guest appearance late in 1957, Brooks faced the issue head-on. He insisted that he had been invited, albeit before the trouble in Little Rock, and that he planned to come. He was escorted to the church where he was to speak by police, and the church was searched for bombs due to anonymous threats. But he began telling his humorous stories, teased and cajoled his fellow Baptists until they joined in his laughter, and then told them of their responsibility for finding a path to racial justice.

He handled his mail as president of the convention much as he had handled his mail in Congress for fifteen years. He prepared several form letters, one for each of the major subjects that concerned his constituents. Since this was in that long ago day before word processors made life so much simpler for public officials, he depended upon his secretary to recognize the type of letter to send in response to each query. If the secretary felt a certain letter deserved his special attention, she would ask him to add a personal final paragraph.

For the hundreds of letters protesting the Christian Life Commission's 1957 report on race, a form letter assured writers that Brooks was well-grounded in the Baptist right to dissent, that he himself had often done so, and that he respected their opinion on this issue, even if it did differ from his own. He reminded them that the convention did not approve the report, that it recognized how divided Baptists were on race and therefore simply received it, but that he believed the report correctly and accurately stated the Christian position on the issue. He ended by emphasizing the report's rejection of violent solutions to the current crisis and assured them that this attitude had his whole-hearted support.

To letters protesting integration in general, and what some considered Brooks's support for that eventuality, he sent a form letter that assured

---

[47]Letter from Ralph Kolb to Brooks Hays, 17 March 1958.

them he was glad to be apprised of their opinion. He reminded them that he too was opposed to forced integration of schools and then used for his own purposes a fact he already admitted privately shamed him: he explained that he had signed the Southern Manifesto. He quickly went on to say that he approved of dissent, both from political and from denominational authority, so long as that dissent was legal and nonviolent. He ended by saying he hoped to lead Southern Baptists to new levels of Christian love and justice.

To letters threatening to leave or divide the convention over any number of matters, primarily racial, he pointed out in a form letter that a new organization based on unanimity on one issue, say race, would soon find itself in disagreement on other issues. The best solution, he said calmly, was to stay together, work together, and encourage diversity. Let local churches decide their own policies on integration. This was of course a very Baptist solution to the problem. It was not the first time, and it would not be the last, that Southern Baptists differed on a basic issue yet remained united in order to achieve higher goals.

Brooks did keep what he called his "crackpot" file of letters, the ones so sick he felt he should not encourage the writers by answering. And there was a file marked "no answer" for those that did not deserve his time. Some people who received an answer to their first letter were filed "crackpot" or "no answer" the second and third times. But Brooks answered thousands of letters as president of the Southern Baptist Convention, just as he accepted every possible invitation to speak at Baptist conventions. His loss in the 1958 congressional race was in part due to the inordinate amount of time he spent on denominational work to the neglect of his political duties at home.

He saw to it that every Southern Baptist Boy Scout who received the God and Country Award and whose local church sent him the boy's name received what appeared to be a personal (but was really a form) letter of congratulations from the president of the Southern Baptist Convention. He sent (form) letters of congratulation to pastors of small and large churches celebrating anniversaries and to youth groups having special occasions. He assured his fellow Baptists who were concerned over gambling, drinking, and pornography that he too was concerned over these problems, but that he did believe in freedom of choice. One letter told writers concerned over alcohol that he had recently appeared before a Senate committee considering a bill to prohibit the advertisement of alcoholic beverages in interstate commerce. He neglected to mention that he allowed himself a drink each night, for his stomach's sake.

He was inundated with letters, some barely literate, calling for laws banning pornography, when in May 1958 Lana Turner's daughter Cheryl Crane killed her mother's gangland boyfriend Johnny Stompanato. Brooks responded to these letters by saying that he agreed that both the church and the government should be concerned with the problems caused by pornography, and he agreed that Hollywood did contribute to juvenile deliquency. He reminded them that the Christian Life Commission had been waging an untiring war against all kinds of immoral social influences.

Some letters concerned issues Brooks simply did not want to address, and he found ways of ignoring these. One, from Mrs. C. C. Stark of Franklin, Kentucky, representing the Council of Church Women of her city, asked him to support a law requiring that the Ten Commandments be displayed in every American public school classroom. Brooks instructed his secretary to tell Mrs. Stark that it came during his absence (which may have been true) and would be shown to him later. The secretary thanked her for giving him the benefit of her views.[48] But other letters touched him deeply, and he not only answered them personally but spent a surprising amount of precious time trying to help petitioners. A letter that arrived in September 1957, at the time of the Little Rock crisis, was from a Texan, a graduate of Baylor University, who had gone on to seminary at Yale and now found Texas Baptist churches afraid to employ him.[49] Brooks wrote to the man, offering his best wishes and his help in locating a job if he could manage it.

More touching was a handwritten letter sent in January 1958 from W. L.White of Wetumpka, Alabama, saying that he wanted to go to seminary so badly he could "taste it" but that with five mouths to feed he could not see a way to do so. He wanted no handouts, he insisted, he would work, but he knew that Baptists had no use for a man without seminary training and felt little sympathy for one who could not pay his own way.[50] Brooks wrote the Alabama Baptist Convention offices in Montgomery to get White's address, which he had neglected to enclose, answered the letter personally, then wrote to New Orleans Baptist Seminary and had officials there contact White about fees and housing.[51] This was indeed a labor of love, above

---

[48]Letter from Mrs. C. C. Stark to Brooks Hays, 30 November 1957.

[49]Letter from Texan to Brooks Hays, September 1957.

[50]Letter from W. L. White to Brooks Hays, 1957.

[51]Letters in Brooks Hays Collection.

and beyond the call of denominational duty. It shows Brooks at his Christian and presidential best.

In April 1958, Brooks made a trip to the Soviet Union, financed by the Southern Baptist Foreign Mission Board at a carefully recorded cost of $1,014.30, "to lay the groundwork for a Baptist peace program in the U.S.S.R." Accompanied by his pastor at Calvary Baptist, Clarence W. Cranford, he took along two Bibles and four New Testaments in Russian and a copy of the 1955 Christian Life Commission's resolution on world peace.[52] Traveling via Copenhagen, he arrived in Moscow at 5 P.M., Thursday, 17 April. On Friday the 18th he walked around Red Square and visited the Baptist Church of Moscow, where he took photographs. On Saturday the 19th he visited the Kremlin and saw the tombs and museums; and on Sunday the 20th he attended services at the Baptist Church. When he arrived there at 8:45 A.M., he found a long line of people waiting to be admitted, 2,000 as it turned out. Only 1,200 people could be seated, so 800 stood. Since Brooks was a layman, despite being president of the Southern Baptist Convention, his address was called a testimony rather than a sermon. At the end of the two-hour service the congregation sang "God Be with You Till We Meet Again." After a Monday morning visit to a monastery at Zagorsk, Brooks left for home on the afternoon of 20 April.

He was just a bit surprised not to hear any protests concerning his visit from the usually anti-Soviet Southern Baptist hinterland. There was, in fact, some indication that Southern Baptists took pride in his trip behind the Iron Curtain. Before going to the Soviet Union, he had received a brutal letter from William Loeb, publisher of the Manchester, New Hampshire, *Union Leader,* warning him not to give respectability to those Soviet killers by visiting their country. "Would you have gone to call on Al Capone and his gang?" Loeb had asked him. "You are doing a great disservice, not only to the Baptist faith but to the United States of America."[53] Brooks had replied to Loeb that his was the only negative letter concerning his trip he had received. He had indeed received a hearty commendation—and would be the subject of a glowing editorial in May—from *Christian Herald* editor Daniel Poling.[54] After the trip only a few radicals

---

[52]Baptist Press report, 18 April 1958.

[53]Letter from William Loeb to Brooks Hays, 19 March 1958.

[54]Letter from Daniel Poling to Brooks Hays, 2 April 1958.

out to exploit anticommunist sentiment for their own purposes, such as comic Tulsa radio evangelist Billy James Hargis, had anything but praise for Brooks's mission.

No sooner had he returned from Moscow than Brooks found himself in the middle of preparations for the 1958 Southern Baptist Convention, to be held in Houston, Texas. One of his dreams was to have President Eisenhower address the convention, something that would give deserved national stature to this meeting of the nation's largest Protestant denomination. He felt that because of his service to the Eisenhower administration during the crisis in Little Rock Eisenhower might agree to honor him with an appearance. He was wrong. Ike declined. Despite this one setback, however, the convention was perhaps the high point of Brooks's work for Southern Baptists. Moves by segregationists to discipline and/or disband the Christian Life Commission were rejected by the delegates; and charges that money used by the Christian Life Commission was tainted were answered and discarded. The Christian Life Commission's report on race relations, "A Call for Racial Reconciliation," was received without approval or disapproval, some accomplishment given the feelings it stirred and the motions to reject it.[55] As a member of the commission, Brooks had helped draft the report, and as president of the convention he helped steer it through to its reception.

As early as August 1957, Brooks had begun talking up the idea of instituting a Southern Baptist commission for the study of world peace. He had helped draft the Christian Life Commission's statement on peace presented to the 1955 Southern Baptist Convention, and as chairman of the commission from 1955 to 1957 he had encouraged further study of the issue. Now as president of the convention, having visited the Soviet Union to dramatize the issue, he hoped to make it a convention project. He had written to Vernon Eagle of the New World Foundation asking for a $10,000 grant and had received a tentative promise from former President Harry Truman to serve as chairman should the convention approve such a commission. When all his carefully laid plans fell through, no grant, no hopes for a funded commission, he went ahead and asked the convention delegates to authorize him to name a committee to study strategies for world peace. This was done. He appointed a nine-member panel, headed by Walter Pope Binns, president of William Jewell College, and commissioned it

---

[55]Hays, *A Southern Moderate Speaks*, 210.

to begin its work. The move was praised on the floor of the United States Senate the following week by Senator Estes Kefauver of Tennessee, who had been the Democratic candidate for vice-president in 1956.

All in all the 1958 Southern Baptist Convention was one of the most productive and peaceful in history. Brooks was given credit, both by liberals and conservatives, for the way he conducted it, avoiding a bitter feud, and assuring delegates that Southern Baptists could disagree agreeably. The *Christian Century* praised him lavishly. This was, it calculated, the most liberal and yet the most harmonious convention in years, all due to Brooks Hays's skillful leadership. Some of the stands he had taken so openly, such as the one on compliance with Supreme Court decisions, might have serious political repercussions for him back home; but if his constituency should learn how well he had negotiated dangerous twists and turns, they would reelect him with enthusiasm. Other denominations, the article concluded, should observe the example Southern Baptists had set and search for leaders with Brooks's combination of Christian devotion and parliamentary grace.[56]

Brooks was elected to a second term as president of the convention, two terms being a tradition, his fellow Southern Baptists recognizing the positive effects he had had on the convention. In his presidential address he strongly supported the Christian Life Commission's efforts at racial reconciliation, refusing to play safe, and he spoke with feeling about the need for Christians to involve themselves in social work. As a boy, he told the mass audience, he had heard preachers say that Christians should despise the world, but he had found on his own that the Bible said God loved the world. "If our Christian doctrines regarding God, the world, and man are to be taken seriously," he concluded with a flourish, "it is apparent that this world is a Christian's workshop."[57] With these words, he summarized his theology and dropped the name of his new book, which would be published later in the year.

After the 1958 convention, the letters protesting his and the Christian Life Commission's racial attitudes, while still vicious, were fewer in number. For those that did arrive, Brooks prepared another form letter. This letter assured those concerned that the convention passed no motion favoring race mixing but merely received the Christian Life Commission's

---

[56]Virgil Lowder, "Southern Baptists," *Christian Century* (11 June 1958): 700.

[57]Hays, *This World: A Christian's Workshop,* 18.

report calling for strengthened "fellowship with people of every race," for reconciliation and brotherhood, which he believed everyone desired.[58] But in this letter he went further than he had gone in his 1957 letter. Now more specifically he concluded, "As president of the Convention, I have advocated that we re-affirm our devotion to justice, which means political rights, *not social aspirations.*"[59] It is obvious what Brooks was trying to do here. In one sense he was going farther than ever before, farther than any Southern Baptist Convention president had gone before, in supporting political rights for minorities. In another sense he was assuring fellow Southerners that he did not necessarily favor meeting all the demands of racial minorities, that he did not particularly advocate the social mixing of the races. The times were confused and confusing, with sides drawn between the Martin Luther Kings and the Orval Faubuses; and men like Brooks Hays, despite their consciences and good will, had to tread softly on the quicksand.

Brooks continued in his second term to be an active and controversial Southern Baptist president. He created a cabinet of Southern Baptist leaders to advise him on matters troubling the convention. In speeches to college, seminary, association, and state Baptist meetings across the convention, he suggested remedies for specific ills. He accepted $100 plus expenses for each address. He served as vice-chairman of a committee appointed by the Executive Committee of the Southern Baptist Convention to investigate conditions at Southern Baptist Theological Seminary in Louisville, Kentucky, when thirteen members of the faculty stood as a unit against the policies of President Duke K. McCall. He made national headlines when he told *This Week Magazine* that he favored holding political elections on Sunday.

A proposal for Sunday voting was on the fall ballot in New York and Florida. In both states, newspaper ads in support of the proposal featured photographs and responses from the president of the Southern Baptist Convention, who happened to be a Congressman, to the effect that "This proposal is entitled to the favorable consideration" of church people everywhere "because it might well increase the number of voters, who would be

---

[58]Brooks Hays, Form Letter sent to those protesting CLC's report, 1958. Brooks Hays Collection.

Ibid.

off work on Sundays, and show that voting is a religious duty."[60] The idea
was also endorsed by James A. Pike, who would be the controversial Epis-
copal bishop of San Francisco, California, during the coming decade. Brooks
was immediately inundated with letters of protest from everywhere in the
convention—Florida, North Carolina, Alabama, Texas, Virginia, West
Virginia, Arkansas, Delaware, Mississippi, even Illinois and the District
of Columbia—most of them damning him for suggesting that voting should
be considered a holy act. One letter from a man in Amory, Mississippi,
whose signature is indecipherable, asked if Brooks advocated "desicrating
the Sabbath" and concluded, "I for one, and am sure many others would
wish that you no longer were 'President of the Southern Baptist Convention.' Your attitude is any think but Christian. You have our PRAYERS. That
you might change for the better."[61]

Brooks knew that he had gone a step too far on this issue and took some
pains in the form letter he drafted to placate bruised feelings. He said that
while he gave the advocates of the proposition the right to quote him, he
felt "my comments . . . were not quite accurately interpreted."[62] This of
course left the impression, by juxtaposing *quote* and *interpret,* that he had
been misquoted, a ploy he had used the previous year when the Religious
News Service told too many people about his Calvary sermon on ecumen-
ism. He went on to say that the use of the term *favorable* was regrettable,
but he did not deny using it. What he had meant to say was that church
members should give the idea of Sunday voting *earnest* consideration. He
had not forgotten and he did respect the fourth commandment, to keep the
Sabbath holy, and he was not urging adoption of Sunday voting. With this
mild apologia the protests gradually died down.

The next major controversy of his presidency, one that broke in the early
autumn of 1958, just as Little Rock Central High School was being closed
down for the year due to racial unrest, just before Dale Alford declared his
intentions to run against Brooks as a write-in independent candidate for
Congress, was racial in nature. Brooks appeared in Chicago in September
as president of the Southern Baptist Convention, along with his Calvary
Baptist pastor Clarence Cranford who was president of the American Baptist Convention, on a program with National (black) Baptist Convention

---

[60]*This Week Magazine,* Brooks Hays Collection.

[61]Letter from Amory, Mississippi, 24 November 1958.

[62]Form Letter sent to protestors.

President J. H. Jackson. Photographs of them smiling, hands joined in a demonstration of Baptist solidarity, appeared in newspapers from coast to coast. Southern Baptists who had long suspected Brooks of being a race mixer now had their proof. The letters that came flooding in to protest this breach of Southern principles were for the most part poorly written in almost illegible cursive, the work of uneducated and usually very old people, but they carried an unusually painful sting.

For the first time Brooks felt ill when reading these letters, and he answered very few of them. Before he knew it, of course, Alford had come into the congressional race against him, and two weeks later he was a lame duck. Now he had to decide whether to challenge the election or go into graceful retirement. He also had to weigh the exceptionally warm condolences of his Southern Baptist admirers against the calls for him to resign as president of the convention. In the end he did not challenge the congressional election, and he did not resign his presidency. At the Virginia Convention soon after his defeat, he was given a standing ovation when he announced that he intended to finish his term. Within weeks eight Baptist state conventions announced their votes of confidence. His head was bruised but unbowed.

His defeat and the subsequent national adulation it brought him actually seemed to give Brooks courage. In January 1959, just a week after he left Congress, the man who had to some degree backed away from ecumenism responded positively to Pope John XXIII's call for Christian unity. The Philadelphia *Inquirer* quoted him: "All Christians share the Pope's concern for Christian unity in a period threatened by materialism and unbelief. I assume that unity rather than unification is the objective." He had learned to cover his flanks, but he had not learned to keep quiet about things that mattered to him. With the story's syndication came more angry letters, and in his form reply he explained that "my comment was more in line with Christian courtesy, and no one would be justified in reading into what I said any more than this."[63] Some papers had failed to include his disclaimer that he supported unity and not unification. To his reply to perennial antagonist Jack Trammell of the Shiloh Baptist Church in Sardis, Alabama, he added a final paragraph. Unity and unification, he said, are different. Unification means amalgamation and ultimate absorption,

---

[63]Ibid.

while unity means a common spiritual devotion to the Christian faith.[64]
Even in these modest steps, however, Brooks was far out in front of a multitude of his Southern Baptist brethren.

The greater multitude of his Southern Baptist brethren, however, were
overwhelmingly proud of their president, a man who always stood for what
he thought was right; and their pride was shared by Protestants and Catholics nationwide. *Newsweek* reported in May 1959 that Brooks was more
popular with Baptists and the national public than he had ever been before. Its report quoted him: "My whole religious philosophy has tried to en-
compass these opposite sides of the same coin: Love and justice." Brooks
was rephrasing a maxim introduced to American religious thought by
Reinhold Niebuhr, one that would be adopted by Jimmy Carter, to the effect that in politics love is translated justice. "It is not enough merely to
help the Negroes," the article quoted the liberated Brooks Hays as saying,
"it is just as important for white people to be learning charity and understanding and love."[65]

Expressions of admiration were becoming so numerous and elaborate
by the middle of 1959 that Marion Hays said, "I've told Brooks that if he
does any thing else to be congratulated for I'm going to enter a rest home
or a nunnery." The Religious Heritage Foundation awarded Brooks its 1959
"Churchman of the Year" honor. Within a matter of months fourteen Baptist institutions of higher learning would confer honorary degrees on him,
one of them a Doctorate of Divinity, most unusual for a layman.[66] He went
to the 1959 Southern Baptist Convention in Louisville assured that he had
unified his denomination and helped negotiate Southern Baptists through
the dangerous currents of the civil rights revolution. He tried and failed
to get Canadian Prime Minister John Diefenbaker, United Nations General Assembly President Charles R. Malik, and President Dwight David
Eisenhower to address the convention; but he presided over a convention
remembered for its progressivism and decency. It was an appropriate way
for a Brooks Hays presidency to end.

---

[64]Letter from Jack Trammell to Brooks Hays, 8 February 1958; letter from
Brooks Hays to Jack Trammell, 25 February 1958.

[65]"Brooks Hays Says It," *Newsweek,* 18 May 1959, 100.

[66]Hays, Conversation with Ronald Tonks, August 1977.

Although he would never again hold denominational office, Brooks would never stop being thought of as Mister Baptist. President Kennedy would think of Brooks as his liaison with Baptists. Both Pope John XXIII and Pope Paul VI considered him the world's foremost Baptist. When Brooks toured west Africa for Kennedy he was received more warmly as a Baptist than as an American public official. In June 1965, he was asked to address the Baptist World Alliance in Miami, Florida, and as the most respected of Baptist elder statesmen he told the audience, "Participation in the processes of government is essential if committed Christians are to meet their responsibilities." He spoke of his trip seven years earlier to Russia and said, "God grant that two mighty nations might build a lasting peace upon the concepts to which both Russian and American Baptists are dedicated."[67] Had he encouraged the move he would have probably been elected president of the Baptist World Alliance.

That same year he was the first recipient of the Southern Baptist Convention's Christian Life Commission "Distinguished Service Award" for social ethics. In presenting him with a plaque at the Nashville meeting, the commission's director Foy Valentine said that it was "in recognition of unique and outstanding contributions to Southern Baptists, the nation, and mankind in the interest of world peace, social justice, and Christian citizenship." In his acceptance speech Brooks said that the wall separating church and state should have gates so that there could be interplay between the two, and he called on his fellow Baptists to get involved in politics.[68] Doubtless he meant politics of a moderate to liberal tone, not the conservative politics some later Baptist politicians would espouse.

Brooks Hays left his Baptists a great life to emulate, but he also left them an exceptionally thoughtful and literate theology. It is amazing, as one reads his diaries, public addresses, and personal comments, how sophisticated his theological opinions were. He taught Southern Baptists a great deal, by word and by example, and he still has much to teach them and the Christian church as a whole, even today.

He gave a lot of thought, for example, to the structure of his church. Here he was ambivalent. He loved its congregational government, its group singing, its dynamic preaching. He was proud to be a member of a church where common men and women had a voice in ecclesiastical policy, where

---

[67]Ibid., October 1977.

[68]Ibid.

the washerwoman had an equal vote with the rich woman who employed her, where the blacksmith could teach the banker in Sunday school. Baptists, he used to say, are at their best on the frontier, where their individualism, lay leadership, and free-form worship work well.

He wrote to one-time Southern Baptist President Louie B. Newton, when Newton solicited his comments for a book to be called *Why I Am A Baptist,* that Baptists must never forget that all their success is due to the fact that their program is of, by, and for people.[69] On the other hand, he knew from his own experience that these virtues can be vices. They can make for mediocrity in worship, preaching, teaching, theology, and positive social action. They can limit Baptists to the geographical frontier and block their passage to other, even more challenging ones. They can cause the kind of violent, divisive controversies that stormed through the convention when he was its president, controversies born of democracy perverted by ignorance. Brooks always seemed on the edge of advocating a stronger Baptist authority, in the hands of educated persons, to avoid controversy and evoke the best in his church; but tradition kept him from saying so publicly.

In most ways Brooks was an orthodox Baptist, despite his disdain for what is so often Baptist ignorance, intolerance, and inefficiency. He was as devoted to the Bible as any Baptist, even if on numerous occasions he dissented from denominational interpretations of key passages. He once confessed to his friend Billy Graham that he found it hard to believe in the doctrine of the virgin birth. He was pleased when Graham told him, "I wouldn't let it bother me," since it was not necessary for salvation.[70] Brooks, by the way, wished Graham's message had included more social gospel and less individualism and salvationism; but he considered Graham a good, eloquent preacher and overall a positive influence. Brooks once admitted that because he was more liberal than his church he found it a challenge to be its president, to lead it forward without losing its support. He often found himself torn between his devotion to the Bible and his respect for modern scholarship. He believed, for example, that some of the florid words attributed to Jesus in the New Testament were not really his words. He questioned the passage "When the son of man returns in His glory to sit upon the throne of his glory with his holy angels, the nations shall gather before

---

[69]Letter from Brooks Hays to Louie D. Newton, 6 November 1956.

[70]Hays, Conversation with Ronald Tonks, August 1977.

him." This he said sounded more like some Southern "Bourbon" politician than like the rural social worker he knew his Lord to have been.[71]

Brooks then had trouble accepting Baptist congregationalism when it placed power in unscrupulous hands, Baptist fundamentalism when it praised ignorance and blinded people's eyes to the heart of the social gospel, and Baptist denominationalism when it kept Baptists isolated from the larger body of the Christian church. He complained that the Baptist emphasis on personal salvation taught people that the conversion experience was the essence of the faith, that it kept Baptists spiritually selfish and immature, and that it failed to send them out into the world to serve their fellowman. He worried about Baptist tendencies toward Biblical literalism and inerrancy, especially when in 1971 the Sunday School Board was forced to dismiss a writer for a new Bible commentary because ignorant rabble accused him of not believing in the inerrancy of the scripture. "I do not believe that the Bible is true in every literal sense," Brooks once said, "and I think it is a great mistake to insist that the Baptist tradition requires that."[72] He said, in fact, that the person who demanded some dogmatic interpretation of the Bible was himself out of step with the Baptist tradition of freedom of conscience and the priesthood of every believer.[73]

Morally Brooks lived up to every traditional Southern Baptist standard but one. He considered marital infidelity inexcusable and was faithful to his wife for sixty years. He was honest in handling his and the public's money and as honest in public statements as a politician could be. He was a family man who felt guilty when he did not spend enough time at home. It was only in his moderate use of alcohol that he violated the Baptist ethic. As the aphorism has it, a Baptist is someone who does not drink—in front of another Baptist. As we have seen, Brooks did not drink until 1940, when after an ulcer almost cost him his life he was ordered by his doctor to have a glass of sherry every evening before bed. Later this became a martini. As an older man, working at Wake Forest's Ecumenical Institute, he would also have a beer with lunch. His drinking was moderate. "Never less than one, never more than two" was his motto. Only once apparently did he ever overdo it. This was at Colonial Williamsburg in 1980. Waiting overlong

---

[71]Ibid., May 1975.

[72]Ibid., September 1977.

[73]Marion Hays, Unpublished manuscript, "How to Live Dangerously and Enjoy It," 13. Possession of the author.

for Mrs. Hays to pick him up for dinner, he lost count and had several drinks and had trouble negotiating the stairs down to the dining room. When she was told that he was a bit tipsy Mrs. Hays said, "Thank God, I thought he'd had a stroke." His few obligatory stabs at supporting alcohol control legislation came to little, and late in life he admitted that he really did not believe in prohibition.[74]

But where he differed most sharply with other Baptists was in his devotion to the social gospel. He called himself a Rauschenbusch Baptist. He told the Southern Baptist Historical Society in 1976, "From the glib way in which some of the zealous ones speak of Jesus in current discussions, without evidencing an interest in the application of his teachings to social evils, doubt is cast on their understanding of his place in history."[75] At a convocation at Western Kentucky University in 1968, eight years before Jimmy Carter's presidential campaign, he told his audience that justice is but another word for love. In his book *This World: A Christian's Workshop* he wrote, "The world cannot be regarded as a secular interference with our individual Christian devotions but as the scene of moral exertions which God requires of us."[76]

Brooks followed the Southern Baptist tradition of opposing sending a U.S. ambassador to the Vatican. The only time he broke ranks with Harry Truman was when Truman tried to appoint Myron Taylor to that post. He believed that this violated the doctrine of the separation of church and state.[77] He was still opposed to the idea when Jimmy Carter finally succeeded in establishing that diplomatic link, expressing surprise that a Southern Baptist would do it and that his pastor, Charles Trentham, would approve.[78] But unlike other Southern Baptists, he approved of communication and cooperation between Catholics and Baptists, and he earned the self-styled title "Southern Baptists' chief ecumaniac."

Despite his deviations from common Southern Baptist assumptions, Brooks was one of this century's truest Baptists. He adopted the best, he exemplified the best, and he inspired the best his church had to offer. When

---

[74]Hays, Conversation with Ronald Tonks, August 1977.

[75]Arthur Schlesinger, Jr., preface to Hayes, *Politics Is My Parish,* ix.

[76]Hays, *This World: A Christian's Workshop,* vii.

[77]Hays, Conversation with Ronald Tonks, August 1976.

[78]Ibid., August 1977.

nominating Adlai Stevenson for president of the United States at the 1960 Democratic National Convention, Eugene McCarthy said, "He made us proud to be Democrats." For a generation of young people coming to maturity in the late 1950s, often disillusioned and occasionally outraged by other denominational leaders and self-appointed guardians of tradition and orthodoxy, Brooks Hays, and often Brooks Hays alone, made us proud to be Southern Baptists.

CHAPTER 6

CIVIL RIGHTS

Russellville, Arkansas, at the turn of the twentieth century when Brooks Hays was a boy growing up there, had a population of 3,000 people. One quarter of that number, large for the Ozark foothills, was black. The blacks lived in what was called "colored town," one of which could be found in every Southern town in those days, and they were for the most part poor and without proper education. Brooks would never forget his earliest impressions of black people, or as polite whites then called them, Negroes. These impressions instilled in him equal measures of pity and disdain—pity for their condition, disdain for their inability to better it.[1]

At the age of twelve Brooks asked his father's elderly yardman, Uncle Nelson, why he preferred the Republican party over the Democratic Party, to which Steele Hays belonged. A curious boy of twelve, interested in politics, would ask such a question. Uncle Nelson told him it was because the Republican party was the party of freedom , while the Democratic party was the party of bondage. Up until that time Brooks had only been told that Republicans were carpetbaggers and scalawags while Democrats represented the little people. Uncle Nelson's answer gave him pause.

He remembered then that, two years earlier, on a train trip to Little Rock, he had been disturbed to see black people standing in the aisle behind a rope that separated them from the white section, while white seats on his side of the rope remained empty. He had not been able to forget the fatigue on one black man's face as he stood there. Now he knew he was a

---

[1]Brooks Hays, *A Southern Moderate Speaks* (Chapel Hill: University of North Carolina Press, 1959) 6.

part of the system that forced blacks to remain lower-class citizens. He would be aware of it all through his youth, through his years of holding office in the party of bondage, until at last he was called upon to break with the past and assert his inner convictions. Late in life he would conclude that his years of conformity, even though he was more moderate than his colleagues, had eventually cost him his seat in Congress—and that he deserved it.[2]

Fayetteville, where Brooks attended the University of Arkansas, was a town of 7,500. Only a tiny minority in that mountain town was black, all of them living in a small ghetto called Tincup. Brooks taught a Sunday school class for needy boys while he was a student; but he taught white boys on Rose Hill, not black ones in Tincup. He did once conduct a seminar on race relations for the campus YMCA; but at its close he and his fellow students, who would one day be leaders of their society, concluded that to speak of giving blacks in Arkansas a better break was star gazing. To entertain any idea of civil rights for them was foolishness.[3]

At George Washington University School of Law in Washington, Brooks was invited to join the Ku Klux Klan and refused to do so, as he would again when he returned to practice law in Russellville. But he would do little in those days, or in the days when he represented his district in Congress, to challenge the Southern traditions of racial segregation and white power. He would recall with some remorse his failing to give blacks their proper representation when he was Arkansas Assistant Attorney General in the late 1920s. Although he knew in one case that $9,000 earmarked for a black school was given to a white school, he let it pass because he knew that to challenge the decision would jeopardize his own budding political career. He would also recall that during his sixteen years in Congress, until the last year, he did not speak up for the rights of black people.

While a young man in Little Rock he did, however, help found the city's Urban League. He also talked with the mayor about employing black policemen, a practice that would not be adopted for thirty years. While serving on Little Rock's public welfare board he insisted that those applying for assistance not be asked their race, and he pushed for social programs that would benefit all citizens regardless of race. As an officer in New Deal

---

[2]Brooks Hays, Public Address, Western Kentucky University, Bowling Green KY, November 1968.

[3]Hays, *A Southern Moderate Speaks*, 9.

programs during the 1930s, he took advantage of several opportunities to help raise wages for black workers. But he did not speak of civil rights for blacks in either his 1928 or his 1930 races for governor or in his 1933 race for Congress because he knew that to do so would hurt his chances for election. Blacks could not vote, and whites would not vote for a man who advocated black rights.

In 1937 the Bankhead-Jones Act, which Brooks had helped formulate and shepherd through Congress, provided liberal credit for tenants to acquire and poor owners to keep farm lands. While it did not specifically aid blacks, it made no distinction between the races, and Brooks was convinced that it had helped black farmers.[4] Also in 1937, at the request of Will Alexander, his superior in the Farm Security Administration, he joined the biracial Commission on Interracial Cooperation. This commission, which was supported financially by philanthropist Julius Rosenwald, was judged by observers to be imaginative, forceful, and successful in its fairly modest program of encouraging interracial cooperation and understanding. Brooks would always recall his participation in it with some pride.

In 1938 he led an unsuccessful but bold movement to abolish the Arkansas poll tax—a dream of his since the 1928 election—and received a commendation for his work from Franklin Roosevelt. This move was aimed at giving a free vote to poor people. It did not mention extending the right to blacks, but Brooks knew that any liberalization of voting rights would help both blacks and whites. The white "Bourbon" establishment, particularly strong in east Arkansas, defeated the proposal. Perhaps partly to appease this element, hoping to run for office again himself, Brooks argued against a congressional act to abolish state poll taxes by federal law, saying that states like Arkansas should be able to take such action for themselves rather than having it forced on them from above. It was for this position, support of liberal reforms but only by state laws, that Brooks came to be known as a "states' rights liberal." This title and the philosophy it represented would stay with Brooks, protecting him from racists but impeding his moral impact, until it became untenable in the late 1950s, left him vulnerable to the fierce winds of black demand and white resistance in Little Rock, and forced him at last to become the champion of black rights that his better instincts had always urged him to be.

---

[4]Ibid., 18.

Despite his care not to be singled out as a proponent of black improvement, Brooks's actions during the 1930s left him with if not a liberal at least a moderate image on racial matters. It would dog his steps and a number of times cause him to take cover from accusations of race mixing. In 1942, when at last he was successful in his bid for Congress, his opponent charged that if elected Brooks would seek to alter the status of Negroes. It was rumored that Brooks was a member of organizations dedicated to the destruction of Southern traditions; he was said to have helped raise the wages of black workers; he was accused of trying to abolish the poll tax in order to help blacks get the right to vote; and he was accused of joining forces with integrationists at the 1939 Birmingham Conference on Human Welfare. As we have seen, Brooks was able to counter the last charge by saying simply that he had been in New Orleans the day his opponent said he was in Birmingham and by reprinting a statement of a Methodist Women's organization that condemned the use of race in political campaigns. He did not say that he had gone to Birmingham hoping to find ways to help blacks, had found instead that the organization was too radical for his tastes, and had left before his name was placed before the body for an office without his permission. He was too near victory to cloud the waters. To have said anything good about race relations might have cost him the election. He was about to win, about to go to Congress, about to grow more cautious.

Once elected to Congress, Brooks went about his job, refusing to make racist statements for popular effect, yet mostly serving the white constituents who reelected him over and over. Even when he spoke for racial justice, he added clauses to protect whites from social upheaval brought about by any sudden changes. A sign of his new caution was his withdrawal from the Commission on Interracial Cooperation. He might have remained a member had the organization not begun to be an agent of racial polarization. An October 1942 meeting in Durham, North Carolina, demanded immediate civil rights for blacks, and a meeting of 300 Southern whites in Atlanta the following April resulted in a statement decrying the Durham statement's violent language and its call for the overthrow of Southern social patterns.[5] Brooks excused himself from the battle, saying that his new Congressional duties prevented him from further involvement. Even when, in June 1943, black and white leaders assembled and formed the moderate

---

[5]Ibid., 197.

Southern Regional Council, Brooks remained aloof. He would not duck the racial issue when he was asked his views, and he would never espouse racist causes; but he made it clear that he was a moderate on racial matters. This allowed him to do a few minor things for blacks without alienating his Fifth District of Arkansas constituency. It would not protect him from intermittent attacks from both sides of the racial polarity.

Brooks always thought he understood black people, their tribulations, their aspirations. He was a personal friend to Russellville sharecroppers and Washington janitors. He preached at black churches. But it is likely that he was treated, as were other white moderates and liberals of the day, to regular performances of what has been called the "Negro Act." He spent little if any time talking with liberal black leaders who might have been able to tell him the truth about black aspirations. As it was, he was surprised when in 1957 and 1958 he at last came face to face with the radical extremes of white and black racism. It was only then that he knew how little he had helped blacks, as a moderate, while keeping on the good side of his white constituents.

To his credit, whether his moderation was wise or not, Brooks did not hide from the issue of race relations. Early in his congressional career he staked out his middle ground, the moderate position that would allow him to practice his moral convictions without losing white support, and held it. On 23 April 1945, he debated Representative Charles M. LaFollette of Wisconsin on House Resolution 2232, the question of whether or not to make the Fair Employment Practices Commission permanent. His address, entitled "The Norton Bill Will Hurt Rather Than Help the Minorities It Is Designed to Aid," was considered significant enough to be included in the *Congressional Digest*. In his remarks Brooks outlined the moderate course he believed Southern leaders could pursue, helping to ease racial tensions, without letting racists bring them down. He argued that fair employment, to be successful, must be voluntarily accepted by the white majority in each state. The South would sooner or later come to see the need for fair employment practices, but federal enforcement of laws passed by Northern politicians would only create the kind of white resistance that would hurt blacks. "Government cannot supply the motive for unity," he said, "it can only supply the mechanics, and if the motive is lacking, no government process will succeed."[6] He went on to say that the nation needed

---

[6]Brooks Hays, "The Norton Bill Will Hurt Rather Than Help the Minorities It Is Designed to Aid," *Congressional Digest* (June-July 1945): 181-85.

to think less in racial than in human terms; that the Negro had more to gain from playing down than playing up his race; and that a force bill would only accentuate the differences between blacks and whites, at first perhaps giving blacks a few minor victories but in the long run only confirming their segregation.

He argued that the proposed bill confused the two functions of government, the regulatory and the promotional, by trying to regulate an attitude when all it could properly and successfully do was promote a new one. He made it clear that he for one did not condone racial prejudice or discrimination, an unusually liberal statement for a Southern politician in 1945; but he covered his flanks by saying that Southern whites were a minority in this country too and that to force them to hire blacks without reference to circumstances would be to discriminate against them.[7] He even made the disingenuous point, which the worst of racists would make well into the 1980s, that a Southern white who then employed only blacks would, under this bill, be forced to fire some of them and hire whites, thus harming the very people the bill sought to help.

He concluded by pointing out, as he often did in talks on race relations in those early days, that no people had made such rapid progress as American Negroes had in the past eighty years. He said that in certain fields, albeit ones considered humble, they were superior to whites and that this bill, by forcing white Southerners to treat them fairly when whites were not psychologically ready to do so, would expose blacks to new waves of resentment and wipe out the gains they had made.[8] Thus spoke, and apparently believed, the Brooks Hays of 1945, at the end of World War II.

By today's standards, of course, this all sounds pathetically conservative, inadequate, and even racist. But for its day, delivered by a Southerner who had to go back to his white constituency for reelection every two years, it was daring. The printed form of the speech was widely distributed, and Americans everywhere who read it were impressed by what they considered its moderate tone, its lack of racism, its well-reasoned arguments. Brooks was pleased and inspired by the response. He would later say that then and there he began to see himself in the role of spokesman for a new, emerging, moderate South, a South that would accept progress and change if it could be sure the fabric of its society would not be torn.

---

[7]Ibid., 183.

[8]Ibid., 185.

He could imagine himself the man of reason and sanity, standing forth-rightly between Southern conservatives and Northern liberals, between whites and blacks, offering a better, a moderate way, and being heard, heeded, and perhaps even chosen to lead the movement toward racial rec-onciliation.[9] He would be *the* Southern moderate. It was this dream, based both on a desire to make a positive contribution to his nation and region and to gain a measure of personal fame, that shaped Brooks's thoughts and actions for well over a decade. It would prove a pipe dream and would leave him vulnerable to racist attacks without giving him a solid base of liberal support. The moderate ground he had staked out in the 1940s would prove to be a field of quicksand in the 1950s. But between 1945 and 1958 Brooks would take his stand there, as the nation's most respected and promising Southern moderate politician.

National concerns with civil rights for black citizens called Brooks into the spotlight once again during the 1940s. President Truman, still reeling from the mid-term Republican victory of 1946 that gave them control of Congress, named a Committee on Civil Rights on 5 December of that year to recommend ways to protect the civil rights of all Americans. The com-mittee reported in 1947, making a number of recommendations, some moderate and some considered radical for that day. Among the ones that raised Southern hackles was the suggestion that federal financial aid be withheld from states guilty of civil rights abuses, a plan Brooks agreed would only make race relations worse in the South. While Truman did not approve every proposal the committee made to him, he sent it intact on 2 February 1948 to what he called "that good-for-nothing 80th Congress," in part to prove that not all Democrats were the racists Republicans had al-ways charged them with being. The Republican Congress failed to act on the proposals, and Truman used their failure to act on behalf of black cit-izens as an issue against them in his 1948 bid for reelection.

The 1948 Democratic National Convention, which after a tremendous struggle renominated Truman, placed a strong civil rights plank in its platform. The plank, which was inspired by the committee's report and a stirring speech by the mayor of Minneapolis Hubert Humphrey, led to a walkout by Southern delegates and to the creation of the Dixiecrat party, with Strom Thurmond of South Carolina as its presidential nominee. On

---

[9]Hays, *A Southern Moderate Speaks,* 32.

the other hand, Truman seemed to have no trouble running on the platform. Retrospect tells us that it was at this convention that the modern
Democratic party, because of its ever more liberal racial policy, became the
minority party in presidential elections.

Brooks took some heat at home for supporting the ticket of Truman and
Barkley. His Sunday school class even threatened to change its name from
the Brooks Hays class to something more in keeping with its segregationist philosophy. Truman carried Arkansas, but significantly enough he lost
the Fifth District. He believed that he owed his narrow margin of victory
nationwide to liberals and minorities who were attracted to the party because of the civil rights plank. He was determined to resubmit the committee's proposals to the new Congress, which was dominated by Southern
Democrats. The party faced open warfare between its left and right wings.
Into the no-man's land between the two armies stepped Brooks Hays.

Brooks believed, perhaps naively, that Southerners would support a
plan to grant equal justice to all citizens, including Negroes, so long as they
could be sure it would not alter their traditional social system. Hoping to
see his party avoid a destructive battle, the South avoid being forced to
change its racial patterns, and the nation avoid a racial crisis, Brooks decided to formulate, sponsor, and shepherd through Congress a plan to accomplish a moderate civil rights revolution. He unveiled his plan in a
speech before the House on 2 February 1949, the first anniversary of Truman's submission of the committee's report, and incidentally his own
twenty-seventh wedding anniversary. Eventually to be known as "The
Arkansas Plan" because Brooks wrote it, the scheme would be hotly debated and both condemned and praised by all sides before it was finally
allowed to die by radicals on both the left and right who refused its compromise.

The Arkansas Plan addressed the four major issues raised by the Truman committee's report: segregation in the armed forces, the poll tax,
lynching, and fair employment. On the first issue Brooks argued that court
decisions regarding interstate transportation were in the process of rem-
edying this form of segregation and that it was therefore legislatively and
socially the least important. He said that the military could and should be
allowed to desegregate its ranks as it saw fit. His solution was to leave it
to the armed forces, just as in other matters he wanted to leave things to
states and municipalities for remedy.[10] He believed that the military would

---

[10]Ibid., 44.

soon be integrated anyway and that legislation would only create resistance to the idea.

As to the poll tax, Brooks had always opposed it and had made several attempts, before coming to Congress, to get Arkansas to outlaw it. Now he suggested that it be abolished in the six Southern states where it still existed, not by congressional legislation but by a constitutional amendment. To do it this way would make it a truly national decision and perhaps let the South know that it was out of step with the rest of the country. He preferred that the states abolish the tax for themselves, but he knew that this would take longer to accomplish than civil rights activities would allow. A constitutional amendment would require a kind of national referendum and would not create the resentment a congressional bill was certain to raise.[11]

As to lynching, Brooks proposed that Congress call on all states to pass their own anti-lynching laws and give enforcement powers to each state's highest ranking law officer. If a state followed this call—outlawed lynching; pursued, tried, and punished offenders; and conducted each trial outside the accused person's home county—federal officials would not interfere with the state's business. Federal agents would move in only if it became apparent that state officials were not acting in good faith. The proposal would also make lynching a personal rather than a racial matter and identify it as a violation of an individual's civil rights.[12]

The fourth, and Brooks believed the most difficult, area of the proposal dealt with fair employment, and here he suggested that the Fair Employment Practices Commission's powers be patterned on those of the board to prevent discrimination against the handicapped. He argued again that forcing fair employment on Southern managers would only lead to resistance and possibly violence. The plan would work better, he believed, if the commission spent its time and energy educating employers in the advantages of fair hiring rather than in applying legal or economic coercion. This part of Brooks's plan was the most strongly criticized because fair employment was such a hotly debated issue at the time.[13] Liberals said the plan had no teeth and was designed to let the South continue its medieval economic system. Conservatives said Brooks was foolhardy to offer any com-

---

[11]Ibid., 46.

[12]Ibid.

[13]Ibid., 48.

promise at all to what they considered an employer's right to hire whom he pleased.

Yet the Arkansas Plan—the San Francisco *Chronicle* gave it that name—was widely hailed as a legitimate compromise to the racial crisis almost everyone saw looming ahead. It was one of the reasons the state of Arkansas came to be characterized as the most moderate of the states of the old Confederacy and the one where public school desegregation might work first. The Atlanta *Constitution* called it a well-reasoned plan that would appeal to what it called the majority of Americans who were moderate on civil rights.[14] Even Georgia's brilliant but conservative Senator Richard Russell, a true power in Congress, announced that he would support it in the Senate as a one-package compromise.

Brooks met with Truman twice to discuss the plan: the first time secretly, arriving through the back door of the White House, the second time as an honored guest. He would say much later that in private Truman agreed with the plan and that he promised to sign it if it passed Congress but that he believed the 1948 election had committed him to a more strident liberal plan and he could not retreat from it.[15] Brooks always believed that had the president not been preoccupied with world affairs he could have convinced him to support the plan openly. He also believed that Truman could have done so without alienating either liberals or conservatives.[16] But there was not enough time or attention, and when the administration announced it could not support the plan, it died in committee. Brooks yielded to reality. He said he knew his plan had flaws but that "half of something is better than all of nothing." The Arkansas Plan, he concluded, was the victim of extremism of both right and left,[17] as would be his own candidacy for reelection nine years later.

The Arkansas Plan competed against other plans. Adam Clayton Powell, Congressman as well as black Baptist minister from Harlem, also introduced a bill in 1949. His proposal advocated creating a national commission to end discrimination in all the areas Brooks had addressed,

---

[14]Atlanta *Constitution,* 7 February 1949.

[15]Brooks Hays, Conversation with Ronald Tonks, October 1977, typeset in 15 parts. Southern Baptist Sunday School Board Archives, Nashville TN.

[16]Hays, *A Southern Moderate Speaks,* 34.

[17]Ibid., 50.

having powers to force state compliance. Brooks was called to testify before Powell's House Committee on Education and Labor on the bill, and he argued that education and counseling would achieve the goals of the bill better than powers to force compliance. Fellow Baptist Powell agreed with Brooks that racial reconciliation was the ultimate goal of all civil rights legislation. However, he also said that without teeth, without a big stick to force recalcitrant employers and state officials to comply, fair practices, and therefore reconciliation, could never be achieved. Brooks said, as he had four years earlier, that force bills invariably hurt the very minorities they are designed to help. He concluded his testimony with a quote from German theologian Emil Brunner: "All suffering is bitter. Suffering that is unjust is doubly bitter. Suffering that is destiny unites. Suffering that is unjust divides."[18] Brooks was as concerned about the suffering of the Southern white minority of the United States as about the suffering of the Southern black minority of the South.

The Powell Bill made it to the House floor, and during the ensuing debate on it Brooks deeply impressed the volatile liberal Congressman Vito Marcantonio of New York. Marcantonio, a champion of civil rights, was known for his fiery rebuttals of what he considered the agents of discrimination. He had long called the Hays Arkansas Plan of "gradualism" merely another of the stalling operations that had held blacks down for eighty years, and in the floor debate he accused Brooks of being just another disciple of Jim Crow. Brooks's answers to Marcantonio's questions were so thoughtful, reasoned, and obviously compassionate that Marcantonio's tone softened, and reporters expressed surprise at the mildness of the debate. While the two men did not agree on every issue—that force bills hurt minorities, that white people had a constitutional right to associate only with other whites—they helped create an atmosphere of mutual toleration that mitigated the angry outbursts of earlier debate.

The Powell Bill passed the House, where liberals were dominant, but its emphasis on force killed it, as Brooks predicted, in the Southern-dominated Senate. Brooks would always believe that his plan, had the administration supported it, would have passed the Senate as well and would have given the country half of something instead of all of nothing. As it was, there would be no civil rights package made law until 1957, and no overall solution to the problems of discrimination until 1964, if indeed they are solved even now.

---

[18]Ibid., 59-60.

Brooks continued, year after year through the 1950s, to offer his non-coercive equal opportunities bill, which continued to be defeated. Anti-lynching bills continued to appear and suffer defeat. No one ever reintroduced the idea of a constitutional amendment to abolish the poll tax. Truman integrated the armed forces by executive order. Blacks remained disenfranchised and without civil rights in the South. In 1952 Brooks would be challenged for reelection for the first time since 1946, by a candidate calling himself a segregationist. As a result of the Arkansas Plan and his well-publicized House debates, Brooks had become known as the nation's most sincere and articulate racial "moderate," a new variation on the title "states' rights liberal." It would give him prominence and respect across the nation but eventually cause him grief in Arkansas and the South.

Brooks always defended Truman by saying that though he disagreed with the administration's civil rights plan he believed that the president was sincerely concerned about the rights of minorities. He even attributed this concern to Truman's "Baptist" faith in the dignity of every individual.[19] But he tried to make it clear, for the sake of his constituents back home, with an eye on retaining his political base, that he believed the proper road to equality lay through more moderate territory. On 8 April 1950, he debated Fisk University President Charles S. Johnson, then co-chairman of the Southern Regional Council, on the nationally broadcast "Town Hall Meeting of the Air." The topic was "What Effects Do Our Race Relations Have on Our Foreign Policy?" While Brooks did not deny that inequities in American life and the strained relations between the races hurt our image abroad, he emphasized the great progress black Americans had made in recent years. From slavery to the levels of 1950, in eighty-five years, no other people anywhere had risen so rapidly. He said that this progress, rather than the racial strife so prominent in current news stories, was the positive signal we should be sending to the world about American liberty.[20]

In 1950 the Minneapolis mayor who had electrified the 1948 Democratic National Convention with his speech in support of civil rights, Hubert Horatio Humphrey, was elected to the United States Senate. Brooks recalled how he hit Washington "like a whirlwind," ready to do battle with

---

[19]Letter from Brooks Hays to Harry Truman, 12 June 1951. Brooks Hays Collection, Baptist Sunday School Board, Nashville.

[20]Hays, *A Southern Moderate Speaks*, 198-99.

anyone on any issue having to do with human rights.[21] He and Brooks met when they were asked to present differing sides of the civil rights argument. Humphrey entered the auditorium late, gave a rousing talk that had the student audience cheering wildly, and then started to leave, having forgotten that there was to be another speaker. Once he had been reminded, he sat down and listened to Brooks. Brooks did not charm or ignite the audience with his moderate talk, but his quiet, reasoned, nonracist dissent from the Humphrey liberalism impressed the Minnesotan, who had expected the Southern Congressman to be a Neanderthal racist. They became fast friends.[22]

Humphrey studied and liked the Arkansas Plan, except he thought it was weak on enforcement. While in public he was ever the strident champion of civil rights, in private he told Brooks that he believed the moderate approach would more likely be successful than his more radical one. Brooks often said that Humphrey was like one of the Old Testament prophets, a man of uncompromising righteousness, and that all he needed was to understand better the sinners he condemned, as the prophets did. He told Humphrey this and offered to teach him, since as he put it he was one of those imperfect humans who could not stand one hundred percent for the Humphrey civil rights program. Humphrey loved it.

In the spring of 1952 Sam Rayburn, fearing that the argument over fair employment might split the party in an election year, appointed Brooks, who would not be a delegate to the national convention, to the preconvention Platform Drafting Committee. He said he hoped Brooks, the well-publicized moderate, could help write a decent compromise plank on civil rights. Fears of a showdown increased when the probable presidential nominee, Adlai Stevenson, said just before the convention that if states did not enforce fair employment the federal government must do so. Brooks and Alabama Senator John Sparkman, who would be a delegate and would be Stevenson's vice-presidential running mate, went to Humphrey. Southern delegates and voters, they felt and told him, would go along with civil rights if the platform did not mention compulsion or enforcement. Hum-

----

[21]Ibid., 65

[22]Marion Hays, Unpublished manuscript, "How to Live Dangerously and Enjoy It," VII-10-13, Possession of the author.

phrey listened to them, respecting Brooks's sentiments on the issue, and in the end agreed that for the sake of party unity he would not lead a floor fight to add those words. With assurance like this from the party's most eloquent defender of civil rights, they proceeded.

Brooks helped write the preliminary plank on civil rights. Even after the official committee met to write the final draft, he stood outside a door of the room and advised Sparkman when he came out for help. The section that Brooks had written personally, on the proper balance between federal and state authority, was approved as presented. As Brooks had planned it, no mention was made in the plank of the F.E.P.C. or of "enforcing" fair employment practices. It did call for federal legislation "effectively" to secure civil rights. This plank was as strong as the one in 1948 without its divisive tone. Without the red flag words, without a Humphrey challenge, it was approved by voice vote.

In spite of their unity, however, the Democrats lost the White House in 1952 for the first time in twenty years. Both Stevenson and Eisenhower had in the final analysis adopted moderate civil rights positions, agreeing for the most part with the Arkansas Plan. But civil rights played only a small part in an election that was won by Eisenhower's more pleasing personality. Under the new president, the nearest thing to a Whig the nation had known for more than a century, civil rights legislation was put on hold. It would be up to the courts to push the cause of minority rights forward. For his part, Brooks began thinking more of world affairs, in line with his new place on Foreign Affairs, and believed his days of dealing with civil rights were over.

Not so. In 1954 the Supreme Court's decision in response to *Brown vs. Board of Education* brought an end to any plan to handle the issue with benign neglect. The focus was no longer fair employment but school desegregation. Eighteen months before that pivotal decree, in the 8 November 1952 edition of the *Saturday Evening Post,* Brooks had been quoted as saying: "Any act of Congress or any order of the Supreme Court abolishing segregation and overriding the states in this vital matter would not only damage race relations but would also tend to cancel out the tremendous and steady gains being made by our Negro citizens." He had not said, good politician that he was, whether such a law or decree would be morally or constitutionally right, just that it would cause social upheaval. Even "one of the most enlightened of Southern Congressmen," as the author of the article called Brooks, saw more loss than gain in a decision that would force integration on Southern schools.[23]

Just a week before the *Brown* decision was announced on 12 May 1954, Brooks testified before the Interstate Commerce Commission that the courts must be obeyed, whether individuals believed their decisions were right or wrong. He had said that as a member of the House Forcign Affairs Committee he had slowly come to see, as never before, how America's segregated public facilities hurt her image abroad. The debate on "Town Meeting" had affected him. He had also suggested a federal law to require integration on interstate coaches, again adding, however, that each state should be permitted to prosecute violators unless it could be proved a state neglected to do so. No one had asked him about school integration, and he had volunteered no opinion on that more difficult problem. At this point his future dilemma was, however, quite apparent. He fully believed that court decisions must be obeyed, not to do so was unconstitutional, but he knew that forced integration would stir a violent reaction in the South.

On 17 May 1954, the Supreme Court overturned the 1896 case of *Plessy vs. Ferguson,* which had legitimatized the idea of "separate but equal" public schools. The Court ruled that there could be no equality in segregated schools and subsequently ordered schools to begin to desgragate their educational systems "with all deliberate speed." The decision sent shock waves through the South, and once more Brooks found himself in the middle of a great national debate. Neither a segregationist nor an integrationist, a man who believed in obeying Court orders but who had to speak for his white constituency, he faced a dilemma.

Congressman Adam Clayton Powell almost immediately attached an amendment to the latest school funds bill denying aid to segregated systems, and Brooks found himself voting against a package he had only recently been working to get approved. White resentment of the Court's decision, and of subsequent congressional attempts to enforce it, grew geometrically, as Brooks had long predicted. Brooks tried to be reasonable. He agreed with the Court that *Plessy vs. Ferguson* was out of date and should be modified, but he considered it dangerous to throw it out completely. He never denied that the Court had final authority to interpret the Constitution or that federal law took precedence over state law, both of which Ar-

---

[23]Virginius Dabney, "Southern Crisis: The Segregation Decision," *Saturday Evening Post,* 8 November 1952, 46.

kansas Governor Orval Faubus would deny; but he did believe that citizens have the right to disagree with Court decisions and that laws are more easily enforced when states rather than the federal government make them. About all he could do at this point, however, was call for mutual trust between federal and state governments, blacks and whites, liberals and conservatives, courts and citizens. He hoped local school districts would, as Little Rock seemed willing to do, propose voluntary plans for desegregation. He hoped for sanity, unity, and peace and kept his fingers crossed.

His voice was one of the few that spoke for such moderation. By early 1956 the South was so up in arms about forced integration that Southern Congressmen wrote a statement of resistance to the Court's decision, popularly called the "Southern Manifesto," and brought it to Brooks to sign. The statement claimed that in school cases the Supreme Court had abused its judicial powers, had illegally encroached on states' rights, and had tried to destroy the South's social system. It said that the undersigned would take every legal means to reverse the *Brown* decision. More than one hundred Southern senators and congressmen would eventually sign it. At first Brooks hesitated, saying he could not sign as long as it contained the words *nullification* and *interposition* and as long as it did not specifically reject violence and say that resistance would embrace only legal means. When such changes were made, Brooks had a major decision to make.

First-term Arkansas Governor Orval Faubus helped him make it. Faubus urged Brooks to sign the Southern Manifesto because if he refused to do so his constituents would consider him a traitor to the Southern way of life and turn to racial extremists for leadership. Brooks finally decided Faubus was right and signed. He knew within twenty-four hours that he had made a mistake. "It wasn't worthy of me," he would say twenty years later, although even then he insisted that it had been not a manifesto but a declaration, since he had helped eliminate the defiance it had at first shown. He signed it, he always said, in order to keep his seat in Congress, and that in order to be a voice for moderation; but he knew his decision had been wrong.[24]

This judgment was confirmed when, not long after the signing, he was in Little Rock campaigning for his successful 1956 reelection and met with a group of forty black ministers. They had always been Hays supporters, they knew they could speak freely to him, and they let him know how dis-

---

[24]Hays, Conversation with Ronald Tonks, August 1976.

pleased they were. He answered all their questions, some of them hostile, and he lamely quoted the Pauline injunction to "let your moderation be known to all men," arguing that he had had to sign the manifesto in order to remain a moderate leader in the House. But he knew, and the ministers knew he knew, that he had temporarily joined the enemy camp. One of the men told him: "I just tell my people that I've seen you slip before and then get back on the right track." Brooks asked their forgiveness, promising to do the right thing the next time, and left the meeting chastened and changed. He would do the right thing the next time, and he would suffer for it; but he would one day say that if his 1958 defeat atoned for the mistake of 1956, "I am one of the happiest men that was ever defeated for office."[25]

The year 1956 proved to be one of the most difficult years a moderate on civil rights could face. It saw Brooks opposing the Eisenhower Administration's civil rights program, itself a belated reaction to *Brown vs. Board of Education*. Republicans were interested not so much in school desegregation as in voting rights, primarily because they felt that if blacks were allowed to vote, the solid Democratic South might be tilted toward the Republican side. Brooks signed, again under severe pressure from conservative colleagues, a petition rejecting the program. He was again disturbed by the decision, particularly because the petition used words like *sinister* and *iniquitous* to describe attempts to extend voting rights to Negroes, and this time he issued a statement that he hoped would clarify his position. He said that his opposition was not to programs of racial justice or school desegregation but to federal dictation of state election processes. He said the Eisenhower proposal was a potential force bill, which could well insinuate the federal government into community affairs. The bill passed the House by a large margin but never reached the floor of a Senate dominated by Southern Democrats and anxious to adjourn for the 1956 election season.

As a delegate to the 1956 Democratic National Convention Brooks could, unlike in 1952, serve on committees, so Democratic Chairman Paul Butler put him to work writing the platform's civil rights plank. Brooks left his own campaign in Arkansas, which seemed safe enough now that he had signed the two anti-civil rights statements, to go to Chicago and try

---

[25]Brooks Hays, Public Address, Western Kentucky University, Bowling Green KY, November 1968.

to persuade nominee-apparent Adlai Stevenson to compromise his strident position on civil rights and hold the party together. He tried to convince Stevenson that not all Southerners were extremists and that with a moderate platform the moderates would be able to keep the South in the party and eventually persuade it to accept integration. Stevenson listened to Brooks, whom he trusted and admired, but he seemed unconvinced. Disturbed by Stevenson's reluctance to compromise, Brooks went to the Platform Committee meeting with a somewhat devious plan in mind to make the civil rights plank moderate without Northern liberals understanding that it was.

In subcommittee Brooks wrote a civil rights plank that called for racial justice without urging support of the *Brown* decision and without reference to federal enforcement of it. Then, according to plan, he and the four other Southerners on the committee voted against it. Northern liberals on the committee assumed that since it was too strong for Southerners it was strong enough for them, and it was added to the platform. There was an uproar when the platform was circulated, and more critical readers noted the omissions. Once again Brooks was a bridge between extremists. He avoided a bloody floor fight by suggesting that the more radical Northern liberals read a minority report on the floor of the convention, by marshaling Northern moderates to speak in favor of the majority report, and by persuading Southerners just to keep quiet. In the end, former President Truman stood to support the majority plank, calling it the best in history, and Convention Chairman Sam Rayburn declared it passed in a close voice vote, denying pleas for a roll call of delegates. Brooks and moderates everywhere heaved huge sighs of relief.

Stevenson again lost to Eisenhower in November, but this time Democrats won both houses of Congress; and Brooks always believed that the congressional victory was due to the party's success in reconciling differences on racial matters. The nation faced four years of a Republican presidency and a Democratic Congress. In general Republicans favored civil rights programs that extended both voting and educational rights. Conservative Democrats, most of them Southerners, stood squarely against all such talk and proposals. Brooks, the Southern moderate, a rare bird indeed for those days, tried to steer the tricky middle course, favoring voting and educational rights, opposing any attempt by the federal government to force the white South to accept them. He opposed the destruction of traditional Southern social patterns by force because he feared that white reaction might threaten what gains blacks had already made. It was lonely in no-man's land.

The year 1957 would prove to be the time of Brooks's greatest agony and highest achievement. It began badly, as he worked for passage of a bill to give federal aid to public schools, worrying constantly that another of those amendments to withhold funds from segregated schools might be attached to it, which would mean he would have to vote against the very bill for which he had worked so hard. As it turned out, the proffered amendment was defeated, which made him happy, but the bill was returned to committee and died there.[26] Then came the 1957 Civil Rights Bill. He wanted desperately to vote for it but could not do so because the House version did not require jury trials for all civil rights violations. The Senate version did require this, and Brooks hoped this version would be adopted. However, in conference the House version, which left it up to judicial discretion whether or not to have jury trials in minor cases, was adopted. Sadly Brooks had to vote against the final version.[27]

His election as president of the Southern Baptist Convention that spring gave him both a greater forum for his ideas and a greater responsibility to represent high moral principles. In August, just before the Little Rock Central High School crisis, he spoke to a convention of 2,500 lay church leaders in Atlanta, Georgia, and in his address made a three-point proposal for Christians in that day of crises. Churches should, he said, let their ministers speak freely on racial issues, trusting them to interpret God's word correctly, without fear of reprisals from racists; they should stand without equivocation for equal justice under the law for all citizens; and they should in every declaration, whatever it might be, emphasize that all problems be solved nonviolently. He did not call for voting rights or desegregation of public schools, and he did not ask churches to admit Negro members. He was still hoping to avoid crises and confrontations. He still seemed to envision a society of separate but truly equal races, with equal opportunities and rights, living side by side but not necessarily together socially, in harmony if not intimacy.

Then in September came the Little Rock Central High crisis, the actions of Arkansas Governor Orval Faubus, the response of President Eisenhower, the National Guard, federal troops, and chaos. Brooks's hopes

---

[26]Hays, *A Southern Moderate Speaks,* 126.

[27]Brooks Hays, *This World: A Christian's Workshop* (Nashville: Broadman Press, 1968) 12.

and dreams of peace and brotherhood through Christian tolerance and political moderation were about to be dashed.

Central High School in Little Rock seemed, before September 1957, an unlikely site for racial conflict. On 22 May 1954, only five days after the U.S. Supreme Court handed down the *Brown* decision, the Little Rock City School Board publicly expressed its intentions to comply with the order. Board members likely expected a rather lengthy period of grace in which to desegregate on a modest scale, but their assumptions soon proved false. In August 1954, the Little Rock chapter of the National Association for the Advancement of Colored People petitioned for immediate integration. While the federal court denied the petition, it did warn the board that it needed to get busy on a desegregation plan, which it did. In the spring of 1955 it presented a plan to the Court.

Little Rock, in 1955 considered one of the South's most moderate cities, perhaps because of Brooks Hays's reputation, was a city of 243,000—75 percent white, 24 percent nonwhite and mostly Negro, and only 1 percent foreign born.[28] The integration of its schools would be a domestic affair, the players all home folks, people who saw each other regularly on the street but did not meet socially. Only two high schools served this large town. Central High, which dominated the state in most forms of academic and athletic competition, the pride of white Little Rock, was all white but had within its designated service area 1,712 white and 200 black student-age persons. Horace Mann High School, the Negro school, had within its service area 328 white and 607 black school-age persons. A proposed new school, to be named Hall High, located in a white suburb, would have 700 white and 4 black school-age persons. Central would thus be the key to any desegregation plan.

Few blacks would be able to go to Hall High when it was completed; few if any whites would choose to go to Horace Mann. A large number of blacks wanted what they considered the better educational training offered at Central. There was bound to be resistance to desegregating Central from whites who could not go to Hall. As it turned out, nine black teenagers, three male and six female, were chosen to break the color line at this school that was considered one of the most beautifully constructed high schools in the nation. All nine had good reasons for going to Central, each was in-

---

[28]Robert R. Brown, *Bigger than Little Rock* (Greenwich CT: Seabury Press, 1958) 5.

terested in a particular course of study that was not offered at Horace Mann, but their appearance brought violence.

The plan submitted in 1955 by the Little Rock school board called for the high schools to be integrated first, beginning in September 1957, then after two years the junior highs and so forth on down, the entire process to take between five and ten years. All members of the board voted for the plan, even the archsegregationist Dale Alford, who was told that this plan was the least the courts would approve.[29] On 24 January 1956, twenty-seven black students of all levels tried to register for white schools and were turned away. In U.S. District Court and later in the 8th Circuit Court of Appeals another N.A.A.C.P. petition for immediate desegregation was rejected and the board's plan was heartily approved, with the program of desegregation outlined in it to begin in the fall term of 1957.

As the date approached, tensions rose. In February 1957, the Arkansas legislature passed a bill calling for the continued segregation of public schools in the state and naming a Sovereignty Commission to enforce its will. Governor Faubus promptly signed the bill into law, and the commission's first act was to lift attendance requirements at any school that might be forcibly integrated.[30] By summer the entire state was tense, with Little Rock a veritable tinder box. The opening day of school, 3 September, was being called D-Day. No one knew what to expect.

Into this explosive scene came Georgia's inflammatory segregationist Governor Marvin Griffin. Coming to Little Rock to address the local chapter of the White Citizens Council on 22 August, Griffin raised funds for segregationist causes, raised tensions in a city already worried about violence, and raised Orval Faubus's consciousness about the pitfalls and potentials of the confrontation to come. Faubus invited Griffin to spend the night at the governor's mansion, and the two men had a long talk, during which Griffin persuaded Faubus that he should use the National Guard to stop the attempt to integrate the schools and thereby prevent the inevitable violence that integration would bring.[31] A week later, on 29 August, when a group calling itself the "Mothers of Central High League" went to court to stop the desegregation scheduled in five days, Faubus stood as a

---

[29]Virgil T. Blossom, *It Has Happened Here* (New York: Harper and Brothers, 1959) 197.

[30]Brown, *Bigger Than Little Rock,* 10.

[31]Hays, *A Southern Moderate Speaks,* 131.

witness for them, testifying that he feared violence if the plan were carried out.[32] The federal judge who heard the appeal of the case on 30 August ordered the schools to open, desegregated as planned, on time. Faubus's warning of violence was widely circulated and, according to Brooks, became a self-fulfilling prophecy.[33]

On Labor Day, 2 September, the Arkansas *Gazette* ran this headline: Little Rock Quiet on Eve of Opening Integrated Schools."[34] The calm, apparent the night before when the paper was printed, would not last throughout the day. That morning Faubus called out the National Guard and assigned them to the Central High area "to prevent bloodshed" by preventing the desegregation of the school. On 3 September, the day the school should have been but was not integrated, a federal judge ordered the school to admit the nine black students the following day. That day the *Gazette* announced that Arkansas' governor was the first American politician since the Civil War to practice interposition, or placing his word above that of the federal government.[35]

On Wednesday, 4 September, National Guardsmen and state troopers, acting on Faubus's orders, turned the nine blacks away at the school steps. A mob of whites, gathered nearby to watch, cheered the action. On Thursday, 5 September, Congressman Brooks Hays arrived in Little Rock in time to read in the papers that Little Rock's Mayor Woodrow Mann said he believed the governor's fear of violence was a hoax perpetrated to prevent desegregation.[36] Brooks came, he would later explain, and he got involved in the affair because he felt duty bound to do so, much the way he would have felt had some natural disaster struck his district.[37] He would work secretly for a week before his part in negotiations became public knowledge.

On Saturday, 7 September, the federal judge once more ordered that the nine black students be admitted to Central, this time on Monday, 9 September. Brooks would remember that throughout the day on Sunday,

---

[32]Brown, *Bigger Than Little Rock,* 11.

[33]Hays, *A Southern Moderate Speaks,* 133.

[34]Arkansas *Gazette* (Little Rock), 2 September 1957.

[35]Ibid., 3 September 1957.

[36]Ibid., 5 September 1957.

[37]Natalie Davis Spingarn, "Mr. Hays of Arkansas Meets His Responsibilities," *Reporter,* 14 November 1957, 250.

8 September, as he spoke at Second Baptist Church in the morning and absorbed vibrations from the city through the afternoon, he felt tensions rising. And so on Monday, 9 September, when Faubus's troops continued to forbid the blacks to enter, Brooks placed a telephone call to Eisenhower's presidential assistant, the man many said ran the White House at that time, Sherman Adams. He would later explain that he made the call because Faubus asked him to do so. Faubus would later explain that he did so because he feared federal agents had tapped his lines and were preparing to take him into custody. Seeing the situation deteriorating, Brooks once again assumed the role he had grown accustomed to playing in civil rights disputes: the role of mediator.

Over the telephone he assured Adams that Faubus was no backcountry racist, that he was an intelligent man who wanted to keep the peace, and that federal authorities should avoid frightening him into the arms of extremists. Faubus in fact considered himself a liberal. As a native of the northwest Arkansas mountains, where there were few if any blacks, he denied any racist feelings or attitudes. He liked to recall how he had helped integrate the state's Democratic party and its state college system. He told Brooks to tell Adams that events were simply moving too fast and that he needed more time to prepare his people to accept change in order to avoid bloodshed. He did not then and would never admit playing for popular acclaim in the crisis at Little Rock Central, a crisis he had helped make.

At first Adams suggested to Brooks that Faubus come to see Ike in Washington. When Brooks reported this to Faubus, Faubus said he would. When told that Adams wanted him to request the meeting, Faubus agreed again. All he asked of Brooks was that he write the message. Brooks sketched out the request, Faubus made only minor changes, and the message was sent. Faubus thanked Brooks for his help. The next day, 10 September, Faubus accepted a summons to appear on 20 September in federal court to explain his use of the National Guard; and Brooks felt a surge of hope that Faubus was about to accept the court's authority. That same day word appeared in the press that the president and the governor were in direct contact, but there was no mention of Brooks's part in the story.[38]

On 11 September Faubus's request for a meeting and Ike's agreement to it were released to the press by White House Press Secretary James Hagerty, with the explanation that Brooks was the mediator of the dispute

---

[38]Arkansas *Gazette* (Little Rock), 10 September 1957.

and would attend the meeting. Whether Faubus had known before this time that Brooks would come with him is not known. Brooks was immediately besieged by newsmen. The *Gazette* said on 13 September that Brooks had been "revealed" as the go-between in the matter and that he was a "personal friend of the president."[39] Already there were seeds of the story that Brooks was on the federal government's side in the dispute.

Brooks knew that he had to avoid upstaging Faubus. All the newspapers were filled with photographs of both men, with Brooks's usually above that of the governor. He knew he had to speak out, to urge reason and calm, but without appearing to take sides. This was the role of a mediator, whatever his private feelings might be.[40] He also knew that he was not a part of either the Faubus or the Eisenhower inner circle, that he could not in the final analysis influence either group. Photographs and films of the meeting between governor and president, which took place on Saturday, 14 September, at Newport, Rhode Island, show Brooks in the uncomfortable space between them, generally talking more with Ike than with Faubus, but careful not to turn his back on either man. He was at the center of the action, yet he was a man without a party. He said later that he felt "like a sparrow that flew into a badminton game."[41]

On Friday, 13 September, Brooks flew with Faubus from Little Rock to Providence, where they spent the night under police protection. Feeling the hostility toward them from the Northern crowds as they arrived, Brooks knew that he would be hated by extremists on both sides of the controversy. But it was too late to turn back, and he would not have done so had he been able. This was the place in history he had chosen for himself. It was his parish. Newsmen asked him if he had made the trip as a representative of the Southern Baptist Convention, of which he was president, and he replied that he came only as Little Rock's Congressman, that no Baptist could represent any other Baptist. Papers carried photographs of him and Faubus, looking frightened, leaving the airport for their hotel.[42]

On Saturday, 14 September, he accompanied Faubus to the meeting with Ike. Faubus would say twenty years later that Brooks had played the

---

[39]Ibid., 13 September 1957.

[40]Hays, Conversation with Ronald Tonks, August 1977.

[41]Brown, *Bigger Than Little Rock,* 38.

[42]Arkansas *Gazette* (Little Rock), 14 September 1957.

part of peacemaker at the meeting. He would also remember, with great bitterness, that Ike had treated him as a general would treat a lieutenant. The most widely circulated photograph of the meeting is most revealing. Ike is flashing his patented grin, seemingly unaware that he is dealing with a matter of grave concern to the nation; Faubus looks sly, wily, like a fox cornered but still looking for a way to escape, concerned for himself; and Brooks looks deeply troubled despite his attempts to smile, a man thoughtfully searching for answers to a problem he knew to be of far-reaching consequences. One has to regret that Brooks was neither governor of Arkansas nor president of the United States.

The meeting lasted two hours, too brief a time considering its gravity, and during that time Faubus and Ike were alone for only fifteen minutes. Brooks and Sherman Adams were with them the rest of the time, Attorney General Herbert Brownell part of the time. Brooks would later say privately to his family that he doubted Ike ever really understood the issues involved, that while he admired him as a man and a soldier and a patriot he considered Ike to be of only average intelligence with a limited attention span. He also tended to believe, from the way he acted, that Ike hurried the meeting because he was anxious to get to the golf course.

From the outset Faubus, playing his familiar tune, asked for more time to prepare his people for desegregation and argued that if he did not have this time there might be violence. Brownell, however, was adamant that the desegregation order must be immediately obeyed. Faubus would much later accuse Brownell of wrecking the conference, of attempting by his uncompromising position to attract liberals and blacks to the Republican party, of planning to run for president himself in 1960. Ike seemed to take the position that things had already been settled, that the courts had spoken, that Faubus knew he must obey. He did not condemn Faubus for calling out the Guard to keep the peace, but he did tell him he had no right to halt the desegregation order. Whether he said this clearly and forcefully enough for Faubus to understand is still a question.

After two hours, with no real meeting of minds, the conference ended. Brooks later said there should have been an afternoon session, but neither side seemed to want one. He said there were too many loose ends remaining, that the men should have worked out a timetable to cover all contingencies, that there should have been guaranteed agreements. No one seemed to want any of these things. The end of the meeting came when Sherman Adams called on Brooks to tell a funny story and Brooks obliged by telling them about "The Alabama Horse Deal" in which two men kept making nice profits by selling a horse back and forth to each other, each

time raising the price. The meeting broke up with laughter, with neither
side understanding that the story was about them, with the court jester
the only person in the room who understood that the meeting had been a
failure. Only he knew that trouble probably awaited them all.

Brooks wrote Faubus's press release, summarizing the governor's ver-
sion of the meeting. Then the two men parted at New York's LaGuardia
Field, with Faubus flying home to Little Rock and Brooks going to Ft.
Worth, Texas, for a church engagement. The media gave credit for the
Newport meeting, which at the moment was thought to have ended the
Central High dispute, to Congressman Hays. *U.S. News* featured him in
its 20 September edition under "People of the Week." The article discussed
Brooks's religious work and his knack for finding compromises between
warring factions, both religious and political, solutions that were some-
how always both moral and practical. He was the one, it said, who per-
suaded Faubus to make the first move and whose friendship with Sherman
Adams had made the meeting possible.[43] He was the man of the hour.

Brooks spoke at three Ft. Worth Baptist church services on Sunday, 15
September; and he was preparing to fly to Oklahoma City for a week-long
Southwide Baptist Brotherhood rally when Faubus called to ask him to return to Little Rock that night. He did so. During the next four days, from
16 September through 19 September, he virtually lived at the governor's
mansion, trying to explain to Faubus that he simply had to comply with
the court's orders, that he could keep the Guard for civil order but not to
prevent desegregation, and that if he did not relent and let the desegregation plan proceed the president might take drastic actions. He said that
the people would admire him more for keeping the peace, and for keeping
the president from sending in federal marshals, than they would for keeping the school segregated.[44] Headlines in the Arkansas *Gazette* announced: "Governor Secluded, Confers With Hays."[45] Only one photograph
of the two men together appeared in the newspaper, and it showed them
smiling but with their hands clenched nervously.[46]

Brooks would later recall his frustration at trying to explain points of
law to Faubus, who was not himself a lawyer, while at the same time ar-

---

[43]"People of the Week," *U.S. News,* 20 September 1957, 14.

[44]Blossom, *It Has Happened Here,* 96.

[45]Arkansas *Gazette* (Little Rock), 17 September 1957.

[46]Ibid., 18 September 1957.

guing alone against the advice of all Faubus's cronies. Faubus was then forty-five years old, Brooks fifty-nine, and Faubus seemed to think of Brooks as a father figure. He also respected him as a religious leader and, being a Baptist himself, referred to Brooks as "my bishop." But in the end the cronies, several of them from racist eastern Arkansas, persuaded Faubus, over Brooks's protests, that the people wanted segregation and they would reelect him ad infinitum if he would resist the order to integrate Central High. Brooks would later say, when he recalled how Faubus slowly turned from him to the racists and opportunists, that at that critical moment Faubus showed not one ounce of moral strength or vision.[47] At last, on Wednesday, 18 September, Brooks realized he was failing and was ready to concede defeat.

He called Sherman Adams to report that he had made no progress, and Adams persuaded him to stay with Faubus one more day. He agreed to do so, but when there was no change he left the night of 19 September for the last sessions of the Brotherhood meeting in Oklahoma City. The next day, 20 September, Faubus's attorneys walked out of a federal court presided over by Judge Ronald Davies of North Dakota when they learned that Davies was about to order the governor once again to proceed with desegregation.[48] This was, of course, an even more flagrant challenge to federal authority than any actions the governor had taken before; and that night in a television address Faubus promised to withdraw the Guard but denied that the court had any authority over him. He admitted that blacks had the right, under the school board's plan, to attend classes at Central; but he said that if they did so there would be violence and that it was his duty to prevent it. He called for a cooling off period so that he could insure civil order if and when the school was desegregated.

The next morning, 21 September, Brooks was preparing to fly from Oklahoma City to Kansas City to attend a dinner honoring Harry Truman when Sherman Adams called to ask him to return immediately to Little Rock. He called Truman to apologize for missing the dinner, and Truman commiserated with him over his ordeal. "That's all right," Brooks said, "you took this kind of heat for eight years. I can take it for eight weeks." "No," Truman joked, "it's harder on you than on me—I can cuss and you can't."[49]

---

[47]Hays, Conversation with Ronald Tonks, August 1977.

[48]Arkansas *Gazette* (Little Rock), 21 September 1957.

[49]Spingarn, "Mr. Hays of Arkansas," 26.

In a letter to Brooks, Truman assured him that he had the former president's sympathies, and he lamented the tragedy that had befallen what he
called one of his favorite states.[50]

No sooner had Brooks returned to Little Rock than Faubus left the city,
heading out for Sea Island, Georgia, for a meeting of the Southern Governors' Conference. Asked as he arrived in Georgia if there would be trouble when black students arrived at Central High and the National Guard
withdrew on Monday, 23 September, Faubus replied that he thought there
would be. Yet there he was, a thousand miles from home, at a time when
he said he expected violence. Back home in Little Rock, Brooks Hays, despite the presence of Lt. Governor Nathan Gordon, was the de facto governor of Arkansas, the only person who would and could represent the city
to the federal government.

Brooks ran the risk of seeming to be against Faubus for the first time
when on Sunday he met with Little Rock Mayor Mann to discuss plans for
the next day. He avoided meeting with N.A.A.C.P. leader Daisy Bates because he opposed her strategy of pushing for a confrontation, using high
school students to press her cause. He asked Mayor Mann if city police could
keep order, and the mayor told him that they could protect lives but not
escort the black students into the school. Since the court would not permit
U.S. Marshals to patrol the area outside the school yet insisted that desegregation proceed, thus helping Faubus create an untenable situation,
all the elements were in place for trouble the next morning.

The day 23 September would always be remembered as a day of violence as the nine black students were spirited into the school through side
doors. A riot broke out in the crowd out front, and black adults in the area
were chased and beaten. There were fights as well in the school corridors
between white and black students. Superintendent of Schools Virgil Blossom came to Brooks and asked him to notify Sherman Adams that he
needed federal troops.[51] Mayor Mann concurred with this request and told
Brooks he needed 150 men. Sadly Brooks did as he was told, although he
opposed bringing troops into the city. Later that day the black students
were removed from school; and on Tuesday morning, at Brooks's request
to Adams, Eisenhower federalized the Arkansas National Guard and sent
in troops from Camp Campbell, Kentucky. On Wednesday, under armed

---

[50]Letter from Harry Truman to Brooks Hays, 24 September 1957.

[51]Hays, Conversation with Ronald Tonks, August 1976.

guard, Central High was peacefully if uneasily desegregated. By this time, sick at heart, Brooks had withdrawn from the process.

"I was a rather lonely person," he later said of the next ten days, as a U.S. Deputy Marshal was assigned to protect his life against well-documented and widely circulated death threats.[52] Billy Graham called and offered to come to Little Rock for a religious rally, but Brooks advised him to wait. "The patient is in a state of shock," he explained to the evangelist.[53] He made a number of speeches to civic groups, always speaking with soft words, knowing that what he had to say would be unpopular. He later explained to friends that he felt like William Howard Taft who, when asked why fat men were so affable, had replied, "We have to be. We can't run fast." Brooks felt he had to be affable, soft spoken, contrite, because he knew he could not outrun demagogues.[54]

He accepted every invitation offered him to meet with groups of every persuasion, and in every case he counseled calm and nonviolence. His efforts were often labeled fence-straddling, and he was often openly castigated for his remarks. Nevertheless, he plugged away at his call for obedience to the law and for reconciliation. On Wednesday, 25 September, he addressed the Little Rock Lions Club, his home chapter, and explained his side of the issue. As the only elected official from the district with national responsibility, he said, he had felt he had to act. "My part in this drama," he told the men, "was self-imposed." He said that had there not been a Newport meeting the conditions would have been much worse. He reminded his listeners that he was a Southerner who had always stood and still stood for Southern principles; but he said that all laws, not just the popular ones, must be obeyed. He deplored the violence, warning that the Soviets would use it to demonstrate the evils of the American system; and he concluded by saying that the issue was no longer desegregation or federal intervention but law and order.[55]

Later he spoke to a meeting of former presidents of the Little Rock Chamber of Commerce. To this group of twenty-six civic leaders he spoke more bluntly. Arkansas must submit to federal regulations. To refuse to

---

[52]Ibid.

[53]Hays, *A Southern Moderate Speaks,* 177.

[54]Marion Hays, "How to Live Dangerously," X-2.

[55]Hays, *This World: A Christian's Workshop,* 93-100.

do so was to declare the law null and void; and Andrew Jackson had demonstrated to South Carolina 120 years before that in a federal system nullification is intolerable. The 1954 *Brown* ruling was *right,* he said, and it was the law of the land, whether Little Rock liked it or not. To resist the courts would only bring more tragedy. He then presented this group with a written statement of support for law and order, and all twenty-six men present signed it. Only one of them disagreed with what Brooks had said, but even he signed. From that day until the end of school in December, Brooks worked with this group to help keep the peace.

The days following the arrival of federal troops were dark ones. Brooks could later recall only one bright moment, one good laugh, and that from the wit of his wife Marion. He had not told her, for fear it might alarm her, that a U.S. Deputy Marshal had been assigned to guard their lives. But she spotted the man who seemed to accompany them to restaurants and church every time they went out, and she asked Brooks who he was. When he confessed, instead of being alarmed she was pleasantly surprised and proud. "It shows your life is worth something," she said happily.[56] Such moments were rare.

Brooks would always be haunted by the enigma of Orval Faubus. He always considered him a bright, promising young man whose fatal moral flaws rendered him both politically successful and ethically bankrupt. He would one day tell an interviewer that Faubus considered the political ramifications of his actions in Little Rock, while he himself did not. Faubus was right from the political standpoint; Brooks was right from the moral one.[57] In the short run Faubus won, as he went on to be reelected governor of Arkansas four times and Brooks was turned out of office the next year. In the long run, historians would determine that Brooks was the undisputed winner. History, as Brooks knew, was the final judge; and he felt, justifiably so, comfortable with the thought that he would be proven right. The only criticism he would make of Faubus was that he proved too timid for the crisis, and "a timid surgeon makes an ugly wound."[58]

Others have made more definite judgments of Faubus, his character, and his actions than Brooks was willing to make. In 1957 the United States Constitution was 170 years old. Nullification had been declared unconsti-

---

[56]Hays, Conversation with Ronald Tonks, August 1977.

[57]Ibid., August 1976.

[58]Ibid., August 1977.

tutional 120 years before during the Jackson administration and confirmed so by a civil war that had ended ninety-two years before. Yet Faubus contended in the Little Rock crisis that state law took precedence over federal law. He said he believed compliance with federal court decisions would lead to violence, yet he used his armed guard not to assure peaceful compliance but to prevent it. There is little doubt that, though perhaps not a racist himself, he saw political benefit for himself in preventing the desegregation of Little Rock Central High School and used a tragic situation to retain and enlarge his political power. He showed cowardice by leaving his state when he fully expected, and perhaps by his warnings of it even helped encourage, violence. In short, there is little good to be said for him. His weakness and demagoguery stand out all the more starkly because of the inevitable comparisons with Brooks Hays, and it is little wonder that the following year he would participate in a scheme to eliminate this source of embarrassment.

Meanwhile, throughout the crisis, Brooks was still president of the Southern Baptist Convention. Except for the time he spent in Little Rock during the trouble there, he continued to do his duties as his church's chief elected official. The controversy at home and his role in it brought him nationwide publicity—he even appeared on Dave Garroway's morning television show—and his mail picked up considerably, both from Baptists and from other concerned persons. The Baptist letters were mixed, but they were in general more critical than supportive, though not as critical as those concerning the Christian Life Commission's report to the convention that year. Little Rock was not, strictly speaking, church business to many of the writers. It was politics.

He continued to attend the various state Baptist conventions around the South, and in most cases he was warmly received, although he had to have bodyguards when he spoke in Miami and Atlanta. One sanctuary where he was to speak had to be cleared and searched before his appearance because of a bomb threat.[59] But only once did any Baptist group ask him to cancel an engagement. He was to speak to the Mississippi Baptist Convention on 13 November, and six member churches opposed his coming, not because of the fear of violence but because they loathed his actions in Little Rock. The state's Executive Committee, led by Chester Quarles,

---

[59]Marion Hays, "How to Live Dangerously," X-4.

refused to yield to the six churches' demand, however, despite the fact that the host church's pastor, Douglas Hudgins, was a raging segregationist. Brooks received a police escort to the church, which was crowded with delegates, not all of whom were friendly to him. The grim-faced president of the convention introduced him tersely with only the words, "Brethren, the president of the Southern Baptist Convention." But what seemed a bad time ended up being one of Brooks's best hours. He began by telling stories of his years with the Agriculture Department, traveling throughout Mississippi. Before long, in spite of their attempts to remain angry with him, even the most bitter opponents in the sanctuary were laughing. No one could resist this good old Baptist boy. After softening them up, he went on to speak eloquently of the need for racial justice and brotherhood.[60] Southern Baptists, despite their grumbling, were proud of their president. His offer to resign from the Christian Life Commission was firmly rejected, and the next year he was reelected for a second term as president of the convention.

On 20 November 1957, Brooks spoke to the Arkansas Chamber of Commerce and outlined a bill that he said he would soon introduce to Congress (HB11219). This bill called for a cooling off period in which there would be no more Court decisions until the social and educational effects of the *Brown* decision were carefully studied. His bill, introduced on 6 March 1958, proposed that a Joint Congressional Committee make this study. It received warm applause in Little Rock, but in Washington it was immediately attacked by the N.A.A.C.P.'s Clarence Mitchell, who accused Brooks of delaying tactics. Brooks tried to assure his critics that the bill was not an act of defiance, that he merely hoped to show the South that lawful change would not destroy its way of life, that he felt it was wiser to change minds before changing customs, and that he believed this was the best way to make black gains permanent. But no one was listening—on either side of the question. There were no cosponsors, the bill was referred to committee, and Brooks had to watch it die.[61]

One might think that this proposal would have reassured nervous Arkansans that Brooks was looking out for their best interests and helped assure his reelection that year. It seemed a shrewd move at the time. In May, at the end of the public school year, federal troops were removed from

---

[60]Hays, Conversation with Ronald Tonks, August 1976.

[61]Ibid., August 1977.

Little Rock, and tensions eased a bit. In June Brooks was reelected president of the Southern Baptist Convention, a fact that played well in Baptist Arkansas. And in July he won renomination to Congress over a blatant racist who sought to use Brooks's work in the Little Rock crisis against him. There would be no Republican challenge in November, and all seemed well. Not so. In November Dale Alford the eye specialist beat the institution that had been Brooks Hays. Despite local and nationwide remorse over this miscarriage of the popular will, the appeal to overturn the election failed, and Brooks prepared to leave office.

In defeat he experienced victory. He received some 3,000 letters of consolation and support. He was widely hailed as a heroic martyr for the cause of racial justice and political decency. Everywhere he went, for church meetings and political rallies, he was wildly cheered, despite the continuing threats on his life. Gerald W. Johnson, writing for the *New Republic,* reminded readers that Brooks still represented fifteen million Baptists and that as a Southern moderate Protestant he would make Pat Brown or John Kennedy or even Adlai Stevenson or Hubert Humphrey a great vice presidential running mate in 1960.[62]

Speaking to the Virginia Baptist Convention, which became the fifth such state convention to give him a standing vote of confidence and commendation, he said that perhaps his defeat in Arkansas might "turn out to be a victory for the whole south."[63] And at a $7.50 a plate testimonial dinner at Washington's Willard Hotel on 18 December, sponsored by the National Committee to Honor Brooks Hays, his friend Senator Mike Monroney said, "A prefabricated sticker may mutilate a ballot but not a record. Brooks Hays has lost nothing. It is his nation and colleagues in the Congress who are the losers."[64] The committee presented him with a scroll saluting him as "educator, statesman, man of courage, man of faith," and—humorously because of the misprint—"human," meaning humanitarian. In response Brooks explained that a statesman must do the will of the majority only so long as it does not violate his own convictions.[65] He said that

---

[62]Gerald W. Johnson, "Brooks, the Baptist," *New Republic,* 1 December 1958, 17.

[63]"New Role and Wider Stage for Brooks Hays," *Christian Century,* 3 December 1958, 1390.

[64]Hays, *A Hotbed of Tranquility* (New York: Macmillan, 1968) x.

[65]Hays, *Politics Is My Parish* (Baton Rouge: Louisiana State University Press, 1981) 197.

a person may and should question a court's decision if he thinks it is wrong, but that the decision cannot be defied. He said that people's hearts must be changed before any change of social patterns can be effective. And he said, "The door that religion alone can open leads to a pure passageway of peace and justice."[66]

This would be the theme of the book he was at that moment writing and would publish early in 1959, *A Southern Moderate Speaks*. Brooks now preferred the title "Southern moderate" to "states' rights liberal." He took his book title from that sentence in St. Paul's letter to Philemon, the one he tried to use to mollify the Little Rock black ministers back in 1956: "Let your moderation be known to all men." He did not also quote the passage from Philemon that advises slaves to remain in that condition. But it is obvious in reading this book that in late 1958 Brooks was still hoping somehow to regain and hold the constituency that for him was the one base of political power, power to do what was best for Arkansas and the South. He continued to call himself a states' rights Democrat, a man who had tried to avoid disruptive, radical racial changes, one who did not approve of revolutionary upheaval. He even quoted Woodrow Wilson's dictum on racial justice: "Time is the only legislator in such a matter."[67] At this point in his career he was more the martyr who would become a prophet than the prophet who would become a martyr.

In his book Brooks freely used phrases such as "we who oppose military enforcement of school integration" and "we of the white south."[68] He quoted a New England friend who had told him, "If I write an autobiography, I shall call it *Up from Abolition*," leaving the reader to unravel this puzzling statement. He said that had the court foreseen the problems its decision would create, it would have handed down a more "perceptive" interpretation; that he hoped it would grant greater discretion to district judges, who better understood local customs, in the future; and that there should be "a national structure which permits major differences and yet provides a basic foundation of principles and programs on which all can agree."[69]

He said that he believed blacks opposed official segregation but in many ways preferred to be socially separate from whites. He argued against lur-

---

[66]Hays, *A Hotbed of Tranquility*, xi.

[67]Hays, *A Southern Moderate Speaks*, 128-29.

[68]Ibid., 218.

[69]Ibid., 220.

ing blacks out of their own neighborhoods to white schools and said that only when the local school could not provide a curriculum a black student needed should he or she be sent into a white district. All in all, though it was considered in its day a moderate treatise, *A Southern Moderate Speaks* sounds today like the thoughts and proposals of a man anxious to remain a Southern politician, one who still hoped the appeal to overturn the 1958 election might be successful, one planning to reclaim his seat at latest in 1960. He said he saw two streams of traffic flowing in opposite directions. "We who are on the white line down the middle have often felt lonesome and frightened," he said, appealing for respect for the moderate cause.[70] He still put his trust in "the churches and local community organizations that will provide solutions to the problems of civil rights."[71]

A Southern Moderate Speaks stirred wide interest and gave Brooks a wider forum than he had ever had before. *Look* magazine carried excerpts from it, along with photographs of the Little Rock Central High School crisis, in an article entitled "Little Rock from the Inside." *U.S. News,* in a piece called "Inside Story of Little Rock," carried seventeen uninterrupted pages of excerpts. In *Newsweek* an article called "Little Rock Postmortem" gave Brooks credit for saving the crisis from even greater tragedy. He was acknowledged to be the "voice of moderation" between Faubus and Brownell.[72]

With such publicity he was asked to write articles on the racial crisis for the *New York Times Magazine* and *Saturday Review.* In the first he said that his defeat may have awakened many moderates to the fact that they must do battle with extremism. He defined racial moderation, his own philosophy, as adherence to equal justice; commitment to the use of lawful processes to revise the 1954 and 1955 Supreme Court decisions to take local needs into account; a search for alternative methods of desegregation so as not to do violence to Southern traditions and values; a desire to help the Negro gain respect, dignity, and economic improvement; and opposition to all forms of racial hatred and violence. He admitted that moderates

---

[70]Ibid., 228.

[71]Ibid., 195.

[72]"Little Rock from the Inside," *Look,* 17 March 1959, 23-27; "Inside Story of Little Rock," *U.S. News,* 23 March 1959, 118-35; "Little Rock Postmortem," *Newsweek,* 23 March 1959, 30.

were few in number, but he argued that they were growing bolder and more articulate.[73]

In the *Saturday Review* piece, Brooks called on his fellow Southerners to recognize that "the dogmas of a stagnant past are inadequate to a dynamic present." Still he argued that North and South have the right to criticize each other. All he wanted was for them to accept their differences and speak to each other with understanding, brotherhood, and respect for legal processes. He still seemed to be hoping for a system in which the South could retain its mostly segregated way of life until its heart changed enough for it voluntarily to grant equal rights to Negroes. And it is evident that he still hoped to play a leading role in the adoption of this system.[74]

In his native Southland, however, it was becoming ever more apparent that Brooks's moderation, far from making him an acceptable leader, was making him an object, perhaps the single most widely recognized object, of polarity. For many people he was a saint, but for just as many he was a demon. When he spoke at the College of William and Mary in 1959, a group of white racists outside the auditorium surrounded him, and students had to move in and circle him and lead him to safety.[75] There were more bomb threats. He once said, only half in jest, that reports had reached him to the effect that Southern women were frightening naughty children with the threat, "Brooks Hays is gonna getcha."

Through it all Brooks retained his cheerful attitude and saw humor in the dark days. When after winning his race for governor of Mississippi in 1960 Ross Barnett said, "We have shown the nation we don't want any of that Brooks Hays philosophy in Mississippi," Brooks likened himself to the woman who won an ugly contest at her church and said, "I wasn't in the race."[76] But all the indicators, in Arkansas and across the South, were pointing away from moderation and toward more confrontation in the 1960s. And Brooks began to see that he would probably never again represent the Fifth District in Congress. He was now too controversial, too hot

---

[73]Brooks Hays, "A Southern Moderate Predicts Victory," *New York Times Magazine,* 11 January 1959, 17.

[74]Brooks Hays, "Out of a Holocaust, National Hope," *Saturday Review,* 6 June 1959, 34-35.

[75]Hays, Conversation with Ronald Tonks, August 1977.

[76]Ibid., August 1976.

for the job. In the South of the day he was unelectable because he was considered a radical liberal.

As early as 1958, just after his defeat, Brooks mused, "It has seemed to me that my own story, particularly my work in race relations, is a story of a lifetime of adventures in that gap between law and custom."[77] Moderation was in eclipse. his was for him the dilemma of the moderate. The liberal would care little for cus-tom, the conservative little for law, at least where race relations were concerned. He would admit, as a very old man, that in his early career he had often slighted black people in order to please whites; and he said that in the Little Rock crisis he had at last done what he had known all along to be right. With a quaver in his voice he would say this was one of the greatest gift he could give to his grandchildren. He recalled the face of the black man on that train to Little Rock, the man who stood while white seats were empty. He recalled not investigating reports that the $9,000 appropriated for a black school had gone to a white one. He recalled years of benign neglect of his nonvoting, nonwhite constituents. And he concluded that if his defeat in 1958 partially atoned for his past mistakes and weaknesses he was "the happiest of defeated candidates."[78]

Others would have more generous assessments of his career and accomplishments. In 1964 the National Conference of Christians and Jews sponsored an appreciation day for him in Little Rock. Mitch Miller (a Jew) led an integrated choir in song. Senator Eugene McCarthy (a Catholic) was the principle speaker. More than 1,000 persons attended, and 500 more were unable to get into the building, all of this six years after Brooks left office. Orval Faubus, still governor of Arkansas, attended the program, as future Republican governor Winthrop Rockefeller. At the end of the festivities Faubus shook hands and said, "God bless you, Brooks."[79]

In 1976 Brooks and Faubus met at the University of Arkansas library to record their memories of the Central High crisis. Faubus said that he had come primarily to honor Brooks because "I've always had the greatest respect for him." Once more he stressed that he had not been a party to Brooks's defeat, and he allowed as how Brooks was the only man in the whole Central High episode who was not in some way or other a hypocrite.

---

[77]Hays, *A Southern Moderate Speaks,* 3.

[78]Brooks Hays, Public Address, Western Kentucky University, Bowling Green KY, November 1968.

[79]Hays, Conversation with Ronald Tonks, September 1975.

Others said one thing and did another, but not Brooks. He stood up and said what he thought. "I think Brooks, without any question, had more courage and more principle about it," Faubus concluded.[80]

Others have said pretty much the same thing. Robert Brown, Roman Catholic Bishop of Arkansas, in his book *Bigger Than Little Rock* wrote of the need during the crisis to get various groups together for talks. "Tragically enough, only one man offered to take a lead in such mediation—Congressman Brooks Hays of Arkansas. From the beginning his efforts to establish harmony have been outstanding." Brooks, he said, took the initiative and helped work out solutions to problems no one else was willing or able to handle.[81] John Buchanan, a one-time Southern Baptist pastor who was a Republican congressman from Birmingham before his work with People for the American Way, has said that in the Little Rock crisis Brooks reminded him of "the founder of my Republican party," to which Brooks replied, "I can live a long time on the momentum of that comment."[82]

Arthur Schlesinger, Jr., once commented—historically inaccurately but nonetheless true to the myth that appropriately grew up around Brooks in later years—that Brooks was defeated "because he believed black children should be permitted to exercise their constitutional rights to attend school in Little Rock," and that his actions were the essence of nobility.[83] And Dr. Martin Luther King, Jr., once introduced Brooks to black leader Walter Fauntroy with the praise, "This is Mr. Hays. He has suffered with us."[84]

What Brooks meant to his church and country is better understood after a careful reading of Andrew Michael Manis's book *Southern Civil Religions in Conflict*. Manis clarifies as few other writers have done the roles of Southern churches, black and white, in the Civil Rights Movement of the 1950s and 1960s. He explains that while Southern whites rejoined the Union during World War I, proving through military and economic sacrifices that they were indeed good Americans, blacks in a sense really joined the Union during World War II, the same way. The First World War led

---

[80]Taped discussion between Faubius and Hays, Brooks Hays Collection, University of Arkansas Library, 1976.

[81]Brown, *Bigger Than Little Rock,* 35-36.

[82]Hays, Conversation with Ronald Tonks, October 1975.

[83]Hays, *A Hotbed of Tranquility,* vii.

[84]Ibid., ix.

Southerners to see the United States as a loose federation of virtually autonomous regions and to conclude that they could retain segregation in their part of it while remaining good patriots. The Second World War demonstrated just as conclusively to blacks that America stood first and foremost for equality and justice and that these ideals must be fulfilled at home as well as in Europe and Asia. Therefore, the American South, black and white, entered the postwar era holding two opposing and inevitably conflicting national visions, two very different civil religions.

What sharpened the South's dilemma and made its resolution infinitely more difficult was Southern piety, the fact that both white and black Southerners were deeply religious. Both sides saw the struggle for civil rights as a battle for their civil religions. It was a holy war either to defend or to change the status quo, and history shows that wars of religion are always bloody. In the South of the 1950s the fight over civil rights had a distinctly religious flavor.[85] Into this battle stepped Brooks Hays. He did not know what it would cost him, but he could have sidestepped it and did not. By accepting his responsibility as Little Rock's Congressman, he became an unwilling but remarkable martyr, impaled on the horns of the Southern dilemma, a white man raised to believe in the white version of Southern civil religion who came to see and understand the black version and who tried to bridge the gap between them. In doing so he became for the mid-twentieth century an elegant epiphany of the Christian faith.

In 1968 the Little Rock Central High School Class of 1958 held its tenth anniversary reunion in Little Rock's Lafayette Hotel. Among its members was Ernest Green, the first black to be handed his diploma from Central, a man who would in 1977 become an assistant Secretary of Labor in the administration of the Baptist President Jimmy Carter. Orval Faubus was pointedly not invited to attend the dinner, while Brooks Hays was its featured speaker. Brooks had within a decade become a hero to the students involved in the Central High crisis. Like the person he called his Master, he had gone from loser to final victor.

---

[85]Andrew Michael Manis, *Southern Civil Religions in Conflict* (Athens: University of Georgia Press, 1987).

THE NATION AND THE WORLD

Brooks left Congress in January 1959, the appeal to overturn his election defeat having failed, with little hope that subsequent investigations would benefit his case, and Dale Alford occupied his seat. At the age of sixty he had to decide what to do with the rest of his life. He later said that he decided almost immediately after leaving office not to run for his old seat in 1960. He no longer needed the thrills or demands of another race. He knew a challenge to Alford would be hard on him, and he feared that, win or lose, it might take some of the glow off his recent moral victory.[1] Knowing that he might now have to return to the practice of law, he applied and was admitted to the District of Columbia bar.

He rejected his first two offers of jobs. The first was from a refugee agency, and he turned it down because he would have had to live abroad and he wanted to remain in the United States. The second, offered by his friend in the White House, Sherman Adams, was with the United States Information Agency. He gave no formal reason for not accepting this job.[2] Then Adams spoke to him about a federal judgeship, the third time in his career that he had been approached about the judiciary; and this time, as before, he was receptive to the idea. But, as before, the Arkansas state political establishment squelched the proposal. He was persona non grata to Faubus, Alford, and the insiders. It would not be the last time he would

---

[1]Brooks Hays, Conversation with Ronald Tonks, August 1976, typeset in 15 parts. Southern Baptist Sunday School Board Archives, Nashville TN.

[2]Brooks Hays, *Politics Is My Parish* (Baton Rouge: Louisiana State University Press, 1981) 210.

feel the sting of their wrath for upstaging them in Little Rock and pulling a "moral victory" out of the defeat they had hung on him in 1958.

Late in April 1959, an offer came that he could not refuse, one the Arkansas establishment could not deny him. The Eisenhower administration, in appreciation for his work in the Little Rock crisis, made him a member of the three-man Board of Directors of the Tennessee Valley Authority. *U.S. News,* in its story of his appointment, identified him as "a Little Rock lawyer and social worker" and emphasized the fact that Ike had picked a "defeated Democrat."[3] A newspaper editor in Mississippi mused, "We don't know how much Mr. Hays knows about flood control or navigation or hydroelectric power, but there's one thing for sure—the Baptists now have access to the largest baptismal pool in all the world."[4] Brooks took the kidding in good humor and allowed as how "the Baptist image is something that I suppose I will never lose."[5] At his swearing-in ceremony in Knoxville he added to this image by quoting Psalm 46:4: "There is a river, the streams of which make glad the city of God." As to being a lawyer, social worker, and defeated Democrat, he made no attempt to deny any of those descriptions, although he would have preferred to be remembered simply as a former Congressman.

The appointment to T.V.A. carried an annual salary of $20,000—$2,000 less than the Congressional salary he had given up—but he found he had far less personal office expense as a federal employee. He and the two other board members discovered that they could divide their work into three almost equal parts. H. D. Vogel was an engineer, and Arnold Jones was a financier, while Brooks was indeed a social worker.[6] The human problems of T.V.A., he said, "just naturally wound up in my area." He traveled extensively, made hundreds of public addresses, and in general dealt with the effects on human life of the great New Deal river project.[7] His appointment was for one year, but at the end of that time he had taken to the work so well that in 1960 Eisenhower appointed him to a full nine-year term. He well could have stayed on until retirement. As it turned out, he stayed

---

[3]*U. S. News,* 4 May 1959, 21.

[4]Brooks Hays, *A Hotbed of Tranquility* (New York: Macmillan, 1968) 173.

[5]Hays, *Politics Is My Parish,* 212.

[6]Hays, Conversation with Ronald Tonks, August 1977.

[7]Hays, *Politics Is My Parish,* 213.

only until February 1961, when the new Kennedy administration offered him a job in Washington.

Two events stood out in Brooks's memories of the months with T.V.A. In June 1959, Steele Hays died. Steele had survived Sallie by almost four years. He had seen his son Brooks elected to Congress nine times, elected president of the Southern Baptist Convention, and elevated to the level of national hero. Now the sometimes stormy but always affectionate relationship between father and son was over. The other memorable event came in 1960, when Brooks represented T.V.A. at a World Power Conference in Madrid, Spain. The thing that impressed him most at the conference was a meeting he attended in his spare time with Spanish Baptists, who complained to him that despite Spanish constitutional guarantees of religious freedom they were still being oppressed by Catholic governmental officials. Although he was a representative of the American government, Brooks prepared a memo on his findings and sent it to the United States embassy in Madrid. Reports from the Spanish Baptists said that as a result of his intervention tensions eased considerably during the next few months.[8]

Brooks found the 1960 presidential election particularly exciting since there was a good chance the Democrats might win for the first time in twelve years. There had been minor, scattered speculation that he might play a part. Rumor had it that Adlai Stevenson, should he be the Democratic nominee, would name Brooks as his vice presidential running mate. As previously noted, Gerald Johnson in the *New Republic* had suggested that with his immense Southern Baptist following Brooks would make an ideal running mate for a Catholic Yankee like Kennedy. But Brooks knew it was all talk. He had lost the one indispensable claim on political consideration, his base of power. He knew also that he would be immobilized by his federal job, forbidden by the Hatch Act from campaigning, unless he resigned from T.V.A. For the first time in twenty years he could not publicly take sides, express his opinion, or make speeches.[9]

He did work secretly, not for the party that had given him his job, but for Kennedy. At the personal request of Washington *Post* editor Phil Graham, he went to Billy Graham and persuaded him not to make a public endorsement of Nixon, thus neutralizing the Baptist influence in the cam-

---

[8]Ibid., 215.

[9]Hays, Conversation with Ronald Tonks, August 1977.

paign.[10] And Scoop Jackson arranged a secret meeting between Brooks and Kennedy, just after Kennedy was nominated in Los Angeles, so that Brooks could advise him on how to handle the issue of his Catholicism among Southern Baptists. Whether Brooks advised him to pick a group like the Baptist-dominated Houston Ministerial Association to address the issue of church and state, a move that may well have won Kennedy the South, is not known. However, it is known that Kennedy listened carefully to Brooks's advice and gave him credit for helping his campaign. At the end of the session, Brooks spoke to Kennedy "as his elder" and advised him, "Win or lose, *enjoy* this campaign." Kennedy laughed and promised to do so, and as Brooks was leaving he heard Kennedy say to Jackson, "That guy has guts."[11] Kennedy was referring to the Little Rock crisis and Brooks's subsequent loss. His brother Ted later told Brooks that Kennedy had once remarked that if he ever brought out another edition of *Profiles in Courage* he would add a chapter—on Brooks Hays.

John Kennedy was of course elected president in November, and his designated cabinet members immediately began offering Brooks jobs with the upcoming administration. Adlai Stevenson, soon to be Ambassador to the United Nations, wanted Brooks to be his deputy, with the rank of ambassador. But Secretary of State designate Dean Rusk, responding to Kennedy's wishes, wanted him at the State Department, to be in charge of Congressional Relations, to sell Congress on State Department –sponsored legislation.[12] Brooks wanted to please the new president-elect, so he expressed his willingness to serve at State, but before his appointment was finally approved by Congress he had reason to wish he had gone with Stevenson to the United Nations.

Orval Faubus and Dale Alford, still fuming about 1958 and now also upset about the fact that Brooks had written letters to his old constituents in the Fifth District supporting Alford's opponent in the 1960 congressional race, reached House Speaker Sam Rayburn with their opposition to the Hays nomination. They had blocked his nomination to the federal bench, and now they intended to block his appointment to State. Rayburn, party loyalist that he was, hoping to keep his congressional Democrats loyal

---

[10]Ibid., September 1977.

[11]Ibid., August 1976.

[12]Ibid., August 1977.

to party policy, slowed down the process of approval.[13] Late in January 1961, after Kennedy was inaugurated, Rusk told Brooks about the opposition and his helplessness in the face of Rayburn's recalcitrance. Unable to get a taxi, Brooks walked the mile and a half from State to Rayburn's office in the snow, a lonely, humiliating trek. He had known Rayburn for thirty years, since his days with the Department of Agriculture, and several times during those years he had taken considerable risks to support Rayburn initiatives. Rayburn had rewarded him by more than once having him preside over the House. But after Brooks's 1958 defeat and the controversy surrounding it, Rayburn dropped him like a stone. Now he seemed ready to end any hopes Brooks had of working in Washington. He would have been happy to see Brooks keep the job in Knoxville the Republicans had given him.

Brooks got in to see the Speaker, but Rayburn told him about Alford's complaint and said bluntly, "He's in, and you're out." Again Brooks suffered humiliation. He made an emotional appeal to Rayburn's party loyalty, knowing that this was something he understood, reminding him of his years of service to Democratic causes, his sacrifices, the risks he had taken to support Rayburn. He said that it would look bad if his own party failed to honor him as the Republicans had done for his efforts to keep order in the Little Rock crisis. At last Rayburn relented, perhaps feeling that Brooks had been disciplined and chastened enough, or perhaps realizing that what he said was true, and promised to let the nomination go through to confirmation. On 1 February 1961, Brooks ended his service to T.V.A. and was sworn in as Assistant Secretary of State for Congressional Affairs.[14]

As one of several assistant secretaries, Brooks attended each morning's briefing with Rusk and the others. He gave advice when he deemed it appropriate to do so. He helped initiate the early stages of such proposals as the Peace Corps, Alliance for Progress, and the Kennedy Disarmament and Foreign Aid Programs.[15] His job was to lay plans for shepherding them all through Congress. He was widely sought as a public speaker, especially in the South, on foreign affairs. At the same time he continued his role as a good humor man, helping break deadlocks and move policy sessions,

---

[13]Ibid., October 1975.

[14]Hays, *Politics Is My Parish,* 119-20.

[15]Ibid., 228.

congressional hearings, and administrative programs along with his aphorisms and stories. One of his most quoted comments, made to Dean Rusk when Rusk complained of inefficiency among his lieutenants, was: "Dean, remember the scripture: Jacob, leaning on his staff, died."[16]

One of Brooks's proudest moments during his ten months at the State Department came on 23 October 1961, when he had a private audience with Pope John XXIII in Rome. The visit was arranged by Monsignor Luigi Ligutti, who had worked with Brooks during the 1930s on rural rehabilitation in the American midwest and was now papal adviser on Rural Church Affairs.[17] Marion Hays shared the audience and, according to Brooks, "she just fell in love with the Pope." When Pope John heard that 23 October was their daughter Betty's birthday, he volunteered to say a prayer for her during his mass, which the Hays family considered a great honor since he chose only one person each day for this special prayer.

The visit was significant not just because Brooks represented the administration but because he was the first man ever to serve as president of the Southern Baptist Convention and visit a Catholic pope. Understanding the symbolic importance of the visit, Pope John told Brooks, "I too am Baptist," referring to John the Baptist whose name he had chosen for his papal title. He also told this Southern Baptist guest, "We are brothers in Christ."[18] In 1966 Brooks would have a private audience with Pope Paul VI and thus become the first prominent Protestant layman and church leader of any denomination to meet both pontiffs. This first visit brought criticism from several prominent Southern Baptist state paper editors, among them E. S. James of the Texas *Baptist Standard*. After James published a highly critical editorial on the Vatican visit, Brooks paid a courtesy call on him in Dallas and with his usual grace and humor explained the reason for the trip and the audience. James showed Brooks a second article he had planned to run, one even more scorching than the first, then reached over and dropped it in the trash.[19]

But by the time he visited the pope, in the fall of 1961, Brooks was growing restless at State. The major problem, as he saw it, was that Ken-

---

[16]Ibid., 223.

[17]Hays, Conversation with Ronald Tonks, August 1977.

[18]Hays, *Politics Is My Parish*, 234.

[19]Ibid.

nedy in fact was his own Secretary of State and encouraged the White House staff to dictate policy, outline strategy, and interfere at will with procedures at Foggy Bottom. Brooks was outraged but had to hold his tongue when, just as he had convinced fellow Baptist and Louisiana Congressman Otto Passman to support a key Latin American foreign aid appropriation, Larry O'Brien ordered him to discontinue negotiations with this prominent conservative. Brooks was told to cancel a meeting with Passman, lost Passman's attention, and subsequently lost his subcommittee's vote.[20] This only confirmed Brooks's suspicion that as long as he remained at State he was and would only continue to be a glorified errand boy.

He appealed to his friend at the Washington *Post* Phil Graham, a Kennedy intimate, and Graham and McGeorge Bundy arranged for him to be transferred to the White House staff itself. When the announcement of his pending transfer came to light, editorials speculated that Brooks was being demoted, that he was part of the shakeup involving Chester Bowls, and so Graham and Bundy persuaded Kennedy to make the extraordinary gesture of attending a special White House induction ceremony for the Southern Baptist who had kept Billy Graham from supporting Richard Nixon. On 1 December 1961, with Kennedy present in the cabinet room, Brooks took an oath administered by his old friend Bolon B. Turner, once his law partner in Little Rock and now Chief Judge of the United States Tax Court. After the ceremony Brooks introduced Kennedy to his ninety-five-year-old mother-in-law and said, "Mr. President, there's an old saying that behind every man's achievement is a proud wife and a surprised mother-in-law. Well, mine is certainly surprised. She thought I'd be President of the United States by now." Kennedy joined in the laughter and seemed genuinely to cherish this and subsequent light moments he had with Brooks and his stories.[21]

For the next two years, until Kennedy's death, Brooks was happy with his work. He relished the security of being part of the president's official family, a security he had really never known before, and he basked in the light of Kennedy's obvious respect and affection. His title was Special Assistant to the President for Congressional Affairs, but with his easy access to the president his role soon expanded. He once explained to a friend that

---

[20]Ibid.

[21]Ibid.

his White House job had to do with relations: Congressional relations, international relations, federal-state relations, church-state relations—"which I don't mention officially"—and just about every other kind of relations except poor relations. He said he had had enough of dealing with poor relations back home in Arkansas.[22]

He also became one of the administration's most important point men on race relations. Now that he was no longer beholden to a Southern constituency yet was still considered a Southern political and religious leader, in some circles a martyr to the cause of racial harmony, he was called on to speak on the subject that under the leadership of Kennedy's brother Robert, the attorney general, was becoming a central theme of the administration. He spoke far and wide, in the South and elsewhere, with a boldness, decisiveness, and conviction he had never publicly displayed before.

In its 7 November 1962 edition the *Christian Century* reported how Brooks had told a ministerial convention meeting in Washington that when the University of Mississippi admitted James Meredith the entire state would sleep better at night. In response to those who accused him of abandoning his well-known moderation for radical integrationism, his famous role of mediation and conciliation for that of provocateur, he said that "the basis of all mediation is moral soundness, and the course I am suggesting is the wisest and best way to serve our beloved southland."[23] He had come a long way since 1957, when he was willing to say only that the Supreme Court's ruling for integration had to be obeyed, despite the fact that it could disrupt Southern society and harm Southern tradition. He went even further in a speech to Presbyterians four days later when he said, "The fraternal kindness of the nineteenth century is not adequate for the dynamic twentieth" century when it comes to race relations. Of administration policy, he said, "We are yielding to the demands of justice, and with the patient cooperation of the minority group we are making progress."[24]

Early in 1963 the Hays family had its own personal experience with the violence, often seen in racial terms, that had begun to frighten so many people. A young black man, needing money, broke into their Washington home while Brooks was away on a speaking engagement and broke Marion's wrist as he manhandled her. That night before going to the hospital

---

[22]Hays, *Politics Is My Parish*, 229.

[23]Charles Kean, "Hays On Race," *Christian Century*, 7 November 1962, 1370.

[24]Hays, Conversation with Ronald Tonks, August 1977.

for a cast she accompanied Brooks to a banquet. She and Brooks deftly played down the racial side of the affair, blaming it on poverty and juvenile delinquency in general. They would respond the same way three years later when a black man mugged them as they walked down the street near their home. And Brooks would sound the same theme even later when in Dallas for a Baptist conference he was robbed at gunpoint by two young black men.[25]

In April 1963, again representing both the administration and his church, with no feeling of conflict, Brooks paid a visit to the west African nations of Liberia, Sierra Leone, and Nigeria. He explained all along the way that he was wearing two hats, one political and one religious, on alternating days. At the same time Robert Kennedy was meeting with Alabama Governor George Wallace to attempt the integration of the University of Alabama, Brooks was meeting with African leaders to explain to them that the United States was making progress in racial justice and equality. He was particularly at pains to compensate for the damage done to the American image in Africa by Louisiana Senator Allen Ellender, who had said on a recent trip to Rhodesia that Africans were not yet ready for self-government. At the same time, he visited Baptist missions and schools, was made an honorary chief of the Zor Zor tribe, and made a generally positive impression. One of his most cherished momentos of the trip was an inscribed photograph of Dr. Albert Schweitzer, presented to him by a mutual friend. It would hang in Brooks's study the rest of his life.

The year 1963, when Martin Luther King, Jr., while waiting to see the president introduced Brooks to Walter Fauntroy with the words "He has suffered with us," was the year of the Civil Rights March on Washington. Brooks would always remember how frightened the White House staff was that extremists of both races might cause violence and set back efforts to achieve a lasting racial peace. He would also recall his relief when, in the finest American tradition and spirit, the black people rallied those whose aspirations the system had not met and peacefully presented their grievances to the people's representatives. It gave him confidence that justice and peace and reconciliation, his goals for the nation, would be achieved.[26]

Despite his trips abroad and involvement in civil rights affairs, Brooks seems to have spent most of his two years in the White House lobbying

---

[25]Ibid.

[26]Ibid.

Congress and meeting with governors and mayors to push Kennedy programs, speaking at an array of luncheons and dinners, and serving as a public relations man for the administration. His reputation as a humorist and storyteller increased during his years in the White House. He made guest appearances on the NBC Tonight Show, both when hosted by Jack Paar and by his successor Johnny Carson. Both times he told his stories and explained that a politician must have a sense of humor to survive the bruises and frustrations of public life. He was featured on a CBS program on humor hosted by Meredith Wilson, and he was given top billing on a long-play record album of Washington humor compiled by Tait Trussell of *Nation's Business*. Sometimes it seemed that in the White House itself he spent most of his time entertaining the president's daughter Caroline with his stories about and drawings of mythical Arkansas forest animals such as the wallipus-wallipus, kingdoodle, gowrow, jimplicute, and side-hill hoofer.[27] Little did he know as he honed his artistic skills through the years that one of his chief duties as Assistant to the President of the United States would be to draw Dr. Seuss like cartoons for a five-year-old girl.

In November 1963, Brooks was asked to make a speaking tour of Methodist college campuses, and he took a thirty-day leave without pay from his White House duties. In the middle of that month he was asked to serve as chairman of the 1964 Brotherhood Week to be sponsored by the National Conference of Christians and Jews. He called the White House to get official approval. To his surprise Kennedy himself took the call from the cabinet room, interrupting a staff meeting, listened to the proposal, and told Brooks to do it. "That's wonderful," he said. "It's good work. You're a good man for it."[28] Those were the last words he would hear Kennedy utter. He was in Lakeland, Florida, on 22 November, preparing to address the student body at Florida Southern College, when he was told that the president had been assassinated. As a member of the White House staff, he was made an honorary pall bearer for the Kennedy funeral and stood near Mrs. Kennedy during the ceremonies in the Capitol rotunda. He wore a borrowed frock coat and accessories.[29]

Brooks was deeply bereaved by Kennedy's death, more so than even he knew for quite some time, and he did not know the new president very well.

---

[27]Hays, *A Hotbed of Tranquility,* 120.

[28]Ibid., 121.

[29]Hays, *Politics Is My Parish,* 236.

He did not particularly care for Lyndon Johnson's image, that of the slick political manipulator, and as a typical Arkansan he had always had to fight the urge to despise Texans. Kennedy's speech writer and confidant Ted Sorensen advised Brooks to stay in the Johnson White House, and Johnson's personal aide Bill Moyers told Brooks Johnson wanted to keep him.[30] Brooks trusted Moyers, whom he had met when he addressed Bill's class graduation at Ft. Worth's Southwestern Baptist Theological Seminary in 1958. Bill had driven Brooks to the airport and asked him whether or not he should accept a job Johnson had offered him, and Brooks had encouraged him to do so, describing politics as a parish. Later Brooks had advised Bill to go to work for Sargeant Shriver at the Peace Corps. Once when Johnson called Bill his protégé, Bill had replied, "Yours—and Brooks's."[31] Now Brooks agreed to Bill's request that he stay with Johnson, but like other staff members he submitted a letter of resignation, to be accepted if and when Johnson saw fit.[32]

Under L.B.J. Brooks continued to hold the title Special Assistant to the President until he became Special Consultant to the President at his own request; but late in life he would claim in self-defense that he really saw little of the new president, that he worked primarily through Moyers.[33] In point of fact, he probably preferred to forget his role in the Johnson White House, for even more than under Kennedy he became L.B.J.'s court jester. A tape recording he made for L.B.J. to listen to in a spare moment, one he says at the outset that might "relax you, Mr. President," still exists.[34] On it Brooks tells funny stories and tries to make "Mr. President" smile a bit at the end of a long, trying day. It was an inauspicious climax to a distinguished Washington career, and Brooks knew it.

Brooks always spoke highly of his boss in public addresses. At a conference sponsored by the Christian Life Commission in Nashville he announced that he would place the plaque given him there next to the one given him by President Johnson; and he added that Johnson would be re-

---

[30]Hays, Conversation with Ronald Tonks, August 1977.

[31]Ibid., September 1977.

[32]Ibid., August 1977.

[33]Hays, *Politics Is My Parish,* 237.

[34]Brooks Hays, Tape Recording, Brooks Hays Collection, Wake Forest University Library, Winston-Salem NC.

membered by the sincerity with which he spoke the word *compassion*. But
by mid-1964 Brooks was making a conscious effort to put space between
himself and his boss. He had already accepted a post teaching at Rutgers
University, and he requested that he be merely a "consultant" to L.B.J.
from that time on. He admired Johnson's dynamism, his interest in disadvantaged people, his determination to right racial wrongs; but there was
a basic difference in styles between the two men, and there was one policy
difference, which he would never identify publicly, that "appeared to be
more substantial."[35] That difference was Vietnam. It has been noted by
Brooks's family that he was disturbed by Johnson's womanizing—he apparently did not know of Kennedy's, which was less open—but the en-
largement of the war in southeast Asia was the most disturbing matter.
Professor Bill Angell of Wake Forest University remembers that once when
in the late 1960s he was complaining about the public criticism of Johnson, Brooks leaned close to him and in a moment of complete candor said,
"Bill, he's a bad man."[36]

Brooks talked with Bill Moyers about his unease in the Johnson White
House, and Moyers saw to it that he got more and more outside assign-
ments. He helped Roy Wilkins's nephew Roger in the Community Relations division of the Justice Department; and though he knew what some
people would say when it was known he was working under a young black
man, he accepted the assignment gladly.[37] He made scores of speeches to
religious groups defending the Supreme Court's 1964 decision against formal public school prayer, explaining that it did not forbid prayer in schools
but merely ruled against making prayer formal or uniform.[38] And he made
still other speeches against efforts to amend the Constitution to allow public school prayer.[39]

In September 1964, he traveled to Europe and became the first prominent Protestant lay leader to have met both Pope John XXIII and Pope
Paul VI. President Johnson had met Pope Paul VI as a statesman, while

---

[35]Hays, *Politics Is My Parish*, 238.

[36]James Baker, Conversation with William Angell, Wake Forest University,
Winston-Salem NC, March 1987. Possession of the author.

[37]Hays, Conversation with Ronald Tonks, September 1977.

[38]Ibid., August 1977.

[39]Ibid., September 1977.

Brooks met him "as a fellow Christian." When Pope Paul told his assistants to take Brooks to a session of the Vatican II Council and the assistants said it would be impossible, Brooks told them that it was possible because the Pope had ordered it and he was infallible. They worked it out. He was deeply impressed by the dignity and solemnity of the occasion. When the Pope learned that Brooks was going on from Rome to Berchtesgaden in Germany for a meeting of European Protestants, he promised to pray for them all.[40]

Brooks made a partial escape from L.B.J.'s Washington that fall when he began a stint as Arthur Vanderbilt Professor of Government at the Eagleton Institute of Politics at Rutgers University in New Brunswick, New Jersey. In 1959 the director of the institute, Donald G. Herzberg, had invited him there as an instructor in the practical art of politics but he had turned down the offer. In February 1964 he accepted. In the fall he became Johnson's "consultant" and promised to come in two or three days each month. He would be paid W.A.E., "When Actually Employed," since Rutgers would be paying him a salary of $20,000 a year.[41] When L.B.J. subsequently broke his word and let another assistant take Brooks's office and some of his papers were lost, the rift between the two men deepened; but he remained Johnson's consultant until 1966, when he left to run for governor of Arkansas.[42]

When he assumed his duties at Rutgers in 1964, Brooks joked with Rutgers President Lewis Webster Jones, who had formerly been president of the University of Arkansas, that they were forming a "government in exile." At a news conference in New Brunswick an interviewer said, "You are a lawyer, a Congressman, an author, a church leader, and now a college teacher. 'Will the real Brooks Hays please stand up.' " Brooks was about to identify himself as first and foremost a politician, a term he held in high esteem; but before he could speak the irrepressible Marion, at his side, piped, "He's just an Arkansas social worker."[43] After the laughter died down, Brooks agreed with her by calling himself an "ombudsman," someone whose job it is to help other people get things done.[44]

---

[40]Ibid.

[41]Ibid., August 1977.

[42]Ibid., September 1977.

[43]Hays, *A Hotbed of Tranquility*, 185.

[44]Hays, Conversation with Ronald Tonks, July 1975.

Donald Herzberg, who wrote the introduction to the book Brooks wrote while teaching at Rutgers, *A Hotbed of Tranquility,* praised Brooks's work at the institute. Brooks and the Eagleton Fellows apparently hit it off right from the start. His classes proved to be informal, irreverent, and of great value to the young political scientists. Brooks provided just the right mix of craftiness, wisdom, and idealism, giving them a firsthand account of the frustrations and rewards of political life. Herzberg also paid tribute to Marion Hays, saying that she really made the time at Rutgers a success. She laughed at all the old stories, loved all the students, and served Brooks well in her traditional role as his "little manager."[45]

In *A Hotbed of Tranquility* Brooks said that this was one of his most cherished periods. His greatest problem, he said, was that he wanted to give every student an A. One of his fellows attached a note to one of his reports saying that he was not proud of his paper but that he had been up all night with his wife who had delivered a baby at 6:00 A.M. He said he was sorry it was a girl because he was planning to name a boy Brooks Hays. Brooks said, "An A + was the best I could give him."[46]

He admitted he was no scholar. He told his students that he had learned from a survey of his fellow law school students, Class of 1922, that the A students were teaching law, the B students were practicing law, the C students were making money in business, and the D students were in Congress.[47] Yet his wit and experience served him well, and he proved to be a highly effective and popular teacher. His contract originally called for him to teach just the one year, but it was rewritten so that he could stay for two. While there he wrote his book, commuted to Washington once a month, traveled to speaking engagements over a wide territory, and was told by New Jersey political leaders that if an opening ever came up they wanted him to run for Congress. Brooks took delight in dreaming of being a Congressman from New Jersey, but the opportunity never came.

He continued to be active in civil rights affairs and a firm advocate of justice and brotherhood. He continued to provoke racists. In Nashville to receive his Christian Life Commission award for Christian social concern on 1 March 1965, he suggested that Negroes *should* appeal to Washington and the federal government for help just as St. Paul had appealed to Rome.

---

[45]Hays, *A Hotbed of Tranquility,* xiv.

[46]Ibid., 187.

[47]Ibid, 187.

Early in 1966 he was invited to address a church rally in Bogalusa, Louisiana, a city that had suffered through a period of high racial tension. Church leaders, such as Baptist pastor Jerry Chance, felt that he would serve as a strong voice for moderation. When the Ku Klux Klan got involved and threatened violence, Louisiana Governor John McKeithan said in a news conference that he thought Brooks should not come. A widely published cartoon showed Brooks arriving at the Louisiana state line carrying a caged dove and McKeithan warning him not to come in and upset his K.K.K. cats, which were howling in the background. The ministers were forced by the threats of violence to withdraw their invitation, and the rally was not held. Later that year, when Brooks did speak to the New Orleans Federation of Churches, the mayor of Bogalusa handed him a personal invitation to visit his fair city.[48] The next year at Williamsburg, Virginia, a delegation of Louisiana State University students gave Brooks a certificate making him an honorary citizen of their state. It was signed by John McKeithan.[49]

In the spring of 1966 Brooks completed his second year at Rutgers and joined a National Council of Churches "Delta Mission" to help relieve poverty in rural Mississippi. While there he received a call from a Jonesboro, Arkansas, attorney named Bill Penix, asking him to return to his home state and run for governor. It was a foolhearty idea, and hindsight would tell Brooks that it was doomed to failure; but for a sixty-seven-year-old man who had wanted so badly to be governor of Arkansas thirty-five years before, it was irresistible. He went to Little Rock and met with his old nemesis Orval Faubus, who had announced he was stepping down after seven two-year terms. Neither man made any promises, but Faubus told his allies that he thought Brooks was the strongest candidate on the scene. He would have to oppose the radical segregationist Jim Johnson in the Democratic primary, and if he won he would face his old friend Republican Winthrop Rockefeller in the general election. It seemed to him possible to win. He would later say that he had no burning desire to be governor, that all he really wanted to do was give young Southern moderates a good example for the future;[50] but the zeal with which he entered the race belays that simple explanation.

---

[48]Hays, Conversation with Ronald Tonks, September 1977.

[49]Hays, *Politics Is My Parish,* 239-40.

[50]Hays, Conversation with Ronald Tonks, September 1977.

Brooks's son Steele, now a justice of the Arkansas Supreme Court, still shakes his head ruefully when this race is mentioned. Despite the time and energy he and his father and so many supporters put into the effort, it was a lost cause from the beginning—and an embarrassment to all concerned. Soon after Brooks declared his candidacy, expecting to be the only moderate in the Democratic race, Arkansas Supreme Court Justice Frank Holt, also a moderate, announced. The moderate vote was to be divided and the Democratic nomination would go to the racist Jim Johnson. As it turned out there were seven men in the race, one of them the Little Rock eye surgeon who had taken Brooks's House seat, Dale Alford.

The New York *Times* labeled the race "lackluster," and Brooks later admitted that it was, explaining that since the polls showed him near the top and the only Democrat who could beat Rockefeller in the general election, he for one was holding his fire, hoping to hold his party together for November.[51] He did raise some issues. He called for state government reform, greater welfare benefits for the needy, water projects throughout the state, and an end to illegal gambling. He ran a good, old-fashioned, progressive race. He was known and respected by voters across the state. The Arkansas *Gazette* said, "No man in the field can match Hays' credentials in government service" and described him as "a national figure, possessing exceptional courage and gifts of articulation."[52] And just before the election, while taking care not to endorse one man, the *Gazette* named Brooks, Sam Boyce, and Raymond Rebsamen as the best three choices to lead the state after Faubus.[53]

But his opponents, particularly Johnson, were able to score points by calling him an outsider, a man with no local address who lived in the Sam Peck Hotel in Little Rock while visiting the state for the election, a man who had lost touch with Arkansas. Johnson accused him of being the candidate of the national administration, "Lyndon's boy," and regularly referred to him as "that old Quisling."[54] Although Steele Hays denies that Brooks's eight-year absence from the state was a decisive issue in the race, there is no question that it played a part, as did his age, his association

---

[51]Ibid.

[52]Arkansas *Gazette* (Little Rock), 20 July 1966, 6-A.

[53]Ibid., 24 July 1966, 2-E.

[54]Hays, *Politics Is My Parish,* 250.

with Kennedy and Johnson, and the lingering bittersweet memories of the Little Rock crisis.

He ran what he considered a disappointing third in the primary. Johnson came in first and defeated the second-place Holt in the runoff, then lost to Rockefeller the Republican in November. Brooks admitted that he too would probably have lost to Johnson in a runoff; but he believed that had he won the primary he would have defeated Rockefeller. He took some comfort in the fact that he ran well ahead of Alford in all six counties of his old Fifth District and 11,000 votes ahead of him statewide.[55] He could and did also boast that he led all candidates among black and young voters. And on election night he told his disappointed supporters, "The important thing is that we see politics as a great adventure in human service." He said that to heal wounds and aid the disadvantaged would bring all of them "real inner peace and happiness." He told them to march on, with or without him.[56]

One of his most avid campaign workers was a Catholic priest named Bruce Streett. Brooks, Steele, and Streett were in fact affectionately known as Father, Son, and Holy Ghost. Streett offered the closing prayer at the dinner that closed the campaign and concluded it: "Lord, this prayer is sponsored by Citizens for Hays, Ed Lester, chairman."[57] Brooks wrote a letter to all his supporters and contributors thanking them for their help and announcing that he and Marion would soon be moving up to Amherst, Massachusetts, where he would be Professor of Practical Politics at the University of Massachusetts. He would also spend four days a month at Rutgers. Both the state of Arkansas and the District of Columbia, it seemed, were to take a back seat. He kept his home in Washington and would live there again, but this was his last farewell to Arkansas.

His professorship at Amherst was supposed to be for the fall semester only, but the Ford Foundation provided funds for him to teach through the spring semester as well. He worked with political science head William C. Havard to organize two graduate seminars, and in his spare time he delivered a series of public addresses. He made $20,000 for the year, the same as his T.V.A. salary eight years earlier and $2,000 less than he had made in Congress ten years before; but he lived in the Faculty Club, the oldest

---

[55]Hays, *Politics Is My Parish*, 250.

[56]Ibid., 253.

[57]Hays, *A Hotbed of Tranquility*, 47.

house west of Worcester, built in 1728, rent free. Its rugged oak rafters were
so low that he had to buy salve to treat his regular head wounds. While at
Amherst, which he thoroughly enjoyed, he addressed the Massachusetts
state legislature and noted that he had never been so honored by the legislature of his own state.[58]

After the year in Amherst, Brooks and Marion returned to their home
in Washington. For a year Brooks involved himself in volunteer political
matters, unable to be lazy in retirement. During that first summer back,
he and a group of like-minded Southerners planned and that November
founded the Southern Committee on Political Ethics, called SCOPE. Brooks
was SCOPE's first chairman, and he was backed by such figures as Hod-
ding Carter, Ralph McGill, and Vernon Jordan. Their professed purpose
was to channel the South's moral and intellectual resources into helping
create in the South and across the nation a more ethical and just society.
SCOPE's first project, which had been the impetus for its birth, was to produce a white paper on the career and programs of Alabama's racist Governor George C. Wallace.[59] In the report was strong, documented evidence
of Wallace's antilabor policies. When Wallace ran for president on the
American Independent ticket the next year, the AFL-CIO used the paper
against him with some effect.

As SCOPE's chairman, Brooks was asked by the House of Representatives to be a consultant as it sought to establish a standard of official conduct.[60] And the Senate Committee on Agriculture and Forestry asked him
to testify on rural Southern poverty. At the hearings he urged the committee to propose a law that no one in America would ever again be hungry. He said that while the food stamp program needed safeguards against
abuse, it was better to err on the side of the poor than to deprive any person
of nutrition. He particularly urged the committee not to let local officials
frustrate such programs.

That same year, 1967, he and his old congressional pal Walter Judd,
now out of office himself, developed the idea of founding an organization
called "Former Members of Congress." They wrote to all such former members as could be found and received a great deal of encouragement. The
group was formally incorporated in 1970 with Brooks serving the first two

---

[58]Hays, Conversation with Ronald Tonks, September 1977.

[59]Ibid.

[60]Hays, *Politics Is My Parish*, 242.

years as its president and thereafter until his death as honorary president. One of his assistants while in Congress, Warren Cikins, served as the group's first director. It worked not only to serve the needs of its members but also to make their expertise available to Congress and the government in general. It has proved to be one of the most impressive success stories of Brooks Hays's career.

And so by 1968, the tenth year since his liberation from elective politics, Brooks was a true elder statesman. Having turned defeat into victory, at seventy he was widely known and respected and free to be as irascible, eccentric, or vain as he pleased without fear of criticism, rebuke, or ridicule. For a time he sported a mustache, which looked truly terrible, and told audiences that he had found an old family mustache cup and decided not to let it lie idle.[61] He even bought a toupee and enjoyed rearranging it about his head, telling audiences, "What God hath not wrought, I went out and bought."[62] But he had his serious moments as well, mostly when he spoke of civil rights, his major concern toward the end of the 1960s. In early 1968 he told audiences that the congressional race in Mississippi's Third District, where black leader Charles Evers had a chance to be elected, was more significant for the nation than the New Hampshire presidential primary. And he praised the report of the National Advisory Commission on Civil Disorders, which spoke out far more boldly in support of civil rights than even the liberals of the 1950s, to say nothing of what moderates like Brooks had done. Gone now was the old Brooks Hays of Little Rock, worried that Southern traditions might be disrupted, and in his place was a Brooks Hays who felt it his duty to represent dispossessed people all over the nation.[63]

In 1968 came an invitation from J. Ralph Scales, president of North Carolina's Wake Forest University, to lead an enterprise dear to Brooks's heart and a challenge to his imagination. Scales wanted Wake Forest to join with the North Carolina Benedictine school Belmont Abbey to found an ecumenical institute that would involve all denominations, but particularly Baptists and Catholics, in joint ventures of Christian dialogue. Brooks would be the institute's director at a half-time salary of $10,000, a furnished apartment in Winston-Salem, and a car called "Old Ironsides"

---

[61]Brooks Hays, Public Lecture, Peabody College, Nashville TN, 13 March 1968.

[62]Baker, Conversation with William Angell, March 1987.

[63]Brooks Hays, Public Lecture, Peabody College, 13 March 1968.

to drive. At the last minute before announcing the project, President Scales, who was already being criticized for the idea, proposed that instead of Ecumenical Institute it be called the Center for Cooperative Christianity; but the old warhorse who would be directing it insisted that it be called by its proper name and let the cards fall where they might. This was done.[64]

From 1968 to 1974, then, Brooks directed the institute, organizing ecumenical sessions for people of various denominations, and taught an occasional course at Wake Forest and North Carolina State. He and Marion joined the campus church at Wake Forest, but he kept memberships at Calvary Baptist in Washington and at Second Baptist in Little Rock. Being on Calvary's role enabled him to serve as vice president of the National Council of Churches in 1970. Southern Baptists were not members.

There could not have been a better choice for director of the first Baptist ecumenical institute than Brooks Hays. He had been an ecumenist most of his life, long before more than a handful of people even knew the meaning of the word. He had been married for nearly fifty years to a Methodist; he had worked with other Protestants, Catholics, and Jews in all kinds of social and religious projects; he had met both of the most recent popes; he had served as president of the Southern Baptist Convention and chairman of the National Conference of Christians and Jews; and he was about to be a vice president of the National Council of Churches. At the National Conference of Christians and Jews' dinner honoring him, 16 April 1964, Senator Eugene McCarthy had compared him to the Catholic saint and social utopian Thomas More. Brooks had just laughed and said he was merely the Southern Baptist Convention's most visible ecumaniac.

He did oppose, until his death, appointing an American ambassador to the Vatican, saying it would make as much sense to appoint one to the Southern Baptist Convention; but he did everything he could to encourage Protestant-Catholic dialogue and cooperation on religious, social, and political issues. When John Kennedy had asked him what kind of Baptist he was, he had told the president that he was an ecumenical Baptist, "a catholic Baptist, with a little *c*." Then he added that he hoped Kennedy was a "protestant Catholic, with a little *p*."[65] His ecumenism had been a subject of contentious debate while he was president of the Southern Baptist Convention, and he had been forced to mute his desire to further Baptist-Cath-

---

[64]Hays, Conversation with Ronald Tonks, September 1977.

[65]Hays, *Politics Is My Parish,* 235.

olic relations. But now as a Southern Baptist elder statesman, as well as a political one, he was free to do as he pleased. He was becoming a prototype for the daring Baptist, secure in his own faith, enjoying the adventure of confrontation with brothers of all faiths.

During his six years with the Ecumenical Institute, Brooks was as true a "tar heel" as a "carpet bagger" could be. In February 1970, Governor Robert Scott appointed him chairman of the North Carolina Good Neighbor Council, later called the Human Relations Council, which dealt with race problems in the state. The announcement of his appointment in at least one newspaper contained the misprint that the council would seek "methods of creating more mob [sic] opportunities for Negroes." Brooks took the work seriously and spoke out at every opportunity for better relations between the races in North Carolina. In March 1970, he told newsmen at a University of North Carolina seminar that the United States could not survive eighty percent affluent and twenty percent wretched and concluded that there would be no social order without justice.[66] He served on the council with distinction until 1974, when he stated publicly that since the new Republican Governor James Holshouser was indifferent to the council's agenda he could no longer participate in its programs.

In 1970 Democrats in the heavily Republican Fifth District of North Carolina approached Brooks about running as their candidate for the United States House of Representatives. He felt the old excitement creeping up his spine, and he longed for one last campaign. However, he declined the offer, saying that he had been a resident of the district for only two years, that as chair of the council he might find a conflict of interest, and that the work at Wake Forest kept him busy. Two years later, though he was still chair and director and only a resident for four years, he let himself be persuaded. Senator Sam Ervin, soon to gain national fame in the Senate Watergate Hearings, made a personal appeal for Brooks to run, and he said yes.

It was a futile gesture, more futile even than the race for governor of Arkansas in 1966, and fortunately the last Brooks would make; but he considered it a worthy project. He was up against the Republican incumbent Wilmer (Vinegar Bend) Mizell, himself a native of Alabama, a former big league baseball pitcher, a Holiness lay preacher, a man whose grip on the English language was loose enough to make him say after one of his

---

[66]*Baptist and Reflector* (North Carolina Baptist Paper), 19 March 1970.

victories, "I am so humiliated." But not only was Mizell popular in his own right, Richard Nixon would win seventy percent of the North Carolina presidential vote that year, Richard Holshouser would be elected governor, and Jesse Helms would be sent to the United States Senate. In short, it would be a Republican year. Brooks knew all this, yet he gave it his all, knowing from experience that losers are often winners.

Citizens for Brooks Hays, in its appeal for funds, cited his positive accomplishments without once criticizing Mizell. A letter to potential contributors, signed by such persons as former North Carolina Governor Luther Hodges and Professor Arthur Schlesinger, Jr., described how he had tried to get Faubus to obey the law of the land and "paid the price of his courage"; how he had served as president of the Southern Baptist Convention and chair of the North Carolina Human Relations Commission; and how he was now director of the Wake Forest Ecumenical Institute. Without using the word *Democrat,* it mentioned that he had worked for Presidents Eisenhower, Kennedy, and Johnson.

All this high praise and Brooks's many honors and accomplishments counted for little. The election was a foregone conclusion. There were a few issues of local interest. Mizell accused Brooks of being anti-tobacco because he had once worked for the reelection in Utah of the anti-tobacco Democratic Senator Frank Moss. Brooks did not respond to the accusation, except to say tobacco was not an issue when he went to Mormon Utah. He in turn criticized Mizell for saturating the district with a "report," which was actually an election document, using and abusing the congressional franking privilege. School busing for racial balance was a national issue that year, and Brooks tried to avoid it; but he answered honestly when asked about it that he considered it an appropriate experiment. When headlines blared HAYS FAVORS BUSING he made no complaint.[67]

Knowing that he badly needed publicity to offset Mizell's superior election treasury, Brooks made a 154-mile walk from one end of the district to the other, getting free press all along the way. When he reached Winston-Salem, Sam Ervin joined him for a walk through the city. When his opponent joked that he walked west to east, downhill, he replied with a grin, "Anyone stupid enough to walk uphill when he can walk down is too stupid to go to Congress."[68] At seventy-three Brooks was not stupid. At the

---

[67]Hays, *Politics Is My Parish,* 267-68.

[68]Ibid., 263.

end of the campaign the shoes he wore on his trek brought $45 at auction. But minds were apparently not changed by his energetic good humor and obvious political wisdom. A poll taken when he addressed a Rotary Club near the end of the race resulted in 131 votes for Nixon and eight for George McGovern; and he laughed with everyone else when someone said that the eight were "Brooks and the 7 waiters."[69] Brooks led McGovern in the district but still got only thirty-five percent of the vote. He was, however, the leading vote-getter on the entire ticket in every black precinct, even running ahead of black candidates. On the other hand, he lost most of the white precincts by large margins, even running behind a black in one of them. He was seen, both by black and white voters, as a liberal on civil rights, not as the moderate from Little Rock days.

The election, his last, was a disappointment, but in the long run it proved valuable to Democrats in the district. Just as his race for governor of Arkansas in 1966, though a loss, resulted in the election of young, progressive Democrats in future years, so his loss in North Carolina's Fifth District in 1972 helped Democrats in future elections. Just two years later Democrat Steve Neal defeated Mizell, partly due to the effects of the Watergate scandal of the Nixon administration, partly due to the fact that Brooks had pulled Democrats together, given them a sense of purpose, and solidified the black vote for his party. Once again, as in so many previous races, Brooks won for his party and country by losing himself.

Now, however, he was truly finished with elective politics. He would laugh indulgently when in 1976, at age seventy-eight, Eugene McCarthy invited him to be his third party vice presidential running mate.[70] It was time to let younger men run the races. But it was not time to retire, not from religious work. In September 1972, he undertook a lay preaching mission in British Baptist and Methodist churches. In October 1973, he accepted a part-time, unsalaried position as lay minister in residence at Washington's Capitol Hill Methodist Church, even though technically he was still associated with the Wake Forest Ecumenical Institute. He told newsmen that while advising young pastor James Archibald's programs to aid the needy and elderly of the area around his home, he would remain a member of the Calvary Baptist Church around the corner, where he would

---

[69]Ibid, 262.

[70]Hays, Conversation with Ronald Tonks, September 1977.

continue to teach the Vaughn Men's Bible Class one Sunday each month.[71] He also continued to serve on civic, educational, and governmental boards and to testify before committees of both houses of Congress on federal-state relations, taxes, and relations between the executive and legislative branches of the federal government, as well as on civil rights.

Brooks and Marion moved from their town house at 314 Second Street S.E. to a flat in the Irene apartment complex on Willard Avenue, just inside the District of Columbia line, in 1977. There he watched the government from a close vantage point. Richard Nixon, who had admired Brooks but had not been admired in return, was gone from the scene, buried by scandal; but he sent Brooks his memoirs, signed with an affectionate note. Brooks spent a long time trying to compose a response, could think of nothing appropriate to say, and finally let the matter drop. He had visited President Gerald Ford as an honored guest at the White House but had little good or bad to say for him. Now, in 1977, a new man occupied the White House, this one a Southern Baptist like Brooks, but for two years there came no invitation to visit him.

During this time, when he was feeling neglected, he told an interviewer that he feared Carter might be wearing his religion a bit too much on his sleeve and hinted that he might be exploiting it. He noted Carter's lack of national experience and worried that right-wing religious leaders might try to use his inexperience and religiosity to gain power for themselves and their causes. It bothered him that Carter taught a Sunday school class instead of merely attending church and using his time for presidential matters. He was shocked by the appointment of an American ambassador to the Vatican. He said he considered Carter's use of the term "born again" a cliche and huffed, "We cannot sloganize ourselves into a Christian society." When Jesus said the words "born again," he was not giving Nicodemus a political shibboleth. Brooks said that when asked if he were born again he always said, "Yes, every day." He said he wished Carter well and hoped he would one day exhibit more dynamic political leadership and more wholesome churchmanship.[72]

Then one day someone suggested to Carter that he have Brooks to the White House for a visit, and Carter expressed surprise that Brooks was in Washington. He had thought he lived in Arkansas. In 1978 he had Brooks

---

[71]*Baptist Standard* (Texas Baptist Paper), 3 October 1973.

[72]Hays, Conversation with Ronald Tonks, October 1977.

in for a visit, bragged on him as a great statesman and religious leader, and made up for the unintended slight. There is a wonderful photograph of the two Southern Baptists, Carter flashing his country-boy smile, Brooks sporting his toupee, posing for posterity. Carter would be the last president Brooks met. He had met every one since Warren Harding, eleven in all, spanning sixty years. He had no great desire, the last year of his life, to meet Ronald Reagan, whom he judged not a very bright man, similar he thought to his Republican predecessor Dwight David Eisenhower.

His health was failing precipitously. In 1980 and 1981 he suffered several minor strokes. At about 2:00 A.M. on Monday morning, 12 October 1981, he got up from bed and went to the bathroom. As he started to get back into bed Marion roused, and he said, "Sorry I disturbed you." These were his final words, almost symbolic of his hope that he not cause pain to family, friends, his fellow man. The next moment he fell dead. He was eighty-three. Marion Hays, who was eighty-five, made coffee and kept a silent vigil until 7:00, when she called her daughter Betty.[73]

Brooks's Washington funeral was held on Wednesday, 14 October, at 4:00 P.M. at the Joseph Gawler's Sons Mortuary. His Arkansas funeral was on Friday, 16 October, at 11:00 A.M. at Little Rock's Second Baptist Church. He was buried in Russellville's Oakland Cemetery. In death he had journeyed back, retracing the steps that took him from the Ozarks to the nation's capital. It is a route many younger Southern Baptists will take, following his steps, at his inspiration.

---

[73]James Baker, Conversation with William Bell, Washington DC, March 1987.

CHAPTER 8

POSTERITY

Once when he was teaching at Rut-
gers, Brooks was asked to give his version of the American Dream. His ex-
temporaneous answer, which of course he could have finetuned in previous
oral addresses, reads like a psalm.

> It is the anticipation that some time
> we will be able to say here is equality
> and freedom, here is brotherhood and justice.

> The dream is of compassion expressing it-
> self in society's concern for those who fall
> by the way in a competitive system.

> It is imagination perfecting the mech-
> ansims of government. It is sensitivity to
> the claims of righteousness in human affairs.

> It is the hope that triumphs here will
> strengthen values shared with people
> around the world.

> It is human kindness so penetrating
> the nation that every man, no matter how
> incapacitated, will feel that he is wanted.

> It is the vision of opened doors of oppor-
> tunity. It is insistence upon government *by*
> as well as for and of the people.

> It is the hope of human dignity made
> secure. It is the longing for acknowledge-
> ment of the human family's oneness.

> It is the vision of a citizenry drawn together

in mutual confidence, facing common evils
and exalting a common faith in God.[1]

As a politician, one of those rare ones who also become statesmen,
Brooks made a valiant effort to realize and help others realize the American Dream. For him in his career as a public servant that meant giving
his people, in church and state affairs, both what they wanted and more
importantly what they needed. He once said that his life was significant
only in so far as he helped other people find the good life.[2] But he understood far better than most politicians that at times he had to follow his conscience and make decisions that, while right and good for his people, would
not please them.

As noted earlier, he loved to say that no one should go into politics who
could not paraphrase St. Paul at Miletus: "Neither count I my *political* life
dear unto myself." He felt that as a representative he should decide the
wisest course for all, not merely represent popular opinion. He believed that
minority rights are often more important than majority rights—more important even for the majority. He never took a poll to determine the way
to vote because with Edmund Burke he believed: "A representative owes
the people not his energy alone but his judgment as well, and he betrays
them if he yields his judgment to their passing opinion." For him political
corruption almost always results from weakness, from the lack of courage
to do what is obviously right.[3]

The source of Brooks's courage, his strength to do in most instances what
he knew to be right regardless of the consequences, was his religious faith.
He was at heart a deeply religious man: a Christian, a Baptist, a pietist.
His faith gave him an inner peace that enabled him to endure frustration,
threat, and defeat. It gave him a capacity to love and to see love's responsibilities, a capacity to surmount obstacles that would otherwise have
trapped him in a world of confusing sounds and signals. His faith was a
call to duty, a call to provide consolation for the weak and judgment for the
strong. It gave him a courage, a daring rarely matched in American political or religious life and almost never in both at the same time.

---

[1]Brooks Hays, *A Hotbed of Tranquility* (New York: Macmillan, 1968) xiv-xv.

[2]Brooks Hays, *This World: A Christian's Workshop* (Nashville: Broadman Press, 1968) vii.

[3]Brooks Hays, Conversation with Ronald Tonks, September 1975, typeset in 15 parts. Southern Baptist Sunday School Board Archives, Nashville TN.

Brooks once said that one of the greatest needs of his time was "the political education of theologians and the theological education of politicians."[4] According to one of his admirers, Arthur Schlesinger, Jr., Brooks's life was "a quest to find ways of relating religion and politics without violating the constitutional separation of church and state," and that Brooks's own memoirs did not begin to reveal the courage this goal required.[5] Brooks believed that his vocation was to serve both his church and his state, to be a theologian who practiced politics and a politician who practiced theology. And he believed that the keys to his success in these difficult and dual ventures lay in the words and spirit of Jesus, "for Jesus dealt with the strong and elemental forces of human life."[6] Jesus was *the* central figure in "this great vocation of building for truth and justice and freedom and democracy—the great rich word in the field of government."[7]

The Little Rock Central High School crisis of 1957 stands out as the pinnacle of Brooks's career, the moment when a man armed with the words and spirit of Jesus served as both comforter and judge, as both theologian and politician, and through his courage rose to be both statesman and saint. During the next year's election he would suffer defeat for his actions; but much later he would explain, "I was not trying to vote a popular idea. I was trying to popularize an idea that had become so much a part of me that I could not rid myself of it." David Broder of the Washington *Post*, naming Brooks his Thanksgiving inspiration the year Brooks died, remembering those words of "this wise and just man," concluded, "Wherever a politician can speak honestly of himself or herself in those terms, the spirit of Brooks Hays will live."[8]

For those of us who either knew or knew of Brooks Hays, the fondest wish can only be that the South and Southern Baptists will produce other leaders with his faith and courage. Such leaders, understanding the true nature and potential of both church and state, would stand with the poor and dispossessed and turn the resources of government and gospel to the

---

[4] Ibid.

[5] Arthur Schlesinger, Jr., preface to Brooks Hays, *Politics Is My Parish* (Baton Rouge: Louisiana State University Press, 1981) viii.

[6] Hays, *This World: A Christian's Workshop*, 72.

[7] Hays, Conversation with Ronald Tonks, August 1977.

[8] David Broder, Washington *Post*, 25 November 1981, A-21.

comfort of the weak and judgment of the strong. Such leaders, unlike many of those who were prominent in Brooks's day and are in our own day, would provide hope that the future can achieve the social and spiritual triumphs that have eluded us in the past and continue to do so in the present.

BIBLIOGRAPHY

PRIMARY SOURCES

I. Books

Brooks Hays. *The Baptist Way of Life* (with John Steely). New York: Prentice-Hall, 1963. Reprint. Macon GA: Mercer University Press, 1981.

Brooks Hays. *A Hotbed of Tranquility*. New York: Macmillan, 1968.

Brooks Hays. *Politics Is My Parish*. Baton Rouge: Louisiana State University Press, 1981.

Brooks Hays. *A Southern Moderate Speaks*. Chapel Hill: University of North Carolina Press, 1959.

Brooks Hays. *This World: A Christian's Workshop*. Nashville: Broadman Press, 1968.

II. Collections

Brooks Hays Collection. John F. Kennedy Presidential Library. Boston, Massachusetts.

Brooks Hays Collection. Southern Baptist Sunday School Board Archives. Nashville, Tennessee.

Brooks Hays Collection. University of Arkansas Archives. Fayetteville, Arkansas.

Brooks Hays Collection. Wake Forest University Library. Winston-Salem, North Carolina.

III. Interviews

Brooks Hays. Interview with Walter Brown. May 1975. University of Arkansas Archives. Fayetteville, Arkansas.

Brooks Hays. Interview with Ronald Tonks. 1975-1977. Typeset in 15 parts. Southern Baptist Sunday School Board Archives. Nashville, Tennessee.

Brooks Hays Family. Interview with James T. Baker. March 1987. Washington, D.C. Possession of the author.

William Angell, Ph.D. Interview with James T. Baker. March 1987. Winston-Salem, North Carolina. Possession of the author.

Steele Hays. Interview with James T. Baker. May 1987. Little Rock, Arkansas. Possession of the author.

IV. Addresses

Brooks Hays. Public Address. Peabody College. Nashville, Tennessee. 13 March 1968.

Brooks Hays. Public Address. "Washington Humor." Album collected by Tait Trussell, 1964.

Brooks Hays. Public Address. Western Kentucky University. Bowling Green, Kentucky. November 1968.

V. Articles

Brooks Hays. "Faith Steadies the Politician." *Christian Century,* 11 June 1952, 698-99.

Brooks Hays. "Inside Story of Little Rock." *U. S. News,* 23 March 1959, 118-35.

Brooks Hays. "Little Rock from the Inside." *Look,* 17 March 1959, 23-27.

Brooks Hays. "Little Rock Postmortem." *Newsweek,* 23 March 1959, 30.

Brooks Hays. "The Norton Bill Will Hurt Rather Than Help the Minorities It Is Designed to Aid." *Congressional Digest* (June-July 1945): 181-85.

Brooks Hays. "Out of a Holocaust, National Hope." *Saturday Review,* 6 June 1959, 34-35.

Brooks Hays. "A Southern Moderate Predicts Victory." *New York Times Magazine,* 11 January 1959, 17ff.

SECONDARY SOURCES

I. Books

Dale Alford. *The Case of the Sleeping People.* Little Rock AR; privately published, 1959.

Virgil T. Blossom. *It Has Happened Here.* New York: Harper and Brothers, 1959.

Robert R. Brown. *Bigger Than Little Rock.* Greenwich CT: Seabury Press, 1958.

Marion Hays. Unpublished manuscript. "How to Live Dangerously and Enjoy It." Possession of the author.

II. Articles

"About Face." *Time,* 15 July 1957, 17.

Harry Ashmore. "They Didn't Want a Man of Reason." *The Reporter,* 27 November 1958, 20-21.

"Attack from Behind." *Time,* 17 November 1958, 22.

"Brooks Hays Says It." *Newsweek,* 18 May 1959, 100.

"Casualty." *Newsweek,* 17 November 1958, 30-31.

"Conspiracy Charged." *Newsweek,* 29 December 1958, 16.

Virginius Dabney. "Southern Crisis: The Segregation Decision." *Saturday Evening Post,* 8 November 1952, 40ff.

"Defeated Democrat Picked by Ike for T.V.A. Post." *U. S. News,* 4 May 1959, 21.

"Election in Dispute." *Commonweal,* 19 December 1958, 306.

"For Congress, A Place to Pray." *U. S. News,* 25 March 1955, 14.

Gerald W. Johnson. "Brooks, the Baptist." *New Republic,* 1 December 1958, 17.

Charles Kean. "Hays on Race." *Christian Century,* 7 November 1962, 1370.

Virgil E. Lowder. "Southern Baptists." *Christian Century,* 11 June 1958, 700.

"New Role and Wider Stage for Brooks Hays." *Christian Century,* 3 December 1958, 1390.

"People of the Week." *U. S. News,* 20 September 1957, 14.

"People of the Week." *U. S. News,* 4 May 1959, 21.

"Portrait." *U. S. News,* 1 April 1949, 28.

Natalie Davis Spingarn. "Mr. Hays of Arkansas Meets His Responsibilities." *The Reporter,* 14 November 1957, 25-26.

"Victory Without Hate?" *Newsweek,* 23 June 1958, 28.

"What Happened in the Election." *U. S. News,* 14 November 1958, 97.

III. Periodicals Consulted

Arkansas *Democrat.* Little Rock. 1948.

Arkansas *Gazette.* Little Rock. 1919, 1928, 1930, 1957, 1958.

University *Weekly.* University of Arkansas, Fayetteville. 1918-1919.

U. S. Department of State *Bulletin.* Washington. 1955.

INDEX